W9-AWY-368

SELF

AN ECLECTIC APPROACH

Randall E. Osborne

Indiana University East

ALLYN AND BACON

BOSTON   LONDON   TORONTO   SYDNEY   TOKYO   SINGAPORE

Second Printing, with References

Vice President, Social Science: Susan Badger
Series Editorial Assistant: Erika Stuart
Marketing Manager: Joyce Nilsen
Editorial–Production Service: Electronic Publishing Services Inc.
Cover Administrator: Suzanne Harbison
Signing Representative: Jack McCanna
Production Administrator: Mary Beth Finch

Copyright © 1996 by Allyn & Bacon
A Simon & Schuster Company
Needham Heights, Massachusetts 02194

Library of Congress Cataloging-in-Publication Data

Osborne, Randall E.
    Self : an eclectic approach / Randall E. Osborne.
        p. cm.
    Includes bibliographical references and index.

  BF697.074   1996
  155.2—dc20   96-17527
                                  CIP

Printed in the United States of America

10 9 8 7 6 5 4 3 2 1   99 98 97 96 95

I DEDICATE THIS TEXT to the five most powerful influences in my life. First, to Mom for all the pep talks, all the strength of character, and all of the wisdom that you somehow managed to get through this thick skull. Second, to Dad for instilling in me a respect for common sense, a motivation to be who I wanted to be, and the single-mindedness that such self-realization requires. Third, to Diane for the years of patient love, the underlying support, and her command of grammar. Fourth, to Joseph for showing me the joy in parenting, the energy in discovery, and the simple pleasure of time spent together. Finally, to my students for serving as my colleagues, giving of themselves to enhance my own learning, and keeping the quest for knowledge burning in me as strongly today as when I started this thing I love called "Teaching."

Contents

Preface

The concept of self has been the focus of psychological research and interest for decades (Wylie, 1974). As investigators continue to narrow their focus on small pieces of the "self" puzzle, however, something is getting lost in the translation. Psychology has become a field of specialization, and that in and of itself is not a bad thing. If, however, the big picture gets blurred by this narrowing of interests, those working within the discipline may fail to see that others are conducting work directly related to what they, themselves, are doing. A unified theory of self will not be possible if the current trend continues. In order to integrate the seemingly disparate findings in the self literature, one must look beyond the data being collected and attempt to address the underlying issues that permeate these studies. Numerous questions must be asked, and the answers may provide insights into the inner workings of this construct called "self." The questions include (but are certainly not limited to):

1. What do the research findings tell us about the processes by which self-concept develops?
2. What do the findings tell us about the processes by which self-esteem develops?
3. What are the differences between self-concept and self-esteem?
4. What are the sources through which individuals gain self-knowledge?
5. What are the consequences of this self-knowledge?
6. How do we explain the individual differences among people in relationship to the self?
7. What are the applications of this understanding of self?

8. What do we gain by understanding the multiple facets of self-concept development?
9. What are the ramifications of self for education and daily life?

These questions tie directly into the concept of an "eclectic" approach to self. One of the main goals in studying self is to understand the development and implications of self-knowledge. If I see myself as "gregarious" and "charming," what implications do those self-images have for my own behavior and the behaviors of others toward me? An eclectic approach will be somewhat different from approaches that have been taken in the past. The *American Heritage Dictionary* defines eclectic as "selecting or employing individual elements from a variety of sources." This text will attempt to do just that. Such a definition clearly does not suggest that an exhaustive and complete review of the self literature will be presented. Such an attempt will not be made within the pages of this book, for several reasons.

First, such a review would be nearly impossible to accomplish. Second, and more important, such a summary of the literature in the absence of a guiding theoretical framework would do very little to add to our understanding of self and the implications of self for the individuals and the other persons that make up their social world. Instead, this text will present sufficient reviews of the applicable literature as it relates to the eclectic theory being outlined to illustrate the integrative nature of self. Research on the factors that influence self-esteem level will also shed light on behavioral patterns of individuals and individual differences in the way these persons perceive their social world. Another summary of the self literature was not needed. Instead, this text takes the current findings and puts this information into a working model of self. Once this working model is in place, it becomes much easier to make predictions about the implications of self for behavior, impression formation, perceptions of others, and self-esteem levels.

As you progress through the book, keep in mind that this approach makes a major assumption about the "self." An eclectic approach to self assumes that understanding the integrative nature of self will shed light on the inner workings of the whole person. If it is understood that self-views directly impact the processing of social information, then much more can be learned about the processes involved in the formation of stereotypes, the development of attitudes, and levels of attitude-behavior consistency. Once this integrative nature of self is understood, it becomes clearer how the construct of self applies beyond the laboratory. Self is a dynamic and "defensive" structure. This means that self develops in such a way as to continuously reconfirm itself. If I see myself as an honest person, I am likely to put myself into honest situations and, therefore, become even more certain that I am an honest person. This cycle of self-perpetuation provides one of the fundamental integrating notions of this text. As you read the chapters, it is an understanding of this concept of "self-defense" that will provide the key insights into the comprehensive theory of self that is being developed.

Each section begins with an introduction that sets the tone for what is to be discussed within the chapters of that section. Once this tone is set, the information in the chapters will provide details that center around both the theoretical/empirical information that is available in the area and possible applications of that knowledge. The chapters end with an integrative section that gives the reader insights into the ramifications of the chapter and brings the information back to the theme of "an eclectic approach to self." The reader is also direct-ed specifically back to the theoretical diagrams to continuously reinforce an understanding of how the information is coming together into a comprehensive theory of self.

Integrating the self literature was a monumental task. So many excellent studies are being done on so many diverse aspects of self that finding a way to whittle it down was challenging. I have tried to present an overall organization for the book that helps the read-er to understand the major themes that a self theory must address. In addition, I felt it was important to avoid the trap of summarizing everything anyone has ever said about the "self." Keeping with the current passion for being health-conscious, I wanted to present a lean and trim integrative text on self. What appears before you is the culmination of that exercise program. I do not present or intend to promote a single theoretical perspective. Certainly some theoretical perspectives will find their way into my writing more than others. Although I do not feel this is necessarily a bad thing, it is not my intention to assume that my way of seeing things is the only way. As literature is cited, summarized, analyzed, and integrated, the reader is encouraged to question other methods by which that same information could be interpreted. What remains when all of the comparisons between theories and findings have been made is a comprehensive theory of self that combines the best pieces of what other theories had to offer.

I would like to thank those professors who took the time to read and comment on the manuscript: Robert Arkin, Ohio State University; Edward R. Sofranko, University of Rio Grande; Paula Niedenthall, Indiana University; Michael Strube, Washington University; Michael Kernis, University of Georgia.

In the end, I hope you, the reader, can recognize the contributions that each of the the-ories discussed made to the eclectic theory that I present. Much of this book is intended to be forward thinking. Although we certainly must focus on findings from the past, the main emphasis is, and must be, on the implications that this theoretical model has for the future. This future I am referring to is twofold. First, it refers to the future of self research. Such investigations must move forward by asking questions about how our models and theories need to be changed and how our own research relates to other work being done within our own discipline and across disciplines. Second, such a theory provides direct insights into the processes by which our view of our "self" not only motivates future behavior but also determines how that future behavior will then be perceived. So, without further philo-sophical delay, let's begin moving forward with our journey toward an eclectic approach to self.

Randall E. Osborne

Introduction

Before beginning with our journey toward a more integrated understanding of self, it would be beneficial to set the tone for this work. An eclectic approach to self must, by definition, be made up of elements from a variety of sources. A significant portion of this text, then, will focus on the variety of information that has been discovered about self and the proposed implications of this information. At every step of the way, however, the goal will always be integration. Human beings are, by their very nature, curious. More of this curiosity is directed toward understanding ourselves than perhaps any other object. We seem to have a need to know why we do the things we do, and why others make the choices they make. "Why did I do that?" is a question we often ask ourselves, and it bothers us when we cannot come up with a satisfactory answer. The self literature has been asking these same questions for decades, sometimes experiencing the same unsettling feeling when the answer doesn't seem to fall directly from the data. Because self is a dynamic entity, it makes sense that a self theory would need to be dynamic and open to change as well. The eclectic theory articulated in the following pages is meant to be just that—flexible and open to change as more research is conducted and new issues are resolved.

But as anyone who has experienced adolescence can tell you, part of the difficulty in articulating our self involves the multiple and conflicting demands that others attempt to place on our "self." Identity negotiation and a smooth transition out of adolescence into young adulthood is directly dependent on our ability to resolve those conflicts and create an integrated conception of self that we and the others around us can live with. Such is the very nature of an eclectic approach to self. Our task as we progress through the following chapters will be to listen to what others have to say about the identity of "self" as a construct and then use our powers of observation to integrate that information. If something doesn't seem to fit into our working model, we won't force it. If something seems to fit, then we will allow it. In the end, what we'll have is an understanding of the consistent characteristics of self and the implications that those characteristics have for human behavior.

Just as adolescents are experiencing a time of storm and stress because so many people are saying so many different things about who they should be, the self literature is experiencing its own adolescence. The field is expanding rapidly, and fundamental additions have been made to our understanding of self and its nature. The chapters that follow are an attempt to bring the lines of research into sharper focus and blend them into an integrative self theory that uses the best that the other findings had to offer. Adolescents who successfully negotiate the multiple demands others place on them provide a model for this text. The eclectic approach will follow this developmental analogy, and then direct our inquiry toward the future implications of this construct called "self."

Self-Concept and Self-Esteem Development, and the Role of Self-Motives

INTRODUCTION TO SECTION ONE

Definitions

"Self" is sometimes an opaque construct. What is considered the currently acceptable definition of self may be as malleable as the ways to measure it. When discussions focus on "self-concept," does that mean the same thing as "personality"? If these terms do not mean the same thing, what are the differences? Another question that complicates the issue involves the role of self-esteem. Is self-esteem one facet of self-concept or is it a fundamentally different construct? Formal answers to these questions have remained inextricable because of the dynamic nature of self. A quick perusal of popular social psychology journals shows the continuing interest in self issues. The wealth of information that has been collected puts the self literature in a great position. The time is ripe for integrating this research into an eclectic theory that can then be used to guide the next questions that the self literature seems poised to ask and answer.

Many of the implications of research in the self literature have not been fully realized because the interconnections among constructs and self-theories have not been delineated. If, for example, the connection between self-concept and self-esteem can be more clearly articulated, then it may be possible to discover self-esteem enhancement methods that would otherwise remain hidden. Current trends in the self literature define self-concept as "the sum total of beliefs you have about yourself" and self-esteem as "an affectively charged component of the self." Despite how reasonable these definitions may sound, they don't tell us very much. Most textbooks and scientific journal articles use the terms "self-concept" and "self" as if they mean the same thing and therefore can be used interchangeably. Such an assumption is false and may be directly responsible for many of the discrepancies in the self literature.

For our purposes, "self-concept" will initially be defined as "the sum total of the attributes, abilities, attitudes, and values that an individual believes defines who he or she is." "Self," on the other hand, is significantly more complicated. In this text, "self" will be defined as "an integration of self-concept, self-esteem, and self-presentations." This means that understanding self involves an awareness of all three of these avenues of inquiry. This understanding must center around not only the beliefs one holds about self or the feelings one has about those beliefs, but also the extent to which those beliefs and feelings influence behavior. Understanding the integration of these facets of self is complicated. The reason that much of the self literature seems divergent, discrepant, or even contradictory may revolve around the fact that self research, by definition, involves all three avenues of understanding.

Questions of Self

An example of a self theory that could be used to guide self related research is Brehm and Kassin's (1993) use of the ABC's of self. In their discussion, they conclude that understanding self depends on exploring the "affective," "behavioral," and "cognitive" facets of self. In order to truly understand "self," research must be directed specifically toward questions involving each of these. First, research must focus on the "cognitive" question, which seeks to understand the processes by which individuals come to know themselves and by which they develop and maintain a stable identity. A related issue involves the processes by which a feature or characteristic becomes a part of the individual's self-concept. Answers to these questions will deal specifically with information processing, cognitive biases, and interpretations of social information. Second, researchers must explore the "affective" question. This addresses the manner in which individuals evaluate themselves, the methods by which self-esteem may be enhanced, and the methods that individuals may use to protect their sense of self-worth. Third, research should specifically address the "behavioral" question. This deals with the manner in which individuals present themselves to others and the methods that are used to regulate behaviors and, thereby, influence the self-presentations individuals make to the other persons in their social world.

These questions serve as the driving force behind the chapters in Section One of this text. The chapters of this section, then, focus on the triadic nature of self. Every effort has been made to clearly distinguish between the term "self-concept" and the term "self." An *eclectic approach* to self will serve as the driving force behind this book. With each segment of material that is presented, attention will be paid to the integrative nature of self. Chapter One deals with self-concept, and Chapter Two deals with self-esteem. The fundamental issue within each of these chapters is the developmental nature of self. The behavioral aspects of self will permeate the book as a whole. A study of self-concept is only one part of what is needed to understand the more complex issue of self. Self-concept can be understood on a much simpler level than the integrated concept of self. Only when we understand the material presented in all of the chapters of this book will we have a clearly articulated image of self.

For now, this text uses the term "self-concept" to mean "the sum total of the attributes, abilities, attitudes, and values that an individual believes defines who he or she is." "Self," on the other hand, will be defined as "the integration of self-concept, self-esteem, and self-presentational strategies that influence the manner in which the individual thinks about, perceives, and responds to his/her social world" (Osborne, 1993c). As more information about self and self-concept are gathered and presented in this text, these definitions will be revised to incorporate the eclectic nature of self that this text is striving toward.

The Role of Self-Esteem

Important to any discussion of self is the issue of self-esteem. Is self-esteem one aspect of self-concept? Is self-esteem something uniquely different from self-concept that has unique implications for a theory of self? Or is self-esteem both a component of self-concept and a driving force behind the construction of self? How these questions are answered will have a profound impact on the eclectic theory of self that is being created. Alfred Adler (1927) argued long ago that individuals do not acquire a self simply through stimulus-response interactions with the environment. According to Adler's view, in order to picture self truly, one must understand that people create their own personality (a term that Adler seemed to use in a synonymous way with self). He called this notion the creative self, which argues that individuals actively construct their own personalities from their experiences and heredity.

Contrary to other more pessimistic thinking of the time, Adler believed that people were the masters of their own destinies. The discussion of self-esteem that is presented in Chapter Two holds this idea as fundamentally sound. If individuals take an active role in their own self-development, then it is also possible (and this text will argue that it is very probable) that they also play a role in the development and maintenance of their self-esteem. Many books on self-esteem seem to assume that self-esteem is mostly handed to an individual by his or her environment (e.g., Coopersmith, 1981; McKay & Fanning, 1987). The eclectic approach to self, however, will view self-esteem as an active, ongoing, negotiation process in which the individual plays a crucial role. For the most part, then, self-concept is a cognitive entity involving the thoughts the individual has about his or her self-images and the manner in which those thoughts are integrated with existing information. Once this cognitive aspect of self is better understood (the task of Chapter One), our discussions will move on to self-esteem, which represents the affective nature of self (the task of Chapter Two). Self-Esteem can be defined as "a relatively permanent positive or negative feeling about self that may become more or less positive or negative as individuals encounter and interpret successes and failures in their daily lives" (Osborne, 1993a).

Why Self-Motives?

At first it may seem odd to include a discussion of self-motives along with two chapters designed to delineate the developmental trends in self-concept and self-esteem. Any discussion of these developmental trends, however, will center around self-motives. What motivates the individual to ask self-related questions? What kind of information will the individual find to be most valuable? What are the individual's goals in social situations? How do self-motives influence behavior and the manner in which self-related feedback is acquired and interpreted? These questions clearly suggest that an adequate understanding of the development of self-concept and self-esteem would be difficult, if not impossible, without considering the implications of self-motives. Many of the behaviors initiated by self-motives have direct and profound implications for self-concept and self-esteem development. Changing some of these self-motives also may be essential if self-esteem enhancement is to be accomplished. Given these premises, then, it seems acceptable, if not logical, to place a chapter on self-motives in the same section as the developmental issues addressed in Chapters One and Two.

CHAPTER ONE

Self-Concept Development

THE DIFFICULTIES OF UNDERSTANDING ONE'S SELF

When we walk by a pond, or a mirror, or a highly polished car, what do we see in the person that is reflected back at us? Do we see a physical being with arms, legs, eyes, ears, nose and mouth? Or do we see an intelligent, thinking, feeling being with wishes, wants, and desires? Understanding who we are is arguably one of the most difficult cognitive tasks that we must engage in on a daily basis. Why must so much effort be expended to answer a question that seems on the surface to be a simple one? Why is it so hard to answer "Who am I"? We should know ourselves better than anyone else can know us, yet we are never surprised when someone says, "I know you better than you know yourself." After all is said and done, one of the most difficult tasks to complete is the self-awareness process. It is possible for people to describe their "self" to someone, then a few moments later describe a seemingly different person to someone else. Does this contradiction mean that one of the descriptions of the self was a lie? No. It simply suggests what we already know. Self is difficult to define because there are so many things that influence it.

"Self" is difficult to pinpoint because it is hard to understand clearly all of the factors that influence our self definition. Benjamin Franklin has been quoted as saying, "There are three things that are extremely hard: steel, a diamond, and to know thyself." The wisdom of those words is readily apparent to anyone who has ever struggled for self-definition. To rectify this problem, it will be necessary to trace the roots of self-concept development. To gain a unified sense of where self is going, it is necessary to take a step back and look at the process that led self to where it is at the present moment. Only when the developmental sequence that leads to self-concept is fully understood can progress be made toward a unified theory of self. Given that self-concept is one of the major features of "self," and that self-esteem is one of the predominant features of the self-concept (Greenwald, Bellezza, & Banaji, 1988) it is reasonable to use self-concept and self-esteem as the starting points on the journey toward understanding self. It should be mentioned, however, that reviews of the self literature suggest that too much emphasis has been placed on understanding the singular self-related construct of self-esteem (e.g., Wylie, 1979; Jensen, Huber, Cundick, & Carlson, 1991). This is not to say that efforts in the self literature should be turned away from understanding self-esteem. Rather, an eclectic approach to self needs to address self-esteem and the myriad of other issues that are relevant to establishing a working theory of self.

THE FOUNDATIONS OF SELF-CONCEPT DEVELOPMENT

Comprehensive reviews of the self literature clearly suggest that self-concept is not fully in place when the child is born (Wylie, 1974; Baumeister, Tice, & Hutton, 1989). This suggests, then, that childhood interactions and relationships must play a key role in the development of self-concept. Parents or primary caregivers play a crucial role in helping the child to create a pattern of self understanding. To the extent that the home environment is stable, the child is free to explore the environment and try out different personas. Before a child can gain a sense of who he or she is, that child must differentiate itself from the surrounding context. Before discussing self-concept development, then, it is important to have a basic understanding of the roots of self-awareness. Through interactions with the environment and the significant others within that environment, children develop an understanding that they are fundamentally different from other objects and persons they come in contact with. According to Tomasello (1993), "when the child is simulating and culturally learning from the adult's attention to herself, she may then use her developing abilities of categorization to begin forming a true self-concept" (Tomasello, 1993, p.177). In this same chapter, Tomasello suggests that the infant can begin taking the perspective of others around nine months of age. This ability to take the perspective of others, then, clearly establishes for the child an awareness of the distinction between self and others. It is at this point, then, that self will begin to blossom.

This serves as the foundation upon which self-concept is built. The degree to which the child is self-aware directly impacts the development of self-concept, self-esteem, and other related self constructs. Sullivan and others called this awareness *self-efficacy*. This is defined as "a person's awareness that he/she is an entity capable of action and the realization that those actions have consequences." In order for self-concept to develop, then, the child must come to understand that he or she can initiate actions. But that is not enough for self-concept development to occur. The child also must learn that for every action there is a consequence. Through these consequences, parents and society attempt to shape the behaviors of children. One example of such a developmental process can be found in the writings of Harry Stack Sullivan.

Sullivan (1953) discussed the process of self-efficacy development, and that discussion is directly relevant to the material being presented here. This sequence in the development of self-efficacy also lends to our understanding of the relationship between self-concept and self-esteem. The first step in the development of self-efficacy is called *conditional love*. This term involves the child's developing awareness that the family relationship is a two-way street. Children must learn that they must contribute something to the relationship if it is going to be successful. Parents teach this concept to their children by assigning them chores, asking for their input into family decisions, making them responsible for dictating their own punishments, and other methods designed to get the children involved in the familial relationship.

As children explore the family relationship, they quickly discover the second step in the self-efficacy process, the growing awareness that some behaviors are considered more positive than others. Children learn this concept through parental reactions to their activities and choices. If a father sees his one-year-old-child put a block back into the toybox, he may praise her for the action, clap loudly, smile broadly, or send any of a dozen other signals to the child, telling her that the behavior was considered to be a good one. A parent just as easily can send a signal to inform the child quickly that a behavior was not well received. Out of this pattern of parental reaction emerges the third step to self-efficacy, which Sullivan called *good-mother/bad-mother*. This involves the child's awareness that sometimes the mother or father acts nice or does good things and other times acts bad or does mean things. A parent might kiss a child on the cheek for trying to say a word, or spank the child for trying to eat the houseplants. If they are going to discover the predictable patterns in their world, children must attempt to integrate these wildly discrepant behaviors on the part of the parent. This can be a confusing time for the child, who is surprised by the wild discrepancies in the parent's behavior and struggles to discover a way to understand when and why mother or father will act "good" and when and why they will act "bad." This search for predictable patterns in the parents' reactions to the child forms a significant part of the parent-child relationship. Vygotsky (1978) and Tomasello (1993) suggest that the major developmental changes in self are initiated by the child's changes in the concept of others. The more the child truly understands about others, the more he or she can know about self.

As the child continues to explore the environment and test behaviors, he will start turning toward the parent and using the parent's reaction as a gauge for the acceptability of the behavior. A boy may walk toward the houseplant all the while glancing over his shoulder to see how mother and father are going to react. This emerging awareness that parental reactions may be dependent upon the child's own behavior leads to the fourth and final step in the development of self-efficacy. This is called *good-me/bad-me/not-me*. The child has now come to understand that mother or father react bad when the child engages in a behavior that the parents find unacceptable. In this manner, children learn that the ways in which people react toward them may hinge directly on their choices of behaviors. This combination of steps, then, leads to a comprehensive awareness in the child that he or she can make choices, engage in actions, and receive consequences from parents and the environment (e.g., Lewis, 1982).

Lewis (1982) suggests that the child's awareness of the existence of his or her self develops from consistency, regularity, and contingency between the infant's actions and the reactions of objects and people in the social world. In this fashion, the child engages in actions and receives feedback. The degree to which a well-articulated sense of self develops, then, depends upon the reactions of others along these dimensions. If the parents, for example, consistently, regularly, and expeditiously reinforce certain behaviors and punish others, the assumption is that the child will consider the rewarded behaviors, and the characteristic traits that might go with them, to be an important aspect of self. The punished behaviors, on the other hand, might signal to the child that such a characteristic of self would not be valued and, therefore, might be relegated by the child to the "not-me."

Although Sullivan did not discuss the concept of "not-me," it seems perfectly reasonable that a child would differentiate between the positive and negative aspects of self and the things that he or she feels is non-definitional about self. A consensus is emerging within the self literature that self is composed of an array of representations (e.g., Markus, 1990; Markus & Nurius, 1986). The diversity of these self-representations is not only interesting but crucial to our understanding of self-schemas and the self-motives that may drive individuals' behaviors (Markus, 1990). Markus (1990) generated a list of such representations including, "the good me, the bad me, the not me, the actual me, the ideal me, the ought me, the possible me, the undesired me, the hoped-for me, the expected me, the feared me, and the shared me." Although all of these could influence behavior to some degree, Markus assumed that only some of them will become focal points for the individual, and with elaboration these become the self-schemas (Markus, 1990). Given the role that others play in the articulation of self, it is reasonable to assume that the good me, the bad me, and the not me would be focal points for most individuals.

The "good me" and the "bad me" seem easy to understand in terms of their relationship to the developing self. But only recent efforts have been directed toward understanding the role that the "not me" plays in the developing self. Aspects in which the individual performs below desired expectations will influence self-esteem in a negative manner. Such a negative impact, however, should only occur if the individual considers those characteristics important to his or her self-definition. If the individual found a certain characteristic unimportant to self, it could be labeled as "not-me" and therefore have little impact on self-esteem (Osborne, 1993d).

It should be readily apparent that this development of self-efficacy is a crucially important part of the process of developing a self-concept. In order for the child to address the question "Who am I?," she must understand how she fits into the environment and the relationship between her behaviors and the behaviors of those around her (e.g., Banks & Wolfson, 1967; Bronson, 1972; Lewis, 1992; Tomasello, 1993). If a child fails to develop this awareness, she will stumble through childhood unable to be successful in social situations. This lack of success is caused by the fact that she hasn't learned to modify her own behavior in response to the expectations of others. It also will be impossible for the child to exert much influence over the perceptions that others have of her. If the child cannot demonstrate an understanding of the connections between her behavior and the behaviors of those around her, she will make many social errors. These social errors then may compound and influence the self-esteem level that the child develops.

Self-efficacy alone, however, does not explain the developmental process that leads to a self-concept. Figure 1.1 outlines the sequence of factors that are involved in the formation and perpetuation of self-concept. The remainder of this chapter is devoted to developing an understanding of the cycle by which self-concept develops, as well as the influence that self-concept exerts over other aspects of self.

FIGURE 1.1   The Self-Concept Development Process

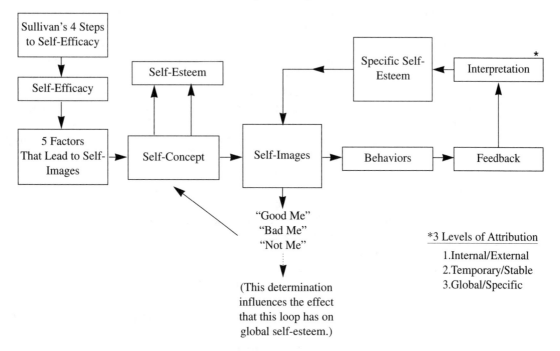

THE DEVELOPMENT OF SELF-IMAGES

Once self-efficacy is established, the child starts actively trying to determine who he or she is. Five separate factors influence the development of self-images within the individual. Each of these factors contributes something to the unique self-concept that develops, but it is actually the combination of the five that most powerfully influences the way individuals view themselves.

The first factor is the *immutable characteristics* that a person is born with. These are unchanging characteristics that influence the way that others perceive us. Obvious examples are race, gender, and body build. These characteristics influence the ways that others act toward the individual in at least two ways. Physical features such as gender carry with them certain expectations that people have about what "that sort of person" is like. Contemporary culture in the United States assumes that girls will be more sensitive, nurturing, and caring than boys, and that boys will be more aggressive, outgoing, and athletic than girls. Contemporary U.S. culture also seems to follow the philosophy that "what is beautiful is good." People who are considered good looking tend to be higher paid, get more promotions, receive more lenient treatment if they commit crimes (Dion, Berscheid, & Walster, 1972; Eagly, Ashmore, Makhijani, & Longo, 1991), and generally feel better about themselves because others treat them better (Langlois, 1986). Are assumptions based on physical features necessarily true? Absolutely not. Do these assumptions influence the way people behave and the expectations they have? Absolutely! In order to truly understand the manner in which other people come to view a person the way they do, it is crucial that these immutable characteristics and the expectations that come with them be kept in mind.

The second factor influencing our development of self-images is the *genetic tendencies* we inherit from our parents, such as intelligence, aggressiveness, and temperament. Although there is no guarantee that if a child's parents are highly intelligent then the child will also be smart, it is certainly likely. Tendencies inherited from parents, however, usually are influenced by the environment as well. Parents who are college educated tend to reinforce intellectual pursuits in their children. If those children then score higher on intelligence tests than other children, is that a function of genetics or the environment, of nature or nurture? The answer to the question is "both." Genetic tendencies can be reinforced and strengthened by the environment (the parents encourage reading and doing homework, for example) or subdued by the environment (the parents do not encourage reading or do not provide an intellectually stimulating environment). This illustrates an important point that is relevant to each of the factors discussed in this section. The behavior that people choose to engage in is a product of not only individual characteristics such as intelligence, but also the environment in which the people are interacting. Lewin (1935) called such an idea *field theory*. This theory worked on the assumption that "behavior is a function of the person and the environment." Just knowing a person's characteristics does not allow perfect prediction of their behavior because environmental influences must be taken into account.

The third factor that influences the development of self-images is the *environmental determinants* that impinge on an individual in either a positive or negative way. Factors such as parental socioeconomic status, intellectual stimulation, being located in rural versus urban areas, and attentiveness of parents determine the richness of the environment for the child's developing awareness of self. Impoverished environments put an individual at a two-fold disadvantage. Not only do these elements determine, to a certain extent, the expectations that others will have for an individual (a concept mentioned briefly before), but they also influence the things the individual is encouraged or expected to exert effort on. Children in poor or impoverished environments may not be encouraged to participate in sports, music, or arts because these things do not help to put food on the table, and they can cost money for the individual to participate in. When calculating the cost of their child's participation in these creative pursuits, poor parents also may not see the emotional and self-worth benefits outweighing the monetary cost. This is conjecture, but evidence has been presented in the literature to support the theory that children raised in lower socioeconomic status conditions are not encouraged to succeed academically. This may be due to the fact that different things seem important to the others in the individual's family structure, and these things then become incorporated as important characteristics to self as well (Baumeister, 1990; Harter & Marold, 1991).

Identity negotiation, the fourth factor influencing the development of self-images, centers on the assumption that at some point all individuals will realize that they cannot be all things to all people. Adolescence has often been described as a time of "storm and stress" (Hall, 1904; Rutter, 1980). But why is this the case? The process of identity negotiation that adolescents go through can be traumatic because they are trying to establish self-concept by articulating who or what they think they are. This is compounded by the fact that the adolescent is not the only one who stakes a claim to this negotiation process.

Parents, peers, teachers, television, and society all exert an influence on this negotiation process by demanding that the individual be a certain kind of person, and the characteristics that are important to significant others become important to self as well (Harter & Marold, 1991). It is entirely possible (if not highly probable) that these multiple demands will be in conflict with each other at some level. It becomes the adolescent's burden, therefore, to attempt to reconcile these conflicts and develop an integrated self-concept that everyone can live with.

The Stress of Identity Negotiation

Identity negotiation is, by its very nature, a stressful process. Society may demand that we fulfill expectations that are so incompatible as to be impossible to co-satisfy. Two conflicting and mutually exclusive demands that society places on individuals are (1) "You must be unique" and (2) "Don't you dare be different." It is easy to see that satisfaction of one of these demands automatically precludes the satisfaction of the other. Society, parents, and peers, however, continue to push for both demands to be adhered to and fulfilled. Is it any wonder, then, that adolescents flounder through the teen years, struggling for self identification? If the storm and stress of adolescence is to be reduced, this conflict of demands must first be reconciled. The real problem is that the people placing these antagonizing expectations on the individual are completely unaware of the fact that they're doing just that.

Even if the individual survives adolescence with a fairly well-articulated sense of self-image intact, the development of self-concept is not complete. It is one thing to have a sense of one's own "self" and quite another to convince others to view that "self" in a similar manner. The attempt to weigh the feedback being directed toward self by others and convey that sense of self to others is called *self-understanding*. This fifth factor in the development of self-images is used by the individual in an effort to further refine a definition for self. When attempting to come to self-understanding, individuals must consider and weigh the feedback being received from others, decide toward whom they should be directing their self-comparisons, and struggle to reach some internal consensus about who they believe they are. This is the culminating step in the initial articulation of a self-concept. When individuals have integrated each of these factors into their working theory of "self," we can say that self-concept is in place. It is extremely important to keep in mind that individuals may not finish this process with a self-concept that is positive. If one aspect of this self-understanding process is overemphasized at the expense of the others, then the self-concept that emerges from this process will be imperfect.

Other attempts have been made to clarify the dimensions important to the development of self. The bulk of the literature appears to focus on those aspects of self compatible with what James (1910) called the "me" dimensions, whereas little attention appears to have been focused on the "I" dimensions of self (e.g., Damon & Hart, 1986; Jensen, Huber, Cundick, & Carlson, 1991). To rectify this apparent paucity of research directed toward the "I," Jensen, Huber, Cundick, and Carlson (1991) propose a hierarchical arrangement of dimensions of self. According to these theorists, self consists of twelve dimensions, including self-esteem, positive self-regard, moral self-concept, self-confidence, self-reliance, self-control, selfishness, self-disclosure, self-as-agent, self-critical, self-identity, and self-reflection (Jensen, Huber, Cundick, & Carlson, 1991, p. 521).

The self-development hierarchy is similar in some respects to Maslow's (1970) Needs Hierarchy but is more expansive. Jensen, Huber, Cundick, and Carlson (1991) state that "according to developmental self-theory, the optimal sequence of personality development is based on stages of self-development" (Jensen et. al., 1991, p. 524). In line with this theory then, self as a global entity can only be understood if the stages of development and the components of self being acquired at each stage are also articulated and understood. This theory also assumes that there is no awareness of self in children younger than one year of age. Once self-awareness is present, however, the theory is not age specific. Three variables are important in the development of self along this hierarchy. First, self-esteem develops and is influenced by different things depending on the stage of self-development the individual is in. Second, the individual will move from external sources of reinforcement to internal sources. Third, there will be some parallel between where the individual is on this hierarchy and his or her level of cognitive reasoning.

As can be seen in Figure 1.2, what emerges from self-development theory is a fairly comprehensive view of the individual's developing sense of self. Once self awareness has been initiated, self-esteem develops next. In tier one, self-esteem is accompanied by positive or negative feelings and is in some ways forced upon the individual by the way he or she is treated during the second and third years of life. According to Jensen, Huber, Cundick, and Carlson (1991), positive feelings about self come mostly from affection and touching. It should be apparent that the self-esteem that develops from such physical contact will be mostly affective in nature. After the development of self-esteem comes the development of self-concept. These authors state that self-concept develops from positive feedback that is more cognitive in nature. Information about "one's body, performance, and other attributes" lends to the development of positive self-concept. From the feedback received from significant others, then, the individual begins to formulate impressions and thoughts about self.

The second tier of the pyramid involves issues of competency and begins with acquisition of self-control. A sense of self-control begins during the preschool years but continues throughout the lifespan. Jensen, Huber, Cundick, and Carlson (1991) suggest that self-control is a necessary precursor for self-confidence, and that self-confidence is analogous to self-efficacy as defined by Bandura (1986). Until the child has entered the formal operations stage of Piaget's Cognitive Theory (1954), he or she will not be ready for the more abstract and complicated self processes of tier two. These processes, called self-reflection and self-identity, require the employment of abstract thinking. In order for the individual to develop a composite summary of his or her behaviors and personality (self-identity), self must be abstractly analyzed across time (self-reflection). At the end of tier two, the individual has developed a fairly complex cognitive model of self and an awareness of his or her competencies.

The final tier begins with identification with others. This identification leads to a sort of empathic concern for others that fosters unselfishness, a moral self, and self-integrity. At the same time that the individual is progressing from more egocentric concerns with self to empathic concern for others, he or she is also moving away from concerns for extrinsic forms of reinforcement to ones that are more internal. With age, then, the individual becomes more concerned with others as well as less driven by physical and pleasure based forms of reinforcement. Jensen, Huber, Cundick, and Carlson (1991) suggest that the self-developmental theory is neither presented as a fully developed theory nor assumed to be fully test-

FIGURE 1.2   Self-Development Theory

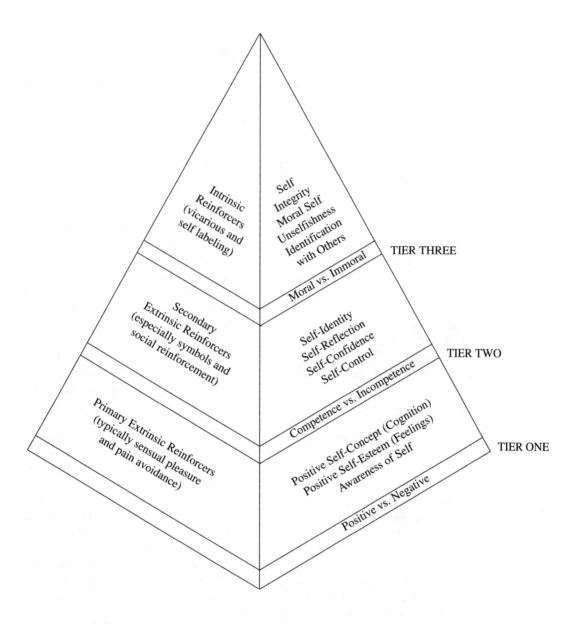

ed. It does, however, seem to move the literature toward a more eclectic approach to self by combining successful aspects of Damon and Hart's (1982) integrative self model, Loevinger's (1976) ego development theory, and Maslow's (1986) needs theory.

Three areas, however, seem to be overlooked within the framework of this original theory. First, its authors spend no time discussing the impact of infant-parental (caregiver) inter-

actions during the first year of life (Tomasello, 1993). Even if it is accepted that self-awareness is not intact until the end of the first year of life, certainly it is developing through significant interactions within that first year. Second, no attention is focused on the perpetuating or cyclical nature of self. A readily accepted consensus in the self literature is that self
and self-schemas, once in place, are used by the individual to create actively, organize, and
interpret experiences (e.g., Markus, 1990). Third, little attention is focused on how low self-
esteem or negative self-concept might develop or what the implications of development in
this fashion would be. The second area of concern will be addressed in the proceeding segment of this chapter; the third concern will be addressed in depth in Chapter Thirteen.

THE CYCLICAL NATURE OF SELF-CONCEPT
DEVELOPMENT

As can be deduced from looking at Figure 1.1, any imperfections in the self-concept may
be perpetuated or even exacerbated by the cyclical nature of the self system (Bandura, 1982;
Lewis, 1979, 1992; Markus, 1990; Osborne, 1993a, 1993b, 1993c). The assumptions that
an individual makes about his own self-concept can directly impact the manner in which
he is perceived by others. If, for example, he has decided that he is smart, he may spend a
lot of time reading books, join intellectual clubs in school, go out for the debate team, and
strive very hard to achieve good grades. How will this person be perceived by others? He
will be seen as smart because he is doing all of the things that individuals assume smart people do. But what if this person decided that he was stupid? The very nature of self-expectations suggests that he will put forth little effort in his classes, avoid scholarly clubs and
organizations, make public displays to announce his lack of interest in intellectual pursuits,
and generally find methods by which he tells one and all that brains don't matter to him.
Others in his social environment who witness these behaviors will readily accept these displays as evidence for his lack of intellect.

This illustrates a fundamental point that will surface several times throughout this text.
Individuals are driven by what is known as a *self-fulfilling prophecy*. This is defined as "the
process by which a perceiver's expectations about a person eventually lead that person to
behave in ways that confirm those expectations" (Merton, 1948; Rosenthal & Jacobson,
1968). In a classic application of the self-fulfilling prophecy, *Pygmalion in the Classroom*,
Rosenthal and Jacobson (1968) wondered if teacher expectations influenced student performance. To test this, the researchers told teachers that certain students (actually students
were randomly assigned to the experimental or control groups) were on the verge of "an
intellectual growth spurt." Eight months after this manipulation was introduced, all students
were given an IQ test. Students in the experimental condition (intellectual growth spurt)
scored as much as 30 points higher than control-group students on the IQ test and were evaluated more favorably by their classroom teacher.

Although the term "self-fulfilling prophecy" often is used to refer to how perceivers'
expectations influence their perceptions of the target toward whom they hold those expectations, a similar process also seems to work in relation to the way a person sees herself
(Schlenker & Trudeau, 1990). If an individual assumes that she is unintelligent, she is likely to engage in behaviors that seem unintelligent (e.g., Harter, 1986, 1988; Higgins, 1987;

Weiner, 1985). She may not study hard because she figures, "What's the use?" Then, due to lack of studying, she receives low grades. These low grades are then used to support the original expectation: "See, I knew I was stupid."

In order to fully understand how a self-fulfilling prophecy works, it might be helpful to view self-fulfilling prophecies as a three-step process (Harris & Rosenthal, 1985). Although intuitively this process will make sense, it is easy to take the steps for granted if they are not clearly spelled out. Individuals translate their expectations into confirming behaviors through the following steps:

1. The perceiver has expectations of the target.
2. Based on these expectations, the perceiver behaves in a manner that is consistent with those expectations.
3. The target unknowingly adjusts his or her behavior in line with the perceiver's actions.

These confirming actions then serve as further evidence for the perceivers that they were accurate in their expectations for the target people. This further motivates perceivers to act in a manner consistent with those expectations. Further behavioral adjustments will be made by the perceivers, and the process continues to cycle. The targets then look to their own behavior and decide, "Since I'm acting this way, I must be this way." (This last point is one example of how information is gathered about self and will be discussed in further detail in Chapter Four.)

Other terms have been used to suggest a similar process, but few of these terms explicitly state that these processes also can influence the way individuals will perceive their own behavior. *Confirmation bias* is defined as "the tendency to interpret, seek, and create information in ways that verify existing beliefs" (Brehm & Kassin, 1993). It is crucial that we understand that these beliefs that drive the confirmation bias process can be beliefs that are directed specifically toward self. The issue of seeking self-consistent information will become vitally important in the next chapter as we discuss the developmental process of self-esteem.

The concept of confirming self-expectations reconfirms an idea that has already been briefly discussed. In the Preface, it was argued that self is a "defensive" structure. This means that self is created in such a way as to perpetuate itself. Self-concept works much the same way. The question that must be addressed in order to understand this self-perpetuating tendency is "Why would such a process take place?" At first glance, it would seem to be significantly more likely that people would try to seek out as much diverse information about self as possible in order to be more accurate in their self-definitions. This, however, is not the case. Human beings are highly motivated to maintain consistent self-evaluations (Tesser, 1988; Tesser & Cornell, 1991). Having our sense of self-security called into question by inconsistent feedback from others is uncomfortable (e.g., Shrauger, 1975; Swann, Griffin, Predmore, & Gaines, 1987). In order to minimize the extent to which disconfirming information is directed toward self, we actively engage in behaviors that are designed to signal clearly to one and all how we would like to be perceived.

This need to be perceived consistently creates a unique bind for self-concept development. Not only does it strongly influence the behavioral repertoire that the person depends on in social situations, but it also makes it very difficult for more accurate information to be accepted by the person or inaccurate information to be rejected (e.g., Osborne, 1993a, 1993b, 1993c; Peterson & Seligman, 1987; Tennen, Herzberger, & Nelson, 1987). If an individual believes that she is overweight, she will perceive and process information about her physical appearance in a drastically different way than if she believes that she is thin. Once an individual has decided where she falls on a particular dimension (such as physical appearance), the processes that are designed to make the self consistent and predictable are initiated, and these processes promote continuing efforts to maintain current self-conceptions (e.g., Greenwald, 1980).

THE POWER OF SELF-IMAGES

This last point leads directly into the next aspect of the self-concept development process outlined by Figure 1.1. Once an individual has a self-concept in place, he or she has a repertoire of self-images that can be salient in any given situation. A self-image is "a role that an individual tries on and negotiates in order to determine that role's appropriateness as a part of the self-concept." The self-image that is activated or being called for in a certain situation influences the behaviors that the person may choose to use. A student may act very differently when sitting in a classroom than sitting at home with her husband and children. The behaviors a person chooses to engage in are usually those behaviors that prior experience has taught the person are expected in that situation or environment. But no one behaves in a vacuum. Whenever a person engages in behavior, someone in the environment will provide feedback about how that behavior is being perceived. If no one else is present in the situation, the feedback may come from within in the form of self-praise or self-deprecation. The major problem with feedback isn't necessarily the information itself. After performance feedback is received, individuals invariably interpret that feedback based on what they think the information tells them about self.

Self-images are not necessarily static elements of the self-concept (Schlenker & Trudeau, 1990). An individual may have an image of himself as a pizza maker while he works for a local pizza place. This image is important as long as he intends to hold down that job. Once a decision has been made to move onto something else (like college or a position in management), the image of self as a pizza maker is no longer important or relevant. If, however, that image is threatened by something outside the person (a layoff or a threat of being fired), suddenly that self-image takes on magnified importance. The self-concept must allow enough flexibility that self-images can be added, taken away, strengthened, or weakened as they become more or less relevant to one's life. The interpretive process outlined in the previous paragraph is an important part of the process by which the self-concept is continually refined according to the changing nature of the self-images that are presently relevant in the individual's life.

This interpretive process, which will be explained in significantly more detail in Chapter Two, culminates with a feeling of self-worth that cycles back onto self-images and causes further clarification of the self-concept. This continuous cycling of the self-concept process allows for significant revision of the self system if new information can be inserted into the cycle. As already mentioned, however, the system is designed in such a way as to make inserting new, perhaps more accurate, information highly problematic. *Belief perseverance* is a powerful force that takes on a life of its own once an individual has reached some conclusion about self or others. Scores of experiments point to the strength of belief perseverance in the face of what seems to the detached outsider to be evidence that should clearly discredit the belief (Anderson, Lepper, & Ross, 1980). One classic demonstration of the power of belief perseverance was conducted by Darley and Gross (1983). In this study, subjects were asked to evaluate a nine-year-old girl in terms of her academic potential. Darley and Gross then simply manipulated whether subjects believed that Hannah came from an upper-middle-class environment or a lower-class environment. As predicted, the results confirmed the expectations. Those subjects who believed that Hannah was from the upper-middle-class environment were more optimistic in their expectations for her academic potential than those subjects led to believe that Hannah came from lower-class origins.

How is it that expectations and beliefs perpetuate themselves? If individuals are asked "Why did you do that?" they may not have a well-articulated answer, but they probably very quickly will come up with an answer. Individuals want to know the motivations behind their own behaviors and the choices they make, so they are continuously asking themselves why they're doing what they're doing. Once this answer or belief has been articulated, a person becomes motivated to remain consistent to such a belief (in a manner that we have already touched on) due to the need to have self be predictable, stable, and consistent. Snyder and Swann (1978) provided evidence to support the idea that individuals not only remain true to beliefs in the face of clearly discrepant evidence, but that they also purposely may seek out information that is designed to confirm the suspicions or beliefs they already hold. These two situations are not exactly the same. It is one thing to ignore or minimize information that is inconsistent with my expectations and beliefs and another thing to actively seek information to convince myself that my beliefs are just and wise. This process of seeking out information designed to confirm existing expectations may have a significant impact on self-esteem, and this connection will be addressed in detail in Chapter Two of this text (Swann, 1985; Backman, 1988; Tice, 1993).

INTERPRETING SELF FEEDBACK

The final step in the self-concept development process is an analysis of the feedback one has received and a possible revision of the self-image that motivated the behavior that has just been evaluated. Once individuals have gathered feedback about their self-image, that feedback is used to assess the extent to which the self-image should continue to be a part of the self-concept. If a person decided that he was a tennis player, engaged in tennis playing with his two-year-old son, and lost, he probably would decide that tennis player is not a particularly good self-image. An individual's assessment as to whether the feedback received about a self-image indicates that the self-image is "good-me," "bad-me," or "not-me" helps to determine if that self-image will be further incorporated into the self-concept or expunged from it (Markus, 1990). If it is decided that the self-image should not be a part of self-concept or is a "bad" part of it, then the effect that the self-image has on self-concept and self-esteem is dramatically different than if the feedback suggests that the self-image is a "good" part of self-concept. Just as a person may try on different hats, individuals try on different images in their attempts to articulate their selves.

A REVISED DEFINITION OF SELF-CONCEPT

Looking back to the accepted definition of self-concept presented in the early pages of this text, we may see an apparent paradox. The reader will recall that self-concept is defined as "the sum total of the attributes, abilities, attitudes, and values that an individual believes defines who he or she is." But an understanding of the cycle by which self-images drive behavior, behavior generates feedback, and feedback initiates self-image revision strongly suggests that self-concept is much more complex and dynamic than this definition suggests. If the self-images that make up the self-concept include those things that an individual thinks she is good at, the things that she feels she is bad at, and the things that she believes do not represent who she is, then a working definition of self-concept must incorporate those differences as well. Likewise, the revised definition of self-concept must include the dynamic or ever-changing nature of this construct.

The following definition of self-concept, therefore, will be used for the remainder of this text. Self-concept represents a "relatively stable but flexible integration of self-images that articulate who individuals believe they are and who they believe they are not." This change in definition may seem minor but it is crucial for establishing the separation between self-concept and self. When individuals refer to "self," the assumption is that they are referring to the core of what makes them the individuals they happen to be. The self is a compilation of the factors outlined in Figure 1.1. But self is not completely static either. Although certainly self is much less open to change than self-images or the self-concept, it is necessary that there be a process through which an individual can engage in self-alteration. Perhaps the easiest way to envision self-change taking place is through the same cycle diagrammed in Figure 1.1. If this is the very process that has creation of self as the eventual outcome, then it must also be through this same process that changes to the core (self) of the individual would take place. This same point, which applies to self-esteem enhancement, will be introduced in Chapter Two and discussed in detail in Chapter Thirteen.

ALTERING THE SELF-CONCEPT

It seems paradoxical that while self literature is filled with information on self-concept development, little effort is paid to self-concept alteration. If it is the case that self-concept is created through a developmental sequence, then change should also be possible through the same sequence of events. Many developmental psychologists believe that children develop through certain phases, stages, or themes (e.g., Bruner, 1964; Erikson, 1963; Piaget, 1959). These same psychologists also believe that one is not necessarily doomed to be a victim of one's background. If this is the case, then it must be possible for individuals to go back and, in some fashion, correct some of the mistakes that were made earlier on in their development. If self is created through a developmental sequence, then shouldn't the same kind of retroactive change be possible? Although this kind of question should more obviously be asked in the next chapter as discussion focuses on self-esteem development and enhancement, the issue is relevant in discussions of self-concept for a very good reason. Self-esteem level is, in part, a direct consequence of the developmental sequence that leads to self-concept (e.g., Neisser, 1992). As such, if self-esteem deficits are to be avoided or corrected, it must be by virtue of redirecting the self-concept developmental process.

A working theory of self-concept as described in this chapter provides the reader with the information that is needed to understand the sequence of events involved in the initial development of self-concept and the early stages of self-esteem. Although this suggests that self-concept and self-esteem are dependent upon one another, they are not parallel processes. An understanding of this point depends on one's ability to understand that setbacks to one's self-concept do not automatically create deficits in self-esteem. How is it that some individuals can have the worst that society could possibly offer dumped into their laps, yet they manage to keep their chins up and keep trudging on? Why is it that others seem to take the slightest self-concept or self-esteem setback and blow it so far out of proportion that it seems that they will self-destruct? The answers to these questions seem very elusive unless one keeps in mind that self-concept influences self-esteem but does not in and of itself create it. As the next chapter will clarify, self-esteem development and enhancement depend not only on the individual's conception of self, but also on a variety of external forces over which the individual may not always be able to exert complete control.

WRAPPING IT UP: WHAT DOES ALL THIS MEAN?

This chapter has presented a broad theory of self-concept development that begins to show the connections between a variety of constructs. An understanding of the global structure and implications of self will come only as the component parts of the self-development process are understood. Questions about how children come to form a sense of self or self-esteem and how transient self-images get integrated into the more enduring structure called self-concept have now been addressed. You, the reader, should now have a more comprehensive understanding of the cyclical nature of self-concept development and have a basic understanding of how this cycle relates to the next topic: self-esteem. Many terms have been presented and defined, and it is easy to fall victim to the similarities between them. But "self" oriented terms have been used without restriction for so long now that the literature is overflowing with self-related adjectives. Such a preponderance of self-related concepts makes finding common ground among the theories difficult at best. The terminology and definitions presented in this chapter are to be used to focus one's understanding of the self process as well as provide a frame of reference for understanding other self-related theories or terms.

The terms self-image, self-concept, self, self-esteem, self-worth, self-regard, self-views, and others have all been used. The terminology can be narrowed down to four vitally important terms that must be understood in order for us truly to say that we understand "self." First, it is important to differentiate between the more restrictive term "self-concept" and the more encompassing term "self." The definitions used in the chapter provide the foundation on which the eclectic theory of self will be built. Second, one must understand the importance of self-images and the roles that these images of self play in the self-concept development process. The description of self-images presented in this chapter, in combination with Figure 1.1, delineates a process through which various self-images are tried on, refined, or discarded in order to continuously refine self-concept. Third, it is crucial to distinguish between self-esteem as a temporary feeling and self-esteem as a motivator of the individual's behavior. Individuals can feel negative about aspects of self without truly suffering from low self-esteem (e.g., Showers, 1989). Likewise, individuals can have only one or two aspects of self that are not as positive as they would like, yet self-esteem can be devastated. This suggests that understanding the self-concept development process will not completely answer all the questions about self-esteem that need to be addressed. Fourth, the reader must understand that traditional views of self-concept may be too restrictive. Even feelings that individuals have about things they are bad at, or that they feel could never be a part of who they are, help to delineate self-concept and lend clarity to the definition of who they think they are (Markus, 1990).

A successful integration of the self literature into what can reasonably be called an eclectic approach requires a thorough understanding of the implications of the self-concept development process. Figure 1.1 provides a schematic representation of the components involved in the developmental sequence that leads to self-concept. It is worth repeating that self-concept is not a static construct. "Static" is used to refer to something that is "not moving or changing." Although most theorists do not explicitly present self-concept as something that does not change, little emphasis is placed on explaining the dynamic nature of the self-system. There certainly are exceptions to this (Self-Perception Theory and Social Comparison Theory are perhaps the best examples of exceptions). Many theories imply a static nature to self-concept development, whereas some theories imply that self-concept is dynamic (e.g., Wylie, 1974; Markus & Wurf, 1987). If an eclectic approach to self is possible, it will only be discovered by exploring the dynamic nature of self-concept and the multiple factors that influence the individual each step of the way.

All in all, the development of self begins as infants experience situations in the environment that signal they are separate from other things within that environment. From the moment children first reach for the mobile hanging above the crib and cause something to move, they are building an awareness of "individuality." Parents can watch as their children engage in activities and movements to see what will happen. As children gain confidence in their ability to successfully make things happen, further and further exploration of the environment will take place. But it is very important for an understanding of self-concept to keep in mind that children's explorations and the reactions that those explorations elicit from others provide them with direct information about their "self" (e.g., Tomasello, 1993). If children continuously struggle to make something happen and these efforts continue to be thwarted, it is likely they will decide at some point that they are incapable of completing the task. If, however, the efforts to engage in behaviors are rewarded (either by successful completion of the desired task or positive feedback from others), they will come to see themselves as industrious. This feeling of competency serves as a catalyst to motivate future behaviors and provides the initial feelings of self-esteem that further influence the cyclical nature of self-concept. In this cyclical way, self-concept and self-images lead directly to a discussion of self-esteem.

CHAPTER TWO

Self-Esteem Development

BACKGROUND INFORMATION

Any discussion of self-esteem invariably will center around the ramifications of low self-esteem. The reader, however, should keep in mind that self-esteem is not something that you either have or you do not. Individuals differ both in quantity and quality of self-esteem. Whereas some individuals seem to have self-esteem to spare, others seem vulnerable to the slightest challenge to their feelings of self-worth. Individuals also differ on the extent to which self-esteem is positively or negatively charged. Individuals who suffer from low self-esteem are assumed to have a self-defeating attitude that can perpetuate the feelings of low self-worth (Brockner, 1983). In contrast to the relatively rational, cognitive nature of self-concept, self-esteem is more emotionally charged. The construct of self-esteem involves the emotional attachments an individual has to self as a whole, as well as the feelings that come from positive and negative evaluations of those images.

But self-esteem, like self-concept, often serves as its own defensive structure. Several recent lines of research have addressed the issue of self-esteem level as a perpetuating cycle (Tesser & Cornell, 1991; Spencer & Steele, 1992; Osborne & Stites, 1994), and the implications that such incessant cycling has for "self" as a global construct must be addressed. As this chapter unfolds, the reader will be reminded of information presented in Chapter One that relates directly to the issue of self-esteem. Likewise, when appropriate, the reader will be informed of information covered in later chapters that will illuminate the integrative nature of this text. Self-esteem development and enhancement cannot be understood without keeping the developmental sequence of self-concept in mind (e.g., Tomasello, 1993). Similarly, self-esteem cannot be fully understood without understanding the implications that feelings of self-worth have on the eclectic nature of self. Self-concept and self-esteem are related constructs that mutually influence each other. They are not, however, two sides of the same coin. There is little disagreement that self-esteem is a central and important aspect of self-concept (Greenwald, Bellezza, & Banaji, 1988), but as self-concept has a unique set of factors and circumstances influencing its development, so, too, does self-esteem. The similarities between the developmental sequences cannot be ignored but, as the reader will soon discover, neither should their important differences be left unexplored.

Susan Harter (1993) perhaps summarized the current need in the self-esteem literature best when she asked "why should we be concerned about self-esteem unless we can demonstrate that it plays a role in individuals' lives—unless we can demonstrate that it performs critical, motivational functions?" This question is the driving force behind this chapter. Research has drawn a fairly powerful connection between self-esteem and cognitive components of the self (e.g., Abramson, Seligman, & Teasdale, 1986; Baumeister, 1990). Certainly an illumination of this connection is critical because of the important role that cognition plays in determining behavior and guiding interpretations of feedback. Before moving to a discussion of these cognitive connections, however, it would be wise to take a moment and consider how to define this entity called "self-esteem."

DEFINING SELF-ESTEEM

Our understanding of self-esteem would be imperfect, at best, if our discussion did not also consider the implications of low self-esteem. The definition of self-esteem that one chooses to use will have a profound impact on the kind of research on self-esteem that will be done. Despite the fact that self-esteem is a critical component of self-concept and self-concept research, there is considerable disagreement about how this concept should be defined. Each definition incorporates information about the affective nature of self-esteem, but differences emerge beyond this point. Osborne (1993b) defined self-esteem as "a relatively permanent positive or negative feeling about self that may become more or less positive or negative as individuals encounter and interpret successes and failures in their daily lives." A well-known social psychology text defines self-esteem as "an affective component of the self, consisting of a person's positive and negative self-evaluations" (Brehm & Kassin, 1993). Harter (1985a) has defined self-esteem as "the level of global regard that one has for the self as a person." Finally, Campbell and Lavallee (1993) define self-esteem as "a self-reflexive attitude that is the product of viewing the self as an object of evaluation." Certainly, all four of these definitions seem reasonable, and any one of them would probably serve the purposes of this text. If self-esteem, however, has implications for the global construct of self that this eclectic approach seeks to find, then the definition of self-esteem that is used gains even greater importance.

For the purposes of this text, it would seem appropriate to use a self-esteem definition that is eclectic in perspective. On the basis of this criterion, Osborne's definition would seem best suited. Several aspects of this definition are important for a discussion of self-esteem. First, of the definitions presented, Osborne's allows for periodic review or revision of self-esteem in the face of new information. Although it has already been argued that self-esteem is designed as a self-perpetuating structure, that does not mean that self-esteem revision is impossible. It is simply difficult. Second, Osborne's definition of self-esteem makes the assumption that self-esteem can fluctuate (within reason) based on the daily successes and failures that one encounters. Self-esteem may not be one global entity but a combination of situational feelings toward self and a conglomerate of self-feelings based on prior experiences and expectations for future performance. The possibility that self-esteem can fluctuate has only recently made its way into the self-esteem literature (e.g., Harter, 1986; Kernis, Cornell, Sun, Berry, & Harlow, 1993; Rosenberg, 1986).

As Kernis et al. (1993) suggest, the stability of self-esteem (sometimes referred to as self-esteem certainty by Osborne, 1993a, 1993b, 1993c) influences cognitive and emotional reactions following feedback. Kernis et al. (1993) suggest that "The hallmark of stable low self-esteem is a chronic dislike for oneself." Although this seems quite pessimistic, the literature supports such a contention (e.g., Kernis, Granneman, & Mathis, 1991). One therefore would expect more attempts to self-protect by the individual with low self-esteem that is unstable than from the individual with low self-esteem that is stable. In the latter case, the individual may be so certain that self is worthless that there is little reason to put forth the effort that self-protection requires. Third, this definition of self-esteem suggests that it isn't just success or failure that determines self-esteem; the manner in which the individual interprets these events matters. Thus, for the purposes of this text, an eclectic approach to self-esteem assumes that: (1) self-esteem revision is possible, (2) self-esteem is a multifaceted construct, (3) self-esteem is a relatively enduring self feeling that nonetheless can fluctuate depending upon situational and individual characteristics, and (4) an individual's interpretations of success and failure play a key role in determining the impact those events will have on self-esteem.

COGNITIVE CONNECTIONS TO AND IMPLICATIONS FOR SELF

BEHAVIORAL CHOICES AND HOW THEY AFFECT SELF-ESTEEM

There is no doubt that the behaviors one chooses to engage in within a given situation directly influence the feedback or reactions one will receive from others in that same situation. But what determines the behavioral choices that a person will make? The answer to this question is directly related to one of the connections between self-concept and self-esteem. Self-concept and self-images can determine the behavioral choices that one makes, but the reaction of others and the impact these reactions have on self-esteem can influence whether that behavioral choice will be made again (McKay & Fanning, 1987; Osborne, 1993a). When an individual enters a situation, certain behaviors may be called for. The extent to which the person chooses to engage in particular behaviors within that situation depends on three factors: situational demand, characteristic certainty, and characteristic importance (e.g., Harter, 1986; James, 1892; Pelham, 1991a). The choices that one makes about how to proceed in a given situation are related to the self-image that is salient (activated) within that situation (Fazio, Effrein, & Falender, 1981). What determines the self-image that will be activated in a given situation? Figure 2.1 illustrates a triangular theory of self-concept

FIGURE 2.1 Triangular Theory of Self-Concept Salience

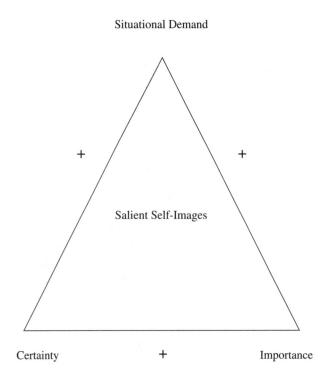

Situational Demand

Salient Self-Images

Certainty   +   Importance

Note: Understanding the images of self that are salient at any given
moment depends upon the integration of situational demands (and the
characteristics that are being primed by that situation), the importance
of that characteristic to the person (or his/her significant others), and the
certainty of the individual about his or her ability to use the called-for
characteristic to satisfy the situational demand.

salience. This theory suggests that three dimensions work in unison to determine the features of self-concept that will be salient in a given situation (partially suggested by James,
1892, and adapted from Pelham, 1991a). Whether these dimensions are present, then, determines whether the individual will choose to behave in a particular way and the impact that
feedback about those behaviors will have on self-esteem.

This triangular theory suggests that the combination of situational demand, importance,
and certainty determines the behavioral choices that individuals will make and the ramifi-

cations for those choices on self-esteem. This theory suggests that the individual must consider and answer the following three questions before making a behavioral choice:

1. What is the situation demanding that I do?
2. How important is this attribute or situation to me?
3. How certain am I of my abilities on the skill that is being called for in the situation and how certain am I of my level of commitment to this situation?

The answers to the above questions significantly impact the aspects of self that will be salient in a given situation and the extent to which the behaviors one chooses to engage in within that situation affect feelings of self-esteem. If the situation is demanding that someone be dishonest, he or she must assess the importance of that dimension to self and the importance of success in this situation to gauge whether or not to enact that behavior. The individual's self-esteem, then, will not usually be affected adversely when the attribute or situation in question is deemed unimportant by the individual (e.g., James, 1892; Harter, 1993a). But importance alone does not determine whether the individual will choose to engage in those behaviors. The extent to which the individual feels competent of his or her ability on the attribute being demanded by the situation or the extent to which the individual is certain that engaging in the behavior is a good idea also affects this process. Harter (1990a) reported robust findings supporting the contention that one factor is the discrepancy between how important the individual judges a domain-specific attribute to be and his or her feelings of competency on that attribute.

Zumpf and Harter (1989) asked adolescents to judge whether one's self-evaluation of appearance determines self-esteem or if self-esteem determines one's self-evaluation of appearance. The answers formed two disparate groups, one endorsing each of the causal options. Although this divergence in causal assumptions is not surprising, the implications of such assumptions may be quite important. Zumpf and Harter (1989) also report that those adolescents who assume that self-evaluation of appearance determines self-esteem feel worse about their appearance, are affectively more depressed, and exhibit lower self-esteem than those adolescents who assume that self-esteem level determines one's self-evaluations of appearance. As already suggested in what Harter (1993a) calls the Jamesian model, self-evaluations in domains the individual has deemed to be important will impact self-esteem. The major qualifier to this, however, is a reminder that this impact is not always positive.

Baumgardner (1990) suggested that low self-esteem individuals are less certain about which characteristics do or do not describe them. It is reasonable to assume, therefore, that this lack of certainty could dramatically influence the behavioral choices that the individual makes. These two lines of research suggest that certainty and importance of domain-specific attributes for the individual can exact quite a toll on self-esteem when there is a large discrepancy between them (Baumgardner, 1990; Harter, 1990a). When all three of these factors are known, then and only then is it possible to predict with a relative degree of certainty what behaviors the person will choose to engage in. When the behavioral choices the individual is making are known, the potential impact those behavioral choices will have for self-esteem can also be understood.

The implications of the integration between situational demand, importance, and certainty should be fairly apparent by this point. The individual weighs the costs and benefits of engaging in particular behaviors in particular situations. But the cost-benefit analysis does not stop at this point. Once a behavioral choice has been made, the individual is committed to that behavior. If the feedback that is received from others about that behavior is positive or the individual engages in self-evaluation and decides that the behavior was positive, then the individual may further integrate that attribute into his or her self-concept and may receive positive self-esteem value from it. If, however, the feedback that is received or evaluated by self is negative, the detrimental impact on self-concept and self-esteem can be dramatic. An understanding of the process by which individuals receive and incorporate this feedback into refining self-concept and self-esteem is critical for a comprehensive understanding of self. One cannot truly understand the self-esteem development process without first understanding the following simple but often overlooked fact: It isn't how an observer interprets the situational feedback someone receives that matters; it is how the individual who performed the behavior interprets that situational feedback that determines the eventual impact that behavior will have on self-esteem.

This means that individuals can interpret situational feedback in ways that may seem inappropriate to the observer. Individuals usually will make attributions for their successes that allow them to internalize them, and will make attributions for failures that allow them to be externalized (e.g., Zuckerman, 1979). But such is not always the case. A tennis player may win a match but stalk off the court as if she lost. To the non-emotionally attached observer, the long face and drooping shoulders of the player may seem inconsistent with our knowledge that she won the tennis match. But the player may be upset by her performance because it didn't live up to some set of expectations that only she would be aware of. In order to understand how this "success" will impact her self-esteem, then, the observer would need to understand the levels on which she is interpreting that "success."

In other words, a success is only a success if the person who engaged in the behavior and received the feedback felt that it was successful. It was mentioned earlier in this text that self-esteem is a defensive structure. Just like self-concept, self-esteem is designed in such a way as to perpetuate itself. Such a point has been made many times by therapists and counselors trying to break the cycle of low self-esteem in their clients. Horney (1950) called such a pattern the "Tyranny of the Shoulds," and McKay and Fanning (1987) refer to the "pathological critic," or "an arsenal of shoulds." This is a very important point because it can help to explain the patterns of interpretations of feedback that individuals may be using and, therefore, may explain how to break patterns of inappropriate interpretations for success and failure feedback.

LEVELS OF INTERPRETATION FOR SUCCESS AND FAILURE

As already shown in Figure 1.1, feedback from others can be interpreted on three levels (adapted from Abramson, Seligman, & Teasdale, 1986; Weiner, 1986). In the original model of "learned helplessness" (generally defined as occurring when prior experience with an uncontrollable event causes the person to feel helpless about and passive toward future threats to well-being), it was suggested that depression could result from exposure to uncontrollable events (Hiroto, 1974; Seligman, 1975; Seligman & Maier, 1967). In a sophisticated reformation of this model, Abramson, Seligman, and Teasdale (1986) concluded it is not just the level of controllability of the event that determines depression but also the attributions the individual makes for such events. Numerous studies on depression show what has come to be known as "depressive attributional style," and this has recently been applied to the manner in which low self-esteem persons interpret feedback (e.g., see Tennen, Herzberger, & Nelson, 1987).

According to these lines of research, three interpretive levels for feedback are used: internal vs. external, temporary vs. stable, global vs. specific. These can create patterns of interpreting feedback that perpetuate the individual's current self-esteem level (e.g., Osborne & Stites, 1994; Tennen, Herzberger, & Nelson, 1987). The first level may be referred to as a locus dimension. With this level of interpretation, the individuals decide whether the feedback they are receiving is because of something internal to their self or something external in the environment. If the individuals receive feedback in the form of an "F" on an exam and that feedback is interpreted internally, then the individuals receiving the "F" are accepting responsibility for it. We can hear this interpretation in the kinds of statements they make about what the grade means. Internal interpretations involve statements like "I got what I deserved" or "I guess I'm just too stupid to understand this." It is obvious that internal interpretations for this kind of failure feedback will have a significant negative impact on self-esteem level. The individuals also may use that information to alter self-concept, perhaps by eliminating "student" as one of the self-images that they had thought described their self.

What happens if individuals, however, interpret that failure feedback externally? In this circumstance, the individuals decide that they received an "F" because "The teacher doesn't like me," "The test was way too hard," or "Someone switched exams with me." These external interpretations for failure will keep the feedback from negatively impacting the individuals' self-esteem. With these kinds of interpretations, individuals create a pattern of attributions for the failure feedback that allow them to reject or minimize responsibility and thereby keep self-esteem level intact.

Success and failure feedback also can be interpreted according to what might be called a time dimension. With this level of interpretation, the individual decides how likely such an event is going to be the next time the same behavior is tried again. The person makes a decision as to whether this event (be it positive or negative) is temporary or stable. If the individual interprets failure feedback as something that was "once in a lifetime" or "a fluke," then this temporary interpretation keeps the failure from impacting significantly on self-esteem. If, however, the individual assumes that the feedback represents something about the behavior that is stable, self-esteem will be significantly affected. Temporary interpretations for failure minimize the negative impact on self-esteem, and stable interpretations for success maximize the positive impact on self-esteem.

Last, the individual interprets the success or failure based on a generalizability dimension. With this level, the person asks questions about how much this feedback tells her about other facets of her life. The questions with this level of interpretation revolve around the significance of the feedback for helping the individual to interpret other facets of self. The emphasis is placed on determining if the feedback should be interpreted in a global or a specific fashion. If she interprets a success as something that is global, then she is likely to experience self-esteem enhancement because it suggests that she can expect that positive outcome to translate into other positive things in her life. But it is just as possible that the individual will decide that the success was something very specific and, therefore, tells her little about future successes. In this fashion, even a success can have very little impact on the positivity of self-esteem.

It should be pointed out that the examples just described do not exhaust the possibilities of how these levels of interpretation can be used by individuals. For each of the levels, interpretations can be made for both successes and failures. An individual can interpret either a success or a failure as being due to either internal or external factors. Likewise, both successes and failures can be interpreted according to temporary or stable causes. And, of course, either success or failure can be generalized in either a global or specific way. Individuals with low and high self-esteem have been found to use differential patterns of interpretation for success and failure according to these three levels. These differences in interpretation can help explain how it is that individuals with high or low self-esteem maintain or perpetuate those levels.

Recent data collected by Osborne and Stites (1994) examine the differences in which success and failure feedback are interpreted based on the individual's self-esteem level. Low self-esteem individuals overwhelmingly interpret success as due to external, temporary, and specific causes. High self-esteem persons, on the other hand, interpret success according to internal, stable, and global causes. Just the opposite, however, is noted for interpretations of failure feedback. Individuals with low self-esteem typically interpret failure feedback according to internal, stable, and global causes, whereas their high self-esteem counterparts interpret the same failure feedback along external, temporary, and specific dimensions. Although the effect that such differential interpretation patterns will have on self-esteem level is obvious, the reasons for such differences may not be so readily apparent.

Why would low self-esteem individuals interpret success feedback in a way that is guaranteed to minimize the positive impact it could have had on self-esteem? Likewise, why would they interpret failure feedback in a way that is destined to impact negatively a self-esteem level that is already low? The answers to these questions seem to revolve around issues of self-protection (e.g., Osborne, 1993b; Swann, 1983; Swann, Stein-Seroussi, & Giesler, 1992) or self-evaluation maintenance (e.g., Tesser, 1988; Tesser & Cornell, 1991).

Research by Tesser (1988) and the resulting self-evaluation maintenance model suggest two antagonistic processes when comparing self to another who is turning in a good performance. If the dimension is highly relevant to the individual's self-definition, then comparison to the good performing other is threatening to self. If, however, the dimension is not particularly self-relevant, self can be augmented by basking in the reflected glory of the other. Tesser and Cornell (1991) make a distinction between self-defense and self-enhancement. Both of these concepts are of critical importance to an eclectic approach to self and will be discussed in depth in Chapter Nine, which focuses on self-enhancement versus self-verification, and Chapter Thirteen, which focuses on self-esteem enhancement. The concept of self-threats and basking in reflected glory will be particularly important in Chapter Six when social comparison processes are discussed.

According to Swann (1983), questions of why individuals seem motivated to verify a self-concept or self-esteem level that seems less than positive to others "all boil down to the same general principle: People seem to possess an inborn preference for things that are predictable, familiar, stable, and uncertainty reducing." This suggests that discrepant feedback strikes the person as disconcerting because it challenges the stable and predictable view of self that he or she was holding onto. These patterns of interpretation of information and feedback perpetuate impressions of self that are already in place. This is quite consistent with Greenwald's (1980) view that self is an "information system" that seeks information that provides a predictable and coherent view of the social world. It seems reasonable to assume, then, that individuals would be highly motivated to engage in self processes including self-deception (as suggested by Gilbert & Cooper, 1985) and self-verification (as suggested by Swann, 1983, and others) that would maximize this predictability.

Swann (1983) goes on to describe the enabling nature of self-verification tendencies. If individuals can seek out and interpret feedback in a manner that perpetuates the impression of self they hold, then "these self-verification processes enable people to create both in their actual social environments and in their own minds—a social reality that verifies and confirms their self-conceptions" (Swann, 1983, p. 34). Recent work by Swann, Stein-Seroussi, and Giesler (1992) further suggests that individuals choose information that is self-verifying with the goal of boosting the feelings of prediction and control they can associate with their self-concept. This suggests that individuals will actively seek out information that confirms self-conceptions. Osborne and Stites (1994), however, suggest that individuals will not only choose confirming feedback, but actively construct such feedback if the reasons for certain behaviors or events seem otherwise ambiguous.

It is difficult to resist the temptation to assume that individuals would always choose to feel better about self if such information were available. Many researchers argue for patterns of "self-enhancement" (Snyder & Higgins, 1988), or "positivity strivings" (Brown, Collins, & Schmidt, 1988; Tesser, 1988). These patterns suggest that individuals are motivated to acquire positive or enhancing information. Although few will argue that this desire to feel better about one's self certainly occurs on occasion, the real question is whether people will prefer to self-verify or self-enhance when both are possible in the same situation. Prior research has argued convincingly that an individual's ability to succeed in social relationships depends upon that individual's ability to recognize how he or she is being perceived by others (e.g., Cooley, 1902; Mead, 1934; Stryker, 1981; Swann, Stein-Seroussi, & Giesler, 1992b). To this end, it is important that individuals be able to acquire feedback that is consistent with their self-conceptions.

If others seem to have views of an individual's self that are at odds with his own, only a few options are available for resolving this discrepancy. First, the person who has received the discrepant feedback could alter his own self-conception to be in line with that feedback. Second, the individual could decide that the person who holds the discrepant view of them is unimportant and should be ignored. Third, the person could attempt to interpret that feedback in a manner that brings it more in line with his self-conception. The key to understanding the impact that discrepant feedback will have on self revolves around asking which of the former methods for resolving the discrepancy is most likely. The answer, for the most part, seems intuitively obvious. Individuals have a strong emotional investment in the conceptions they hold of their selves (Greenwald, 1980). Because of these emotional investments, it is highly unlikely that the individual will reject those prior self-conceptions in the face of discrepant feedback. It is also unlikely that the person will just reject that discrepant information out of hand. If the person providing the feedback holds any importance to the individual being judged, then the feedback being received will be considered important as well. The only method by which individuals can still assign importance to the feedback and keep their self-conception intact is to interpret that feedback in whatever manner is necessary to allow self-concept to remain stable.

The fact that self-conceptions are cognitive representations of self that integrate self-images, prior experiences, and past behaviors also suggests that the self-concept can be used by individuals to predict how other people will respond to them in the future (Swann et al., 1992b). If self-concept represents all that a person has been prior to the present moment, then it is very reasonable for that individual also to believe that others will see him as the same person in future interactions. This expectation of predictability and control not only explains the behavioral choices persons will make, it also explains why individuals will attempt to interpret discrepant feedback in self-consistent ways.

If a person believes that he is a worthless person, he does not want feedback from others designed to convince him that he is great. As counter-intuitive as this may sound, the finding has proven to be quite robust and applies to the type of evaluations the individual will seek (e.g., Swann, Hixon, Stein-Seroussi, & Gilbert, 1990), the interaction partners one may seek (e.g., Swann et al., 1990), and marital commitment (Swann, Hixon, & De La Ronde, 1992). Individuals usually assume that all a low self-esteem person needs is a pat on the back. This is similar to the current ideological war on drugs that chants "Hugs not drugs." Although the sentiment in that slogan is admirable, the idea of such a campaign working to eliminate drug problems is a fairy tale at best. Likewise, one cannot expect to alter permanently an individual's self-esteem level with hugs or words of praise. Self-esteem enhancement will not be successful if the suggested enhancement strategies simply attempt to put bandages on the problem. Just as hugging a child will not cure the problem that led to the drug use in the first place, praising a low self-esteem person will not break the patterns of interpreting success and failure feedback that are perpetuating that low self-esteem level.

Lecky (1945) was the first to argue that individuals are motivated to confirm their self-conceptions whether those self-conceptions are positive or negative. Why, then, has it taken so long for this view to be incorporated into theories of self-esteem development and enhancement? To a certain extent, the problem has been twofold. First, there has been difficulty in replicating some of these earlier findings (Dipboye, 1977; Shrauger, 1975). It now seems that most of the problems with replication centered around issues of what aspects of self are being measured, how those aspects are being measured, and whether it is a matter of what kind of feedback the individual will choose, use, seek out, or prefer. Second, there is a resistance to the apparently pessimistic notion that people suffering with low self-esteem are doomed to such a pattern and, to a certain extent, may be one of the major causes of their own negative feelings (Andrews, 1991). If people seek out and interpret feedback in such a manner that it is destined to perpetuate their cycle of self-disgust, then they must take some responsibility for their feelings.

But these issues miss the main point. Low self-esteem persons do not interpret success and failure feedback in a manner designed to make themselves feel bad. They interpret the feedback in the only way they can to reconfirm the only thing they know about their self. It is not that these individuals are gluttons for punishment. If they felt that they could truly trust positive feedback or live up to the expectations that go with being seen as a positive person or a person with self-worth, they would take that feedback and be pleased to get it

(Swann, Pelham, & Krull, 1989; Osborne, 1993b). As it becomes apparent that interpreting success and failure feedback in patterns that perpetuate current feelings of self-esteem is a defensive move, it seems less difficult to accept the point. Why would low self-esteem persons be wary of allowing someone to convince them that they are "great"? Because allowing their self to be put on a pedestal means they have a whole lot farther to fall should they fail in the future than they would have if they simply allowed themselves to stay where they are (e.g., Tice, 1991, 1993).

If an individual feels incompetent or worthless, then allowing himself to be put on a pedestal puts him in a very precarious position for many reasons. For one thing, the individual probably has very little experience with engaging in behaviors that are designed to exude or perpetuate an impression of social competency. Because of the behavioral patterns discussed earlier as "self-fulfilling prophecies," the individual may engage in behaviors that give off the impression that his newly acquired status was "a mistake." Also, if others accept this as truth and then engage in behaviors designed to displace the individual from the pedestal that he inappropriately acquired, he is going to fall and hit bottom hard. It should be easy to understand why an individual may be unwilling to put himself in such a dangerous position. The individual may also resist such placement because he may doubt his ability to live up to potentially escalating expectations (e.g., Tice, 1993). When the very definition of one's self is at stake, it pays to err on the side of caution. In this manner, the low self-esteem and the consistency and predictability that come with it are comfortable.

WRAPPING IT UP: WHAT DOES LOW SELF-ESTEEM REALLY MEAN?

Given the assumption that self-esteem significantly impacts human cognition, emotion, motivation, and behavior (Campbell & Lavallee, 1993), questions of what it means to have low self-esteem must be addressed. Although disagreements exist about how to define, measure, or enhance self-esteem, there seems to be little disagreement that self-esteem is an issue of critical importance. Some, in fact, have argued that self-esteem may be as close to a "social vaccine" as society will come. This suggests that a potential cure for societal problems such as alcohol and drug abuse, teen pregnancy, violence, and child and sexual abuse would be enhancing the self-esteem of the citizens within that society (California Task Force to Promote Self-Esteem, 1990). If it is the case that one of the major causes and potential cures for serious societal ills is self-esteem, then further research into the development and potential enhancement of low self-esteem should be considered a priority.

For quite some time, assumptions were made that low and high self-esteem individuals simply differed on the extent to which they had positive or negative feelings toward self (see Wylie, 1974, for one of the earliest comprehensive reviews of the self literature). This "valence view" of self-esteem suggests that self-esteem is either something that you have (the presence of positive valence) or you do not have (the presence of negative valence), and those who are high in self-esteem have managed to acquire it. A further extension of this kind of logic, therefore, would also suggest that it would be possible to make low self-esteem persons feel better about their selves by "giving" them the positive valence and, therefore, the self-esteem that they are missing. But as self-esteem research flourished in the late 1980s and into the 1990s, perceptions of what it means to be low or high in self-esteem have started to change. One of the most significant findings to come out of this wave of research was the revelation that individuals with low self-esteem do not necessarily possess negative self-views as much as they lack positive ones (Blaine & Crocker, 1993).

This thought, which at first blush may seem to contradict the statements made at the beginning of the previous paragraph, helps to clarify further what is meant by low self-esteem. If low self-esteem individuals are simply overburdened with negative thoughts, then self-esteem enhancement would simply consist of counterbalancing the negative with positive. Any individual who has tried to help someone with a self-esteem problem will be quick to point out that tossing positive things at low self-esteem persons is often futile. It isn't just that low self-esteem persons are lacking in positive information. They also have a fundamentally different way of processing information about self (Osborne, 1993b), may interpret success and failure feedback in such a way as to perpetuate the feelings of low self-esteem (Osborne & Stites, 1994), have different motives that they are trying to satisfy (Tice, 1991, 1993), and may act in ways that are designed to confirm their negative self-views rather than just seek out positive feedback (De La Ronde & Swann, 1993; Swann, 1983, 1987, 1990). All of these findings support the contention that low and high self-esteem individuals differ in fundamental ways and that these fundamental differences must be addressed and eliminated if self-esteem enhancement is going to be successful.

Many of the issues raised in the first two chapters seem to center on what motivates individuals with high or low self-esteem to be the way they are or to do the things they do. Although at some level individuals are not completely free to determine their self-esteem level or initiate actions based upon those levels, their motivations must play a crucial role in determining the likelihood that certain persons will make certain choices. Many of the differences between high and low self-esteem individuals seem to center on differences in self-motives or how those self-motives are fulfilled. Not only will an understanding of these motives and their applications shed light on the differences between persons with high and low self-esteem, it will also provide information that could be quite crucial in initiating self-esteem enhancement methods. Before moving on to a discussion of sources of self-knowledge, then, an overview of the role self-motives play in the development of self-concept and self-esteem will be presented.

CHAPTER THREE

Self-Motives

DEFINING MOTIVES AS THEY APPLY TO SELF

Before discussing the breadth and implications of self-motives for the actions of individuals high and low in self-esteem, it behooves us to define what is meant by a "motive." Although a standard textbook definition might suit our purposes (e.g., the *American Heritage College Dictionary* defines a motive as "an emotion, desire, physiological need, or similar impulse that acts as an excitement to action"), we are specifically interested here in motives that are mental in nature. Our definition of "motive" must also allow for the dual direction of the action. What is meant by "dual direction" is a suggestion that motives do not just excite action; they also direct it (e.g., Trevarthen, 1993). This dual aspect of motives is critical to the application of motives to self. According to Trevarthen (1993) "Motive . . . designates a mental function that is cause and director of movement and, at the same time, a seeker of information to direct and confirm movement—to make it work for a purpose." This expanded view of motives applies directly to the eclectic approach to self being advocated in this text. Self is not simply a reactive entity. Self directs action as well as seeks information. The motives that underlie self, then, may serve to explain many of the actions the individual engages in as well as what information the person will seek.

Another consequence of motives involves the role they play in perception (and self-perception). Certainly the self-related motives one is trying to respond to will influence the type of information one seeks, and the manner in which that information will be perceived or interpreted (e.g., Trevarthen, 1993). Attempts have been made to understand the role that motives play in the development of cognitive abilities (e.g., Fodor, 1983), but Trevarthen argues that few attempts have been made to understand how motives influence the development and integration of self (Trevarthen, 1993). Several premises come from this skeletal analysis of motives as they apply to self: (1) self-motives initiate exploration in the individual, (2) self-motives initiate behaviors that are purposeful and directed, (3) self-motives cause the person to be selective about what information he or she will attend to, perceive, and integrate, and (4) self-motives play a crucial role in the perpetuating nature of self-concept and self-esteem outlined in Chapters One and Two in this text. Because motives influence not only the behaviors that will be initiated but also the type of information that will be sought or accepted and the manner in which that information will be interpreted, they play a crucial role in maintaining self-predictability and consistency.

Wertsch (1991) reminds the reader that human communication and interaction require an understanding of "sociocultural" voices. This suggests that an understanding of motives is critical to an understanding of human interaction. If motives underlie much of self-related behavior, and much of self-related behavior occurs within a sociocultural context, then understanding those motives will not only clarify self but social interactions as well. For the purposes of this text, our concern will be on understanding the ramifications of self-related motives, but the generalizability of this understanding should not be ignored. It is valuable to keep in mind that all individuals involved in a social interaction are being directed and driven by their own self-motives. To understand human beings and their developing selves, then, one must understand the major self-motives that guide their actions and influence what information/feedback will be sought and the manner in which that information/feedback will be interpreted. Our attention now must be turned toward elaborating what major self-motives might underlie self-related behaviors and choices and articulating the ramifications of these motives.

MOTIVES AND THEIR MEANINGS

Even a superficial search of the self literature reveals a preponderance of self-motives. Trying to sift through such a mountain of terms is troublesome at best. A partial list of such motives includes: need for achievement, need for affiliation, need for approval, need for autonomy, need for comfort, need for dominance, need for influence, need for intimacy, need for power, self-appraisal, self-enhancement, self-evaluation, self-protection, and self-verification. Although each of these potential self-motives would be completely appropriate for discussion in this text, the eclectic nature of the text would be unjustly served by doing so. Certainly many of the motives just listed may be subcomponents of others, and additional motives may have mutually compatible effects on self.

Understanding self-motives and the influence they have on self does not require an exhaustive treatise on this list. Instead, it seems appropriate to select those self-motives that have generated the most discussion in the literature and that seem to have the most global impact on self, self-related behaviors, and the manner in which the individual will process information about self, including self-verification (and the related construct of self-protection), self-completion, self-enhancement, and self-assessment (most important, appraisal of self through reflected appraisals). What follows, then, is a brief explanation of these major motives and a short summary of the impact these self-motives have. The reader will note that several of these motives also have entire chapters of this text devoted to them.

SELF-VERIFICATION

Understanding self-related motives is only possible to the extent that the reader also understands the reasons individuals have for being driven or directed by these motives. Some motivations, like hunger or thirst, are quite easy to comprehend. Most individuals are clearly aware that they need to eat in order to survive. Thus, when the individual is moved to get up off the couch and go to the kitchen to fix a meal, few questions are raised about what might have motivated such actions. If someone is seen eating food, the assumption is made that he or she is motivated by hunger. The remarks individuals make sometimes, however, suggest that the motives that underlie such obvious behaviors as eating are not always as clear as they would seem. What if Rick were overheard saying, "I don't know why I'm eating. I'm not even hungry"? In this case, the assumptions we made about the motivation behind Rick's behavior were proven to be wrong. If it is possible that even deficit driven behaviors such as eating, drinking, and sleeping can sometimes be guided by other, more subtle motivations, then it is easy to understand why getting a handle on self-motives can be challenging.

Hormuth (1990) argues that many theories of self-motives make the same underlying assumption about the nature of self. Understanding the validity of this assumption, then, will be critical to our discussion of self-motives specifically, and our understanding of the eclectic nature of self in general. Many of these theories assume self-concept is stable and that there is a "unidirectional drive toward further stabilization and maintenance of the self-concept" (Hormuth, 1990). Many theories also assume that individuals are motivated to protect and enhance self-esteem (e.g., Darley & Goethals, 1980; Zuckerman, 1979). But it seems inappropriate to discuss protection and enhancement motives as if they were two sides of the same coin. Indeed, recent work by Baumeister and others suggest that protection and enhancement motives are distinct, although sometimes these motives may overlap in influencing behavior (e.g., Baumeister, Tice, & Hutton, 1989; Shrauger, 1975). Self strategies like self-handicapping (Jones & Berglas, 1978) seem to involve both protection and enhancement motives. Indeed, successful self-handicapping appears to accomplish both protection and enhancement for the individual (Baumeister, Tice, & Hutton, 1989; Jones & Berglas, 1978).

Some theories, such as self-verification (e.g., Swann, 1983), assume that self-protection is a primary motive underlying self-related choices. "Self-verification theory assumes that people strive to confirm their self-conceptions to bolster their perceptions of prediction and control" (Swann, Stein-Seroussi, & Giesler, 1992). This is quite consistent with widely accepted theoretical frameworks in the social psychological literature (e.g., Heider, 1958; Kelly, 1955; Rodin, 1986). Although self-verification and self-protection are not one and the same, it seems reasonable to conclude that self-protection is a motive that may be initiated if individuals' attempts to self-verify are met with resistance or if the individual has suffered some form of self-related threat.

This text will work from the assumption that one of the major motives underlying self-related behaviors and choices is self-verification. The ubiquitousness of this need for predictability and control has already been well documented in the preceding chapters of this text. It is understandable that individuals experience discomfort if their views of self are challenged, called into question, or in some fashion threatened. To alleviate such discomfort, individuals may seek out (e.g., Swann, Pelham, & Chidester, 1988), actively elicit (e.g., Swann & Read, 1981), and prefer self-related feedback that verifies or confirms existing self-views even if such confirmation is at the potential expense of feeling better about self (e.g., Swann, Stein-Seroussi, & Giesler, 1992; De La Ronde & Swann, 1993).

Although self-verification and self-protection are usually discussed as separate entities, this text will assume that one of the fundamental reasons that individuals are motivated to engage in self-verifying strategies is for purposes of self-protection. This assumption, of course, will be put to the test in Chapter Nine when self-verification is discussed in greater detail.

SELF-COMPLETION

For the purposes of this chapter, we will assume that individuals are usually driven toward what Wicklund and Gollwitzer (1982) called "self-completion." This theory assumes that human behavior is directed toward "self-defining goals." This is critical for understanding self-motives because Wicklund and Gollwitzer assume that individuals strive toward their goals, in part, through motivational processes (Wicklund & Gollwitzer, 1982). Hormuth (1990) draws upon some of this work in trying to articulate the processes involved in self change. Hormuth suggests that theories about self that pit self-predictability against self-change as motives underlying self and related behaviors are inadequate. The inadequacy of such theories derives, in large part, from the oversimplification that results (Hormuth, 1990).

As already outlined in this eclectic approach to self, individuals are driven by complicated motives. It should be obvious by this point that individuals are not driven by the same motives at all times, nor are different individuals driven by exactly the same motives. When self-change seems possible or probable given circumstances, the individual should be more motivated to attempt such change than when circumstances suggest that attempts to change would be likely to fail. Contrary to Hormuth's (1990) analysis of self-completion theory, however, the eclectic approach to self assumes that individuals will strive toward self-completion in situations that are relatively free from self threats. If, however, behaviors designed to aid self-completion could expose the individual to direct threats to self, it is assumed that the individual may choose to self-protect (or self-verify) instead.

Hormuth summarized self-completion theory in the following manner: "self-completion theory sees humans as actively constructing their identity through the manipulation of elements in their environments in a social context" (Hormuth, 1990). This theory assumes that individuals play an active role in the formation of their own identity, and it allows room for choices to be made. In this sense, individuals initiate actions that may be specifically geared toward resulting in feedback from others that support the identity they are striving to build. This, of course, is quite consistent with the definition of "self-motives" as outlined in the previous section of this chapter. In this regard, self-completion theory is not fundamentally different from self-verification theory; they both assume that accuracy of others impressions toward self is valued. Where self-completion theory assumes that the individual may be motivated to pursue self goals across a variety of situations and circumstances, however, self-verification theory would seem to assume that such attempts to self-complete will be initiated only in the absence of self-related threats or if the individual's level of self-esteem is high enough to counter such threats. Another major motive underlying self and self-related behaviors, therefore, may be self-completion. Rather than arguing whether individuals will self-verify or strive to self-complete, then, the eclectic approach to self (especially Chapter Nine) will ask, "When will individuals strive to self-complete and when will they strive to self-verify?"

SELF-ENHANCEMENT

Tesser and Campbell (1983) argue that self-evaluation maintenance is another self-motive that underlies self-related behaviors in social situations. According to this model, individuals are motivated to acquire and/or maintain positive self-evaluations. This is similar to self-enhancement theories that suggest individuals prefer feedback from situations and others that maximize the positive feelings attributable to self. Tesser and Campbell (1983) maintain that human beings are motivated to accomplish two goals through self-evaluation maintenance. First, the individual strives to stabilize self. Chapter Two already suggested that individuals may find self-uncertainty to be particularly distressing, and therefore they should be motivated to engage in behaviors designed to acquire information and feedback that stabilizes self. Individuals are also motivated, however, to enhance their self-esteem.

These two goals need not be viewed as conflicting or incompatible (e.g., Baumeister, Tice, & Hutton, 1989). Osborne (1993a, 1993b, 1993c) argues that these two goals may be fulfilled sequentially. That is, individuals may be driven to stabilize self before attempts will be made to enhance self-esteem. This would be convergent evidence for what Swann and his colleagues refer to as self-verification (e.g., Swann, 1983, 1987; Swann, Stein-Seroussi, & Giesler, 1992). Even if self-maintenance (self-verification, self-protection, etc.) is the standard motive, individuals will be motivated to engage in self-enhancement to the extent that some feedback is received that threatens to lower self-esteem below its baseline level for the individual. Such conflicting self-related feedback would be interpreted as directly threatening to self and would, therefore, motivate the individual to action necessary to restore the balance. In this case, self-enhancement would be required to restore that balance. It is important to note that self-enhancement need not mean that the individual will end up with a self-esteem level higher than when the attempts to alter self started. In this scenario, then, self-enhancement could be motivated by the self-protection motive. Likewise, Tesser and Cornell (1991) suggest that under certain conditions such apparently diverse self-motivations as self-affirmation, self-evaluation maintenance, forced-compliance dissonance, and attributions that result from learned helplessness may be driven by the same underlying process.

It has also been suggested that affect may serve as the underlying method of exchange for these self-motives (Tesser & Cornell, 1991). Certainly this assumption is consistent with the eclectic approach to self as outlined in this text. Given that self, self-concept, and self-esteem all appear to have predictability, stability, and consistency as a fundamental need, it stands to reason that affect would be aroused not only when that stability is threatened (negative affect such as sadness or mortification), but also when the stability is restored (positive affect such as joy, pride or relief).

A third major self-motive, and one that emerges from the self-evaluation maintenance model, then, is self-esteem enhancement. This tendency toward self-enhancement is also well documented within the social psychological literature (e.g., Alicke, 1985; Beggan, 1992; Gilovich, 1983; Schlenker, Weigold, & Hallman, 1990), and individuals have been shown to use a multitude of processes for achieving self-enhancement, including self-hand-icapping (Berglas & Jones, 1978), basking in reflected glory (Cialdini, Borden, Thorne, Walker, Freeman, & Sloan, 1976), and downward social comparisons (Hakmiller, 1966; Wills, 1981). Self-handicapping has already been described in some detail in Chapter Two; basking in reflected glory and downward social comparisons will be discussed in detail in Chapter Five.

SELF-ASSESSMENT

All of the motives outlined thus far in this chapter share the underlying assumption that individuals are driven by a need to assess self. Certainly individuals' behaviors seem consistent with such an assumption. Individuals could be expected to strive for clarity in self-definition because such clarity feeds the fundamental need for predictability human beings seem to value so highly (e.g., Simon, 1990). The self-motives already presented in this chapter deal only indirectly with issues of self-assessment; yet self-assessment is presumed to underlie such complex processes as self-perception, which is discussed in Chapter Four, and social comparisons, as outlined in Chapter Five. Both of these chapters deal with the methods that individuals use to gather knowledge about self. Although the methods by which individuals gather knowledge about self are also important in understanding (and are related to) methods of self-appraisal, the two sources to be discussed are important enough to warrant separate discussion. Let us now turn our attention to a fundamental method by which individuals draw conclusions about (or assess) self: self-appraisal.

ELEMENTS OF THE APPRAISAL PROCESS

The method by which individuals appraise self is not really as clear-cut as one might first believe. If an individual wants to know how he or she is coming across, all he or she has to do is ask. Right? The appraisal process is known to be more complex than this, and the complexity of the process, to a certain extent, also helps to explain how the process can lead to errors in self-evaluation. It is sometimes the case that the resulting erroneous assumptions about self are overly critical or dramatic. The appraisal process comprises three elements, and errors can be made within each that will influence the overall self-evaluation that emerges from it. These elements are self-appraisal, actual appraisal of significant others, and reflected appraisals (Felson, 1989).

An individual usually has some intuitive notion of how she thinks she is doing. This intuitive awareness, however, is generally not enough for the person to feel self satisfied. Cooley (1902) suggested that "I," or self, is basically a feeling and, as such, cannot be discussed or defined without suggesting the feeling. This suggests that an individual cannot ponder her abilities without the issues of feelings about those abilities naturally being raised.

The individual, then, is motivated to gather evaluative feedback by which to judge that ability. Of course, what the individual is actually seeking is some degree of confirmation of her own self-evaluation from significant others. If the appraisals are not spontaneously offered by these significant others, the individual will request them or engage in behaviors designed to elicit them. Before these appraisals are incorporated into the self-evaluation process, however, the individual reflects those appraisals back on self through a process of perceiving what she thinks the other person is thinking of her.

It is obvious that many errors can be made as self-related information is processed through these three elements. First of all, the individual can have intuitive feelings about her abilities that are either too grandiose or too pessimistic. When this person then seeks appraisals from significant others, these appraisals may be perceived in a biased way by the very person who sought out that appraisal in the first place. Felson (1989) suggested that such a process involves the individual assuming the role of the "generalized other." Generalized other (as first suggested by Mead in 1934) basically means "the attitudes of a group." Thus, reflected appraisals are influenced most strongly by general attitudes and assumptions of how the general person would perceive the individual's self, rather than the perceptions of any single significant other (Kenny & Albright, 1987). Although for the most part this certainly seems reasonable, it seems doubtful that a generalized reflected impression would carry more weight than the reflected impression of one's parent, spouse, teacher, or best friend. Overall, individuals imagine how people in general will perceive the self they are projecting. If, however, very specific feedback is directed toward that self from a significant other whose opinion the individual values, surely that reflected appraisal, whether the individual has perceived it accurately or not, will have a substantial impact on self (Felson, 1981a).

THE IMPORTANCE OF FEEDBACK FROM OTHERS

The concept of reflected appraisals brings to mind images of shimmering pools, mirrors, and other smooth surfaces that reflect images of our self back to us. Although as a scientific concept reflected appraisals are not nearly that poetic, they do play a crucial role in helping the individual to take a look at what his or her self "looks" like. The word "looks" is in quotation marks to stress the fact that the images of self we receive through the process of reflected appraisals do not, and need not, center strictly around issues of physical features. The manner in which an individual gathers information pertinent to self-evaluation, self-revision, and self-assessment plays a pivotal role in determining the answers the individual will receive for his or her self-related questions. If an individual wants to know how he is doing, the answer will depend, at least in some significant degree, on whom he asks the question. His parents may say he is doing fine, a competitive friend may say he is doing poorly, and a disinterested teacher may say there is room for improvement.

What if the individual receives all three kinds of feedback from the significant others from whom he is seeking reflected appraisals? The need for self-certainty becomes important again. For the most part, the individual is left with three options when such discrepant appraisals are being reflected back at self. First, the individual can choose one appraisal and value that at the expense of the other two. Which of these appraisals he picks, then, will determine whether pride or mortification is felt. Second, the individual could choose the reflected appraisal that is consistent with his own appraisal of self. In this manner, the individual can remain consistent with self. Third, the individual could choose to collect more information by seeking out reflected appraisals from more significant others. As this new information is coming in, the individual can choose the appraisal that is most common. If the individual chooses this route for dealing with discrepant reflected appraisals, he essentially is reserving judgment until more self-relevant data are collected. The overall goal of the reflected appraisal process is to be perceived in a manner that is consistent with the image of self one had hoped to convey.

The need for accurate self feedback has already been well documented within this text. But how is an individual to garner accurate feedback on self-relevant issues when different people are providing him with different answers? He probably can't. To a certain extent, we must ask whether it even matters if the feedback received from others is accurate. If we consider the feedback from an individual to be important, then it matters to us regardless of whether it is eventually proved to be accurate or inaccurate. If an individual sees himself as a potent lover, yet his girlfriend considers him a cold potato, he will become concerned with that discrepancy whether he agrees with it or not. As already discussed, a lack of consistency between our own images toward self and the images that others have of our self creates a pattern of discomfort that must be eliminated in some way. Duval and Wicklund (1972) suggest that awareness of this discrepancy between the self and the standard will lead to either attempts to reduce the discrepancy or attempts to avoid the situation. If the individual who is providing the person with feedback is an important source of information, that discrepancy cannot just be ignored (nor is it likely that the situation can simply be avoided).

Even if significant or important individuals in a person's life do not specifically provide feedback information, the individual may make assumptions about what he or she thinks that feedback information might be (Felson, 1981a). This process of bouncing our self off others and interpreting the feedback that is either actually received or imagined is an important source of knowledge about the self (Baldwin, 1897; Cooley, 1902; James, 1890; Mead, 1934). Charles Cooley wrote about the looking-glass self, and such a term still has relevance to how individuals gather self-relevant information (Cooley, 1902, 1964). Cooley's concept was meant to suggest that one's self-feelings (self-esteem) come partially from imagining how one's self appears in the mind of someone else. In other words, our self-esteem is partially determined by the way we believe others perceive the entity we refer to as our "self." This social self is a representation in the individual's mind about what he thinks others see, feel, and think about when looking toward that individual.

Cooley suggested that "in imagination, we perceive in another person's mind some thought of our appearance, manners, aims, deeds, character, friends, and so on, and are variously affected by it" (Cooley, 1902, p. 184). If the individual assumes that others see his self the way he had intended to project it, then the self feeling that results is positive. If, however, the person assumes that there is a large discrepancy between the image of self he meant to project and the image of self that others are reflecting back, negative feelings toward self will result. Cooley described this process of reflected appraisals as a three-step process. First, the individual imagines how his self appears to the other person. Second, the individual imagines how that other person is judging that appearance. Third, a self-feeling such as pride or mortification will result, depending on whether the imagined judgment by the other of the self being reflected is positive or negative. It is important to stress that the event that moves the person to experience pride or mortification is not the actual reflection of self but the effect that the person imagines that reflection is having upon another person's mind.

This illustrates a very fundamental point that has come up several times before within the pages of this text. Self-evaluation and the manner in which individuals interpret self-relevant feedback need not be accurate to be influential. If the individual believes that another person has a negative feeling toward him, that is really what matters. The subjective reality that an individual is using to evaluate and make sense of the world is more important in predicting what he or she will do than what, in actuality, may be a more accurate reality. If Sara believes she is talking to her mother when, in fact, she is talking to a door, it doesn't matter that the therapist knows that the door is a door. The therapist will be able to help Sara only if she can discover the reasons that Sara is interpreting the situation the way that she is. If Sara believes that the door is her mother, then that is just as real to her as anyone else's belief that the door is a door. Likewise, if Sara believed that Jane didn't like her, it really wouldn't matter how Jane truly felt about Sara because Sara's behaviors would be based on the assumption she has already made about the feelings that Jane has toward her. This pattern of making assumptions and having those assumptions guide behavior reiterates the important concept of "self-fulfilling prophecies" discussed in Chapter One.

Cooley also argued that "there is no sense of 'I', as in pride or shame, without its correlative sense of you, or he, or they." A significant degree of who a person believes herself to be is determined in relation to the other significant individuals in her life. These others, whom we have designated as significant others, become the mirrors off which we reflect our self-images and try to discover how our self is being perceived by others. Cooley called this kind of self the "social self" because it involves those aspects of self that can be verified by normal observation. The impact that the social self has for self as a whole, however, cannot always be readily observed. If the individual feels negative about the reflections of self she believes are coming back from those significant others, then self-esteem is likely to be affected in a negative way. This suggests that self can develop only within a social context (Mead, 1934).

This idea that self is a developmental phenomenon is reflected in Mead's assumptions about the nature of self as an entity. According to Mead, the self "is not initially there, at birth, but arises in the process of social experience and activity" (Mead, 1934, p.135). This concept was postulated earlier by Cooley (1902) when he used the term "social self." Similarly, Sullivan (1953) held that an individual only becomes an individual in a social context. The feedback directed toward self from others and the information the individual specifically requests about self from others are not, however, automatically incorporated into the self. Remember that self is a protective structure that must evaluate and weigh the consequences to self of accepting any individual piece of feedback information. Because individuals are so protective of their self, an integral part of the self-concept arsenal is the process of interpreting feedback in a fashion designed to keep that information from dramatically impacting self (Osborne, 1993d).

Cooley (1902) suggested that self becomes a "citadel" of the mind that protects whatever treasures one hides within. These treasures, it seems, would be those aspects of self about which the individual is quite certain or that are considered important to self-definition. This makes reflected appraisals a potentially double-edged sword because the person feels motivated to ask questions about how self is being perceived by others; yet the very answers she may be seeking can threaten the stability of self that is so treasured (e.g., Cooley, 1902; Swann, 1983; Brown, 1993).

IMPLICATIONS OF REFLECTED APPRAISALS

The concepts of reflected appraisals and looking-glass self show up only occasionally in social psychology texts these days. Are such concepts missing from contemporary texts because they no longer seem to be an important part of the self-development process? Or are they missing because they have become such an integrated part of the self literature that the processes are taken for granted? It seems from the literature that has been cited thus far that the idea of reflecting appraisals off significant others is alive and well. The very ideas of self-verification, confirmation bias, self-fulfilling prophecy, and the protective nature of self-concept and self-esteem support the notion that individuals value the opinions of significant others in relation to self, but that these valued opinions are incorporated only to the extent that they do not directly threaten self-consistency. None of this is meant to suggest that self change cannot or does not take place. The ramifications of reflected appraisals center around the degree of discrepancy between the image of self that was intentionally projected and the image of self that one assumes is being reflected back from the appraisal partner.

If there is a high degree of discrepancy between the image of self projected and the image of self reflected back, that very discrepancy can be interpreted as a threat to self. This is similar to the description by E. Tory Higgins (1989) of self-discrepancy theory. This theory discusses the impact of perceived discrepancies between self-concept and expectations on self-feelings. Since this concept integrates so perfectly with reflected appraisals, it will be discussed here rather than on its own. Self-discrepancy theory suggests that there may be differences between the individual's actual self, who that individual thinks he ought to be, and who that individual thinks it would be ideal to be. If there is a large discrepancy between who the individual thinks he actually is, who he thinks he ought to be, and who he would hope ideally to be, negative self-feelings can result. To the extent that the gaps or discrepancies between the actual, ought, and ideal selves are too large, low self-esteem can be the result (Higgins, 1989; Higgins, Bond, Klein, & Strauman, 1986). Although Markus and Nurius (1986) use the term "possible" selves, they discuss a similar connection between possible selves and self-esteem.

If the self as the individual actually perceives it is at odds with the self as the individual feels obligated to be or the images of self that some significant other thinks the individual "ought" to have, guilt, shame, and resentfulness may follow (Higgins, 1989). This directly involves the reflected appraisal process because the individual may use the reflective process to draw conclusions about what she thinks some significant other believes she "ought" to be like. Even if these assumptions or conclusions are in error, the perceived discrepancy will have a negative impact on the individual's self-esteem. The degree of discomfort the individual experiences is a function of two factors (Higgins, 1989). First, it is influenced by the magnitude of the discrepancy between the "actual" and the "ought" self. If the discrepancy is large, the impact on self-feelings will be dramatic as well. Second, the degree of discomfort is influenced by how aware the individual is that the discrepancy exists. If the discrepancy is blatant and very accessible to the individual, it can serve as a kind of constant reminder that she is not living up to some expectation. These daily reminders of that discrepancy can cause it to grow and take on even more importance in the mind of the individual.

Carver and Scheier's (1981) self-regulation theory is based on the simple assumption that increasing focus on the self will also increase the extent to which that self is compared to standards. These standards are similar to the concepts of "ought" and "ideal" selves, and the implications of this theory are directly relevant to any discussion of reflected appraisals and self-discrepancies. Scheier and Carver (1988) suggest that individuals monitor the extent to which they are being successful in reducing the degree of discrepancy between self and standard. If the individuals decide that they are making adequate progress toward reducing the discrepancy, then outcome expectancy will be favorable. Outcome expectancy is the degree to which the individual believes that continued efforts to reduce self-standard discrepancy will be successful. If outcome expectancy is favorable, the individual will be motivated to continue self-standard discrepancy reduction efforts. If, however, outcome expectancy is unfavorable, the individual will not be motivated to continue discrepancy reduction efforts. Duval and Wicklund (1972) had already suggested that if efforts to reduce the discrepancy between self and standard fail (and a negative outcome expectancy anticipates such a failure), then the individual will become motivated to avoid the situation in which the discrepancy exists.

Duval, Duval, and Mulilis (1992) argue that high levels of self-focus in combination with a favorable outcome expectancy lead to increased efforts to match self to the standard when self-discrepancy is high. Likewise, high levels of self-focus in combination with an unfavorable outcome expectancy lead to increased efforts to avoid the situation when self-discrepancy is high. These findings suggest that the degree of discrepancy between self and standard does not, in and of itself, determine whether efforts will be made to reduce the discrepancy or avoid the situation. Individuals who believe that there is a high likelihood that their efforts to reduce the discrepancy will be successful are willing to engage in such reduction efforts. Those individuals who believe that their efforts to reduce self-standard discrepancies will fail may be motivated to avoid the situation.

This leads directly back to Chapter Two. Low self-esteem persons may have learned, because of prior experience, that the chances of their reducing self-standard discrepancies are low (e.g., Blaine & Crocker, 1993). For this reason, they may prefer to avoid situations in which this self-standard discrepancy is salient. But what are these individuals to do if avoidance of those situations is not possible? The information already presented suggests that these individuals would then become motivated to interpret the self-standard information in whatever manner is necessary to reduce the discrepancy. For low self-esteem persons, the self-standard discrepancy is likely to be one in which they are receiving feedback that is more favorable than self-views. If they believe that efforts to bring self in line with that more favorable standard will fail, they will not be motivated to engage in efforts to attain the standard because there would be too much at stake if such attempts were unsuccessful. The real problem with self-standard discrepancies for an individual with low self-esteem is that the standard is usually so much higher than the person's views of self that efforts are made to eliminate the discrepancy by bringing the standard down to the self rather than bringing the self up to the standard.

For the low self-esteem person, it is much simpler and safer to reduce the discrepancy by avoiding the situation. If avoidance is not possible, the individual will engage in efforts to reduce the discrepancy. Prior experience, however, has taught the low self-esteem individual that efforts to reduce self-standard discrepancies will probably not be successful. The individual therefore finds it easier to belittle the standard (through inaccurate interpretations of feedback and the other processes discussed in Chapters One and Two) than to bring self up to the standard. The negative cyclic pattern of low self-esteem can be further understood, then, by keeping self-regulation theory in mind. High self-esteem persons, on the other hand, tend to have favorable outcome expectancies, and they usually will be motivated to reduce the discrepancy between self and standard when such discrepancies are made salient to them (Duval, Duval, & Mulilis, 1992). Until the high self-esteem person has become certain that outcome expectancy has become unfavorable, she will continue concerted efforts to reduce the discrepancy by bringing self in line with the standard.

WRAPPING IT UP: WHAT DOES ALL THIS MEAN?

Obviously self-related motives play a crucial function in the development and maintenance of self-concept and self-esteem. Although dozens of self-motives have been suggested within the literature, a select few of them seem to have far-reaching implications for self as described within this eclectic approach. The self-motives that underlie a certain behavioral choice also play a critical role in determining how feedback about that behavior will be interpreted and, therefore, can further impact self. Several of these motives (in particular self-verification, self-enhancement, and self-assessment) will be discussed in later chapters. Each of these motives builds upon the process of self-appraisal as briefly outlined in this chapter. Since the appraisal process provides such a critical foundation for self-motives, a few moments should be spent summarizing what is now known about self-appraisals and the implications such appraisal attempts have for the individual.

Self-discrepancies can result from the reflected appraisal process, and they can also influence this appraisal process. Once it is suspected that a discrepancy between self and standard might exist, a predictable pattern of behaviors will follow:

1. If individuals feel that a discrepancy might exist, they will be motivated to initiate the appraisal process to determine if that assumption is accurate. If they believe they are being viewed differently by some significant other than they would like, the most obvious method by which they can verify the validity of that belief is by reflecting the self-image in question off that significant other and interpreting the image that is reflected back. A crucial part of this process is the danger inherent within it. Interpreting the images of self that seem to be reflected back from significant others is always a risky business because those interpretations need not be accurate. Because of the motivation individuals have to be perceived in a manner consistent with their own self-conceptions, a negative cycle can be started with one erroneous interpretation. Reflected appraisals and self-discrepancies, then, feed directly into the eclectic approach to self that this text is presenting.

2. If the reflected appraisals coming back lead individuals to determine that a discrepancy between self and standard does exist, the individuals will engage in initial efforts to reduce those discrepancies. These initial efforts may include engaging in follow-up behaviors to give the individual who is providing the standard further information on which to base the reflected appraisal, or it may involve simple verbal efforts to promote a more favorable comparison of self and standard on the part of the individual who is providing the reflected comparison.

3. After these initial discrepancy reduction efforts have been completed, individuals engage in an assessment of outcome expectancy. At this point, they assess the degree to which these initial reduction efforts have been successful. From this initial estimate, the individuals extrapolate about the ultimate success of these discrepancy reduction efforts. If this assessment leads to a favorable outcome expectancy, the individuals will be motivated to continue the discrepancy reduction efforts. If, however, the initial assessments lead to an unfavorable outcome expectancy, the individuals may be motivated to avoid the situation.

4. The individuals' self-esteem level also has been shown to affect this process. If there is a relatively high degree of likelihood that discrepancy reduction efforts will be successful, then both low and high self-esteem individuals should put forth the effort that such reductions require. If, however, the degree of discrepancy between self and standard is quite high (even if that means that the self is viewed much more favorably than the standard), low self-esteem individuals may feel that their self-consistency is threatened. When these threats occur, the individuals are motivated to reduce those threats through self-verification. These steps, then, can explain how and why low self-esteem individuals might be motivated to reconfirm a conception of self that is blatantly negative. To the extent that the individuals feel they cannot safely achieve a more positive standard without threatening the fragile self-consistency that they have established, they will not make attempts to self-enhance to that higher standard.

5. Finally, individuals experience discomfort when discrepancies between self and standard are made salient. To the extent that individuals feel positive about their chances of reducing that discrepancy, positive efforts will be made to bring self in line with the standard. If, however, the discrepancy is too large, or the individuals suffer from low self-esteem, the discomfort experienced may be so large as to prompt the individuals to avoid the situation altogether.

This eclectic presentation of information related to self-discrepancy suggests that multiple options are open to individuals when discrepancies between self and the standard have been made salient. The determining factors as to which of these options will be chosen include: the magnitude of the discrepancy, the initial assessment of outcome expectancy favorability, the self-esteem level of the individuals, and the degree to which avoidance of the situation in which the discrepancy is made salient is possible. Possible contributing factors might also be the importance of the standard to the individuals, the certainty of the individuals about their ability to reach that standard, and the degree to which the situation demands that individuals be held accountable to that standard. Each of these contributing factors as well as the overall impact of the factors that determine the method the individuals will use to reduce self-standard discrepancies must be researched further, and the implications of this research for an eclectic approach to self must be addressed.

Table 3.1 summarizes the major self-motives discussed in this chapter, the goal of each motive, and behaviors that might be expected because of that motive. The reader might note that several of these motives appear to include some aspects of the others. The presentation of self-motives in this fashion is not accidental. Although dozens of self-motives are described in the literature, only a few major ones appear in this text. The rationale for choosing the four that are presented is twofold. First, many of the self-motives in the literature (e.g., need for dominance, need for intimacy, and need for power) are much more similar to personality characteristics than overall self-motives. It was decided, therefore, to include the more global self-motives that appear to have more significant implications for self as a whole. Second, the self-motives chosen are not mutually exclusive. That is, the motives are not clearly distinct and separate. Some situations may activate several of these motives at the same time, and being able to decipher and predict what the behavioral implications of such multiple activation would be is of fundamental importance to this eclectic approach to self. If it can be determined when individuals will operate according to each of these principles, a much clearer picture of self and behavior will emerge. It is also for this reason that self-verification and self-enhancement warrant a separate chapter later in this text.

This chapter also elaborated the steps of the appraisal process involved in self-assessment. Only when these steps of the self-appraisal process are kept in mind do the differential behaviors of individuals experiencing self-standard discrepancies make sense. One overall point to keep in mind is that not all individuals experiencing self-standard discrepancies will be motivated to try to achieve that standard. If the standard is higher than self, the individual may be motivated to bring self up to the standard to the extent that a favorable outcome to those attempts is expected. If, however, the standard is set too high above self or the expectancy outcome is unfavorable, the individual will either avoid the situation, thereby avoiding the discomfort, or attempt to bring the standard in line with the self.

WRAPPING IT UP: INTEGRATION OF SECTION ONE

Summing up the first three chapters will provide a framework in which to view the rest of this book. In order to understand the implications of self-concept and self-esteem for the life of the individual, it is necessary to understand the developmental sequence that has led the individual to hold the self-views and self-feelings that he or she does. Self-concept and self-esteem do not develop within a vacuum. The person's social environment is a critical determining factor in the outcome of both processes. If the child has a stable, predictable, and positive environment in which to explore questions like "Who am I?," "What am I good at?," and "What do I want my life to be like?" then a stable self-conception will probably result, and positive self-esteem will serve as the guiding evaluative component of that self.

If, however, the individual is learning to define self in an environment that is hostile, unpredictable, neglectful, or abusive, he or she will learn to protect self by locking it away within a pattern of interpretations for feedback that keeps everyone at bay. Such individuals have only superficial relationships, call very few persons "friend," are mistrusting of others, and seem to despise every facet of their self. Developing a healthy view of self requires the freedom to actively explore the environment, test the limits of one's abilities, learn that effort is a good thing, and realize that success is not just defined as perfection. Overly

TABLE 3.1

Self-Motive	Goal of Motive	Behavior/Outcome
1. Self-Verification	Protect self and/or maintain stable self-concept	Behavioral strategies (such as self-handicapping) may be used to protect self from threats or reestablish stability following a threat.
2. Self-Completion	Define self and self-defining goals	If self change seems likely to succeed, self-enhancement and other methods for self-change may be employed. If self change is unlikely to succeed, self-protection will be initiated.
3. Self-Enhancement	Acquire or maintain positive self-evaluations	Self-enhancement will be used to return self-esteem to base-line levels following a threat, increase positive perceptions of self, and maximize positive mood.
4. Self-Assessment	Clarify self and accurately assess how self is doing	Self, other, and reflected appraisals all may be used by individual to self-evaluate, revise self, and engage in self-assessment with the outcome impacting self-esteem.

demanding parents teach their children that anything less than perfect is a failure. Neglectful parents teach their children that effort doesn't matter. Abusive parents teach their children that they are not worthy of respect and that they better take from the world what they can because it will never give things to them freely. Although certainly all readers shudder to think that such parental strategies are used, the overwhelming number of teenagers, adolescents, and adults with poorly articulated self-concepts and dramatically negative feelings toward self cannot be ignored.

If the developmental sequences of self-concept and self-esteem are understood within the framework of this eclectic approach to self, however, methods of breaking the impact of such negative styles can be discovered. Children must learn to see their self accurately and be able to articulate who they are as well as who they are not. Self-concept is a cognitive representation of who the individual thinks he is or is not. Self-esteem involves an evaluative interpretation of how one feels about those things that he or she is using to define self. Self-esteem serves as an information processing strategy that the individual uses to analyze social and self-related information, and it is this process that determines the amazing impact that low self-esteem has on the life of the person suffering its consequences. Low self-esteem doesn't just involve feeling negative about one's self. It also involves a process of interpreting information in patterns that (1) perpetuate negativity, (2) set the person up for failure, (3) minimize the impact any positive information could ever have, (4) keep the person from putting forth the effort that being socially successful would require, and (5) establish the limits on what the person thinks he or she is or will ever be capable of doing.

Patterns of self-fulfilling prophecies can work for or against the person. If someone has decided that the individual is a good person, then that individual will act toward that person in patterns that will ultimately verify that expectation. But the pattern does not have to work in a positive manner. If an individual has a negative impression of the person, he or she is just as likely to act in ways that initiate behaviors to confirm that negative expectation. The labels that others use to place parameters on the individual are particularly distressing because the individual may not know what labels are being used to define them. If these labels cannot be discovered, then the labeled individual cannot engage in behaviors designed to convince the labeler that the labels are wrong. Even if the individual finds methods to discover and counter those labels, the power of self-fulfilling prophecies might keep that label in place despite all the labeled person's efforts to tear them down.

The self-motives that drive individuals to act in certain ways are also of profound importance in the eclectic approach to self. Self does not develop in a vacuum, and it certainly does not develop without any conscious control on the part of the person whose self is in question. Individuals can engage in purposeful behavior designed specifically to portray an image of self to others, to gather information from others that relates to self, and interpret incoming feedback and information in a fashion necessary for protecting self. Certainly some individuals will choose some self-motives more than others, and some self-motives may be automatically activated under certain conditions. It has already been suggested that individuals with low self-esteem would be likely to engage in self-protective (self-verifying) behaviors much more often than individuals with high self-esteem. Despite this difference, however, certain situations may seem so threatening to self that even the high self-esteem individuals will initiate self-protective processes. Under other conditions still, individuals are motivated to acquire self-related information that is veridical. In these situations, both high and low self-esteem persons are motivated to articulate, clarify, and understand their own self. As already pointed out, though, low self-esteem persons find such veridicality difficult because they become accustomed to interpreting self-related feedback in a fashion designed to perpetuate self and self-esteem at current levels.

The eclectic approach to self, however, provides an optimistic path by which self-articulation can be enhanced. To the extent that the individual can be induced to further articulate the self through more realistic interpretations for success and failure, self-esteem enhancement becomes possible. The eclectic approach to self assumes that self-concept and self-esteem develop as defensive (meant in terms of self-protection) structures, and understanding this point clarifies much potential confusion. As the best aspects of the current research in self and self-esteem are incorporated into this eclectic approach, the implications of an eclectic theory of self will continue to be clarified. The implications of an eclectic understanding of self-concept and self-esteem for daily life, education, perceptions of others, and future self research serve as guiding principles throughout the remainder of this book. If the developmental processes of self-concept and self-esteem are understood, then self-esteem enhancement becomes possible, methods for reducing prejudice and discrimination may be discovered, techniques for enhancing education can be illuminated, and the ramifications for individual differences in self-concepts can be explored.

Sources of Self-Knowledge

INTRODUCTION TO SECTION TWO

Section One provided information on the developmental processes that lead to self-concept, self-images, self-esteem, and revisions of each of these. But questions still linger about the overall nature of self. If, as Chapter One suggested, self is an active, dynamic structure, it seems reasonable to assume that individuals are usually in a state of seeking information relevant to self. Individuals must (1) delineate a place in the world, (2) clearly articulate what self is and what it is not, (3) build some overall sense of self-worth, and (4) succeed in a variety of social situations. In order to carry out these tasks successfully, an individual must actively seek out information related to self and incorporate that information into existing self-views. Answering questions related to self-articulation is an important step in progressing toward an eclectic theory of self. Indeed, an eclectic approach to self would be incomplete without information centering on the methods that individuals use to gather self-related information.

A word of caution is in order at this point. Just because an individual is seeking out information related to self does not necessarily mean that the individual wishes to change that self. Remember from Section One that being viewed consistently is a powerful self-motive. Individuals have a strong need for others to perceive them the same way that they perceive themselves. Simply seeking out self-information is not an indicator of the person's willingness to alter self. To some extent, it may be appropriate to ask why individuals seek out self-related information from others at all. Others also are trying to have their self perceived consistently. How, then, are we to know whether others are viewing us the way they are because we did not articulate our sense of self clearly enough, or because they can gain some of their own sense of self predictability from viewing us the way they do? In order to understand the answer to this question, it is important to bear in mind that there are two different kinds of answers that individuals can be seeking when they ask the question "How am I doing?"

Individuals may ask the question because they truly want to assess their ability, determine strengths, identify weaknesses, and work to eliminate those weaknesses. Other individuals can ask the same question but mean it to be completely rhetorical. If Joe asks his wife what she thinks of the new car he bought, he doesn't really want his wife to tell him that he is "too old to be driving a one seat sports car with a convertible roof." What Joe does want to hear is how much she likes it, how young it makes him look, and how glad she is that he bought it. Part of the battle in understanding what someone hopes to gain by seeking self-related information, then, is determining whether they are seeking feedback to confirm their own feelings about self (self-verification) or whether they genuinely want to know how they are doing (self-evaluation or self-assessment). Which one of these goals (or self-motives) individuals hope to satisfy will directly influence the extent to which the feedback they receive will have a positive or negative impact on the self.

When individuals provide each other with self-relevant feedback, at least two motives could be involved. First, the individual truly may want to help the other person articulate a sense of self. If Simon asks Jane how she is feeling today, he might actually want to hear Jane's answer. If Jane seems depressed or confused, Simon's goal when asking may be to help Jane puzzle through her dilemma. But it must also be kept in mind that part of our own self-definition comes from the predictability of those around us. If I know that I can always count on Bob to be there when I need a friend, then I may seek him out when things are troubling me. But what if I go to drop my burdens on Bob's shoulder and he slams the door in my face? Likewise, part of Bob's self-definition may come from the fact that I always cried on his shoulder when my life hit rough spots. Maybe Bob incorporated this fact into his self-definition by labeling himself as "a helpful person."

Now, if I decide I can handle my problems on my own and stop burdening Bob with them, I may be altering my own self-concept purposefully, but I also may be altering Bob's accidentally. It is entirely possible, then, that Bob will engage in behaviors designed to bring out my tendency to burden him with my problems because such behaviors on my part confirm his views of who he is. It is also possible, therefore, that Bob will resist my attempts to change my own self-views because they may force his to change in the process. This need for self-consistency on the part of both individuals involved in the relationship can become problematic. If the information the individual is seeking about self cannot be provided from one outlet, the individual may turn to other sources to provide that information. Probably dozens of theories have been postulated about the methods by which individuals seek out knowledge or information related to self. Likewise, just as many theories probably have been postulated about how individuals then incorporate that information into their working definitions of self.

Our concern is not with summarizing all of these theories. With an eclectic approach to self, the task is to sift out those pieces of information that are most relevant to an overall theory of self and focus efforts in those areas. Specifically, we will address four sources of self-knowledge. Two of these sources, self-perception and social comparison, have enjoyed long, fruitful years as theories of how individuals acquire self-knowledge. The other two, culture and organismic approaches, have recently begun to receive more attention. It will become apparent as the chapters progress that none of these sources of information is mutually exclusive from the others. We will first discuss them as separate entities and then spend some time articulating and clarifying the connections among them.

Lewis (1982, 1992) suggested that an active "world" view of the child necessitates not only a belief in self but a belief in self-knowledge as well. An eclectic theory of self would be remiss if it did not include a look at major sources of self-knowledge. Along with such a belief, however, also comes an obligation to articulate the implications and applications of self theory for the individual. This text will end with applied chapters that integrate an understanding of self and self-knowledge with self-esteem enhancement, daily life, and educational settings. An application of an eclectic theory of self will also have implications for developmental theories. Lewis expresses concern and dismay that "the study of the ontogenesis of the self in social development has received little attention" (Lewis, 1992, p.21). Lewis cites several reasons that such an ontogenesis has been slow in coming to the self literature. One reason is that most self theories are passive in nature, assuming that the individual plays little (if any) role in determining his or her self. Another reason is that the literature shows little agreement as to what is meant by "self." The reader will immediately note that this lack of consistency in defining "self" has already been lamented within the pages of this text. Lewis suggests that a developmental perspective must include an understanding of the development of self.

The titles of Chapters One and Two should suggest to the reader that the author of this text agrees with the analysis that Lewis provides. A true understanding of the developmental nature of the human being seems impossible without some understanding of how self develops within a social context. This includes understanding the active role that the individual plays in the development, articulation, and maintenance of his or her own self. Social psychologists should be quite interested in an analysis of the ontogenesis of self because it is influenced by and has an impact on the individual's social interactions. This discussion, of course, is one of the foundations upon which the eclectic approach to self is built. The sources of self-knowledge that are discussed in the following chapters follow this eclectic emphasis by focusing on factors both within and outside the individual. Once these dualistic influences are better understood, our attention will be turned to an application of this understanding.

CHAPTER FOUR

Self-Perception

BACKGROUND INFORMATION

Sources of self-knowledge can often be less than obvious. It is all too easy to forget that a multitude of forces both internal and external to the person influence the knowledge that person will hold about self. Perhaps of equal importance with understanding where self-knowledge comes from, however, are questions of the implications that self-knowledge might have for self and others. Several reviews of the self literature have suggested what these sources of self-knowledge seem to be (Wylie, 1974, 1979). Contemporary views of self-knowledge are probably best summarized by Jones (1990) who states, "we are encouraged, if not gently nudged into remembering, that interpersonal perception involves not only getting to know others but also getting to know ourselves."

Jones suggests that relevant self-knowledge comes from five sources. Several of these sources have already been suggested in this text, and the remainder of these sources will appear in this and later chapters. In order truly to understand the self that an individual calls his or her own, these relevant sources of self-knowledge must be understood, and they must be included in an eclectic approach to self.

First, as this text has already suggested, learning about self is, in part, a matter of self as others see it. This concept was clearly articulated in the section on reflected appraisals and forms an important part of the identity negotiation process. Since self is, by its nature, a social construct (e.g., Cooley, 1902; Mead, 1934), it must also be the case that the self creation, negotiation, and maintenance processes must involve a reflective component. Self predictability will, to a significant degree, be dependent upon having others perceive self in the manner in which the individual had intended it to be perceived (e.g., Swann, Stein-Seroussi, & Giesler, 1992). If there is some discrepancy between the images of self the individual had hoped to project and the images that were actually intended, the individual is motivated in some way to alleviate those discrepancies (e.g., Higgins, 1989). If these discrepancies cannot be eliminated, severe consequences to self may result, including lowered self-esteem, unpleasant emotional symptoms, and in extreme cases possibly depression (e.g., Higgins, 1987; Strauman, 1989, 1992).

Second, individuals learn about self by comparison to what they have done in the past and analyzing what they are currently doing. This concept has been hinted at in other sections of this text but most closely relates to the topic of this chapter, self-perception. This involves using self as a norm or standard by which an individual makes judgments about that self. If an individual has always been honest in the past, she may decide that the fact that she just behaved dishonestly might be informative about self. It is also common for the individual to use self as a standard to which other individuals' behaviors are compared. Perceivers tend to assume that others who behave like them are responding to situational constraints, but it is assumed that others who behave quite differently from self must have very different self characteristics (Ross, Green, & House, 1977).

Third, individuals assume that the decisions they make in relation to self and others are reasonable and rational. This, however, is not always the case. Just as Ross, Green, and House suggest (1977), individuals may make what they assume to be rational assumptions about self and others that may not always be so rational. Because individuals might be more aware of their own inner thoughts and feelings than they can be of the inner thoughts and feelings of others, it is possible for mistaken assumptions to be made. If John is preparing to go to the front of the class and answer a question, he may look to others going before him to see if they are as nervous as he is. If these individuals are good at disguising their fear, John may erroneously assume that he is the only one who is nervous. This assumption, then, may cause John to become even more anxious about the task. This also suggests that comparisons to others may serve as important sources of self-relevant information when individuals want to know how they are doing. This concept, called social comparison (Festinger, 1954) will be discussed in depth in Chapter Five.

Fourth, the degree to which our beliefs or behaviors seem consistent or distinctive in relation to our past behaviors and the behavior of others often is used as a source of self-knowledge. If a person engages in behaviors that are contrary to her beliefs or that seem "out of character," that discrepancy (or dissonance if you will) will motivate either a change in behaviors or a change in assumptions about self (Festinger, 1957; Kelly, 1967). This reinforces a fundamental point that has permeated this entire text: self is a structure that is motivated not only toward understanding but toward consistency and stability as well.

Fifth, it is possible that individuals have no more information to base judgments of self on than others who may be observing them (Bem, 1972). Although when it first appeared this idea flew directly in the face of other theories of attribution that were still popular at the time (e.g., Festinger, 1957; Kelly, 1967), Bem's research clearly suggests that, at certain times and in certain situations, individuals may be forced to make determinations about self simply from the behavioral information they have available about their self. This suggestion that our own behaviors may serve as information sources for our own self-definitions forms the core of Bem's self-perception theory (Bem, 1972).

Jones and Nisbett (1976) suggest that actors and observers have equal access to certain kinds of information relevant to why the actor has behaved in a particular way. The caveat is that observers and actors do not have access to all the same information. Jones and Nisbett argue that actors and observers do (or can) have equal access to what is referred to as "cause" data and "effect" data. If this is the case, then individuals truly may be just as likely to draw conclusions about self from their own behaviors as others would be. Tellegen (1991), however, suggests that research indicates that the anti-trait movement in personality sparked by Mischel's (1968) scathing critique of personality psychology has "run its course." Although actors and observers do not have access to all of the same information, and thus cannot be expected to draw exactly the same conclusions about the actor, that does not mean that personality is an illusion. Kenrick and Funder (1988) as well as Tellegen (1991) suggest that the tendency to use uninformed observers in personality research may have actually fueled much of the anti-trait debate. If observers are used who actually know the actor, that observer truly may have access to most of the same information about the actor that the actor herself possesses. In this fashion, informed observers have sometimes been shown to agree substantially on characteristic ratings of actors' personalities (Tellegen, 1991).

Festinger's cognitive dissonance theory (1957) assumed that individuals are aware of their internal states, moods, attitudes, motivations, and so on. If this is the case, then engaging in behaviors that are dissonant or discrepant with those attitudes would create a state of discomfort he called "dissonance." When individuals experience dissonance between what they think or feel and how they have behaved, Festinger believed they would be motivated to alleviate that dissonance. Several methods for alleviating the discomfort would be possible. First, individuals could eliminate the discomfort by changing the attitude to be in line with the behavior. Second, the individuals could alleviate the discomfort by in some way changing their perception of the behavior. Third, individuals could relieve the dissonance by deciding that they had no choice but to act the way they did. Fourth, dissonance could be reduced by minimizing or rationalizing the discrepancy. Fifth, dissonance could be reduced by adding cognitions to support the behavior.

As can easily be deduced from this description of dissonance theory, there is a connection between self-perception and cognitive dissonance. Bem disagreed that individuals always have accurate or unambiguous information about their internal states, attitudes, motives, and so forth. If this information is not available, the individuals may look to behaviors to determine how they are doing. The behaviors they witness may lead them to make certain inferences about the self. If these inferences are inconsistent with internal attitudes and feelings that are clear, then dissonance may result. In effect, what at first seemed to be irreconcilable differences between two theories have come to clarify when dissonance will and will not take place. If the individual has sufficient justification for the behavior ("I said I like Republicans because I hoped to get invited to the party"), then dissonance will not result. Likewise, any self-perceptions of that behavior will tell the individual little about self. If, however, the individual does not feel that sufficient justification was present, dissonance may result and the individual may wonder "Why did I do that?" This assumption that dissonance and self-perception may result from different circumstances was confirmed in research done by Fazio, Zanna, and Cooper (1977).

Fazio and his colleagues discovered that dissonance is activated when individuals behave in ways that are greatly at odds with the feelings, attitudes, and so forth. If, however, the behaviors are only mildly discrepant from their internal standards, the tension associated with dissonance will not result. In these situations, the individual who wishes to make some kind of self-assessment may turn to self-perceptions to gather information with which to make inferences about the self. From this background information, then, it is possible to conclude that self-perceptions are most likely to be used when little information is available with which the behavior can be compared or in cases where there is a mild discrepancy between internal self characteristics and behaviors.

Self-perception theory is based on the assumption that individuals do not learn about self just by asking for or reflecting in the self-oriented opinions of others. To some extent, individuals cannot remove perceptions of their own behaviors from their evaluative judgments about how they are doing. Even if someone reflects an appraisal back to a person that he is doing a good job, there will be some judgment as to the validity of that reflection based on that person's interpretations of his own behavior. It is extremely important at this point to remind the reader that these assessments of one's own behavior may not be accurate. Individuals can be quite adept at deceiving self by distorting information, seeking out specific kinds of feedback, or engaging in automatic processes designed to maintain self-consistency or self-enhancement (e.g., Gilbert & Cooper, 1985; Langer, 1978; Nisbett & Wilson, 1975; Swann, 1983).

A student may listen politely as someone comments about her prowess as a student. How this feedback impacts self, however, depends in part on whether the individual believes it, based on her own interpretations of herself as a student. Would an individual prefer reflected appraisals or to infer evaluations from assessments of his or her own behavior? When reflected appraisals are possible, an individual will probably prefer such an evaluative method because the information may carry more weight when it comes from someone else. This assumption, however, must be tempered by the fact that the reflected appraisal only seems valid to the extent that the individual feels that the person doing the reflecting has some degree of expertise to be doing so.

If a tennis player wants to know how she's playing, she wouldn't want to ask someone who is not a tennis player because that person's standard of excellence may be so far below her own. The feedback that one is seeking will not mean a great deal if it comes from someone who is not in a good position to be making the judgment (e.g., Frank, 1985; Goethals & Darley, 1977; Miller, Turnball, & McFarland, 1990). Likewise, looking at one's behaviors in an attempt to make inferences about the self makes little sense if the behaviors one just engaged in were dictated by the situation. Multiple factors influence the development of self, and the individual is only one small part of that developmental process. If an individual chooses to engage in certain behaviors, then he or she will receive both feedback from others and some impression as to how to judge those behaviors for him or herself.

The complicated task for the individual becomes deciding how much emphasis to place on all the various sources of self-knowledge. The decision that one makes about which source of self-knowledge to pay attention to will, without question, have an impact on the self that develops and the feelings of self-worth that are attached to it. Choosing a self-knowledge source, of course, is certainly not an either/or process. At certain times and in certain situations, reflected appraisals (as suggested in Chapter Three) may be the most appropriate method for gathering self-relevant information. But it is just as likely that other situations would demand that an individual gather self-relevant information by judging his or her behaviors on their own merits without outside feedback. Chapter Four, therefore, presents summative information about self-perception as a source of self-knowledge and sets the tone for a discussion of social comparison processes in Chapter Five.

THE MECHANICS OF SELF-PERCEPTION THEORY

Few persons would find it surprising that self-analysis can serve as a source of knowledge about the self. When individuals engage in behaviors, they are not ignorant of the impact of those actions, nor are they able to completely withhold some degree of self-evaluation of those behaviors. It seems perfectly reasonable, therefore, to assume that individuals learn as much about themselves from observing their own actions as they do from reflected appraisals. This suggestion, that individuals learn from observations of their own actions, serves as the foundation for self-perception theory (Bem, 1972). Bem's conclusion that one can glean information about self from the same actions that others may be using to make inferences about one's self seems both logical and simple.

The extent to which individuals will turn to observations of their own behavior, however, depends partly on the ambiguity of the other feedback about self that they may be receiving. If an individual lost a tennis match and was booed off the court, she wouldn't have to analyze her own behaviors in too much detail to determine that she had played badly. But it is just as likely that the individual could be unclear as to how she performed and may turn to reactions from the crowd to clarify the success of the performance (e.g., Bem, 1972). It is also the case that the observation of one's own behaviors can serve to solidify the feelings that come back to self. If a person is laughing heartily with friends, it is reasonable for that individual then to assume that he must be happy (e.g., Bem, 1972; Jones, 1990).

Bem (1972) suggests two main postulates for self-perception theory, and then warns the reader that he is not trying to argue that the individual can gain information about self through observances of his or her overt actions only. According to Bem (1972, p. 5):

1. Individuals come to "know" their own attitudes, emotions, and other internal states partially by inferring them from observations of their own overt behavior and/or the circumstances in which this behavior occurs.
2. To the extent that internal cues are weak, ambiguous, or uninterpretable, the individual is functionally in the same position as an outside observer, an observer who must necessarily rely upon those same external cues to infer the individual's inner states.

These are important points for Bem to make because they delineate when individuals will and will not turn to observations of their own behavior for gathering information pertinent to the self. Unlike a behavioristic account, which would assume that an assessment of situational reinforcement contingencies would account for all behavior, Bem assumes that this is the case only part of the time. When internal cues are strong, clear, or interpretable, an individual will simply analyze those internal cues to make inferences about self. "My stomach is growling; I must be hungry." During those times when self-evaluation is desired (or dictated by situational circumstances), yet internal cues are weak, missing, or unreadable, individuals are left little choice but to examine their behaviors within the context of the situation in which it occurred and then make inferences about self from the outcome of that analysis (Bem, 1972, 1981).

Bem (1972) argues that demanding situational pressures eliminate the possibility that individuals will infer anything about self from their own actions. If a situation demands that a person behave in a particular way, then that individual will not make judgments about self based on those behaviors because they were not freely chosen. If, however, multiple response possibilities are available, the person may assume that he is an aggressive person if he chose to engage in an aggressive response. "Sufficient justification" becomes the central element to this self-perception process. If the individual feels that he had sufficient justification for the behavioral choices that were made, he is likely to infer little about personality from those "forced" choices.

As early as 1965, some researchers were contending that actors don't necessarily have the advantage over observers in understanding the behaviors the actors are engaging in (Bem, 1965). In these early writings, Bem argues that individuals, like the observers, must rely on perceptions of their own behavior and the context in which it is occurring to make inferences about the self. Given the attribution literature that was popular at the time, Bem's assumption that individuals have little awareness of the internal states that might be motivating their actions was radical and somewhat unpopular. But as time and further research has revealed (Vallacher & Wegner, 1987), depending on contextual factors and actors' representations of their own behavior, individuals do sometimes look to their behaviors to answer questions about who they are.

Compared to the cognitive dissonance theory, which was popular at the time that Bem proposed self-perception theory, Bem's assumption that individuals have little awareness of their internal states seemed contradictory. As the research progressed, however, Bem provided the seminal statement on when individuals will infer self by observing their own actions. "Individuals come to know their own attitudes, emotions, and other internal states partially by inferring them from observations of their own overt behavior and/or the circumstances in which the behavior occurs" (Bem, 1972, p. 2). When "internal cues are weak, ambiguous or uninterpretable," the individual must turn to what can be noted in inferring those internal states (Bem, 1972). Thus, in these times of ambiguity, the actor, like the observer, must look to the behavior to infer what otherwise could not be known.

Olson (1990) suggests that there are similarities between Schacter's (1964) theory of emotion and Bem's (1972) description of self-perception theory. Both of these theories involve the individual looking back over experiences and making judgments about relevant behaviors. If an individual wants to know what emotion he is experiencing, he may look to situational cues to provide the answer. Likewise, an individual wanting to know how she is doing on a given attribute may look to the situation and her behavior within it to provide answers to that question. If the individual discovers that compelling factors within the situation could have prompted or caused the behavior, then few inferences about self will be drawn. If, however, the individual discovers that little in the situation can account for the behavior, inferences will be drawn directly to the self. "I acted aggressively, so I must be an aggressive person." Bem suggests that individuals may ask questions about environmental contingencies when trying to decide whether a communicator believes his own message. In a similar vein, Bem reminds the reader that if one now applies the postulates of self-perception theory to this same example, one arrives at the hypothesis that the communicator himself might infer his own beliefs and attitudes from his behavior if that behavior appears to be free from the control of explicit reinforcement contingencies (Bem, 1972, p. 6).

In a classic experiment, Valins (1966) also provided evidence for the assumption that situational cues can sometimes determine internal states of knowledge. Valins gave male subjects false feedback of their responses to pictures of seminude females. In this manner, he was able to give them feedback that either sounded like their heart rate had sped up or slowed down in response to the picture. Not surprisingly, subjects rated the individuals in the pictures as more attractive when they had been given feedback falsely suggesting that they were attracted to the female depicted in it. In this manner, Valins was able to show that something as apparently private and internal as emotional states can be pushed in various directions by situational parameters.

Bem concludes his review of self-perception theory by suggesting that social psychology as a field take a different approach in the assumptions it makes. Bem argued that social psychologists had been making the assumption that everything is glued together until it is proven otherwise. This means that social psychological theories assume, for example, that attitudes predict behavior perfectly until the evidence proves that assumption to be incorrect. Bem implies that we might make just as much, if not more, progress if the field were to adopt a view that "nothing is tied together unless it is proven otherwise." If this is the case, then the +.30 correlations between traits and behaviors lamented by Mischel (1968) would be less discouraging. Has time proven Bem's suggestion to have been a sound one? A superficial review of the literature with an eye toward the implications of self-perception theory may provide the answer.

IMPLICATIONS OF SELF-PERCEPTION

The ramifications of self-perception theory are sometimes difficult to uncover. The implications and impact of self-perception theory have been profound in some respects and almost hidden in others. Certainly most theorists now agree that individuals do garner some sense of self from watching what they do. But as Brehm and Kassin (1993) remind the reader, a crucial question must be asked. Is it the behavior itself that is important for determining the implications of the action for self or how the individual interprets that behavior? Certainly discussions from other sections of this text would support the notion that interpretations are what matter (e.g., Chapter Two's discussion of levels of interpretation of success and failures and the implications for self-esteem).

Vallacher and Wegner's (1985) action identification theory has been cited as evidence to support the notion that the individual's interpretation of his or her behavior is what matters. This theory assumes that individuals identify their behaviors in either high-level or low-level terms. High-level descriptions of behavior are in general, global, and abstract terms. Low-level descriptions are more mechanical and involve more specifiable components of the actual behavior. I, for example, am writing this textbook. In low-level terms, that means I am typing computer keyboard keys in a particular sequence in order to form words, combining words in order to form sentences, and so on. In high-level terms, I am trying to articulate action identification theory to you within the framework of enhancing your understanding of the eclectic nature of self. Certainly these are very different descriptions of the very same behavior.

The extent to which an individual describes or thinks about his or her behaviors in low-level or high-level terms can affect the self-perception process. Low-level descriptions of behaviors are mechanistic and uninformative in terms of self. High-level interpretations, on the other hand, can be very informative about the self and therefore may prompt self-perceptions. Individuals who tend to think about their behaviors in high-level terms, then, may use self-perceptions more often as a method for drawing inferences about self. If individuals tend to think about and describe behavior in low-level terms, however, very little information about self can be gathered in that manner. These individuals, then, may turn to other methods of acquiring self-knowledge, such as social comparisons (to be described in depth in Chapter Five) or other sources.

Another implication for self-perception theory has come out of research on overjustification (e.g., Lepper, Green, & Nisbett, 1973; Pittman & Heller, 1987). This concept suggests that rewarding someone for performing an otherwise enjoyable activity may diminish the intrinsic (internal) motivation the person has for performing the task. An individual may work very hard hauling around chunks of marble because the sculptures he carves from them give him great pleasure. Would the same person, however, find the same task as intrinsically rewarding if it were a required part of his job? Numerous experiments have shown that extrinsically rewarding a previously intrinsically rewarding behavior or task can diminish the degree to which the individual continues to find the behavior intrinsically rewarding (e.g., Deci & Ryan, 1985).

This, of course, can have profound implications for self-perceptions. If an individual is rewarded for engaging in a behavior that she found intrinsically rewarding anyway, what happens when the individual uses that behavior to draw inferences about self? Remember that these inferences will be based not only on the behaviors the individual engaged in but also the situational context in which those behaviors occurred. A student who finds doing research intrinsically rewarding may lose some of her enthusiasm for it when she is doing the same work for a course grade. It becomes increasingly difficult, in this manner, for the student to continue to claim that she is doing research because she finds it to be an intrinsically interesting thing to do. (There seems to be a mindset in American culture that suggests we shouldn't get paid for doing something we would have done anyway. An extension of this mindset also suggests that if we do get paid for doing something, we probably wouldn't have done it for free.)

Self-perception theory has been implicated in helping behaviors. (e.g., Strenta & DeJong, 1981). Certainly some individuals consider helping others to be an important part of who they are. One need look only as far as the local soup kitchen or Goodwill Store to see individuals helping others for apparently selfless reasons. It certainly also is the case that being labeled as "helpful" by others can impact one's self positively. But what happens if individuals are rewarded for helping or pressured into helping through applications of guilt? As the research previously summarized on overjustification would suggest, individuals who are coerced into helping or rewarded in some way for helping would be less likely to infer from those behaviors that they were "helpful." In these circumstances, then, helping would have very little positive impact on self and, in certain cases, could even have a detrimental impact. An individual who, through observing his behaviors, decides that he helped someone in order to impress his date may come to question what kind of person would choose to help for such a selfish reason. The resulting impact on self could be quite negative.

Brehm and Kassin (1993) suggest that self-perception theory could have implications for compliance techniques. In an adaption of Freedman and Fraser (1966), these authors suggest that the "foot-in-the-door" compliance technique may work because the individuals observe their own behavior and then draw inferences about "what kind of person is likely to engage in that kind of behavior." With this technique, individuals are asked to perform a small request. Given the smallness of the first request, most subjects comply. At some later point, these same individuals are asked to perform a significantly larger request. Self-perception theory would predict that those individuals who refused the smaller request also would refuse the larger one. Likewise, those who agreed to the smaller request would be more likely to agree to the larger request as well. When the individuals are asked to do the large request, they are likely to look back on past instances in which they were asked a favor. In this manner, the individuals who agreed to the first request have that behavior as evidence of the fact that they must be the kind of people that help. Those who refused the initial request, however, can look to that as evidence that they are not the kind who agree to favors.

All of these suggested implications for self-perception theory relate back to the most often mentioned concept of this text. Individuals are motivated to maintain self-consistency or congruency, and one method by which that consistency can be maintained is by making current decisions based on previous behaviors. If the situation is new, however, past experience may tell the individuals little about what inferences to make about self. In these instances, self-perception can still take place. It might also be argued that the more ambiguous the situation, or the less prior experience the individuals have with the situation or behavior in question, the more likely it is that self-perceptions will take place and self-inferences drawn from them.

WRAPPING IT UP: WHAT DOES ALL THIS MEAN?

Self-perception theory has been implicated in a variety of social-related behaviors including action identification theory, the implications of overjustification, patterns of helping behaviors, and compliance techniques. Although this list of theories related to self-perception is certainly not exhaustive, it does provide insights into how self-perception theory relates to an eclectic approach to self. This text is concerned not only with the manner in which individuals gather information and knowledge about self but also with the ramifications of that knowledge for self (Backman, 1988). Individuals are clearly motivated to maintain consistency between their self, their behaviors, and the manner in which those behaviors are perceived or interpreted by others. To the extent that precise self-knowledge is not always known by self, other sources must be available by which that information can be gathered. One method for acquiring this all important self-knowledge is by turning to the same information that others use to make inferences about self: one's behaviors. After all, actions occasionally speak louder than words.

But what is one to do when the behavior has not been performed yet or an evaluative standard is missing? In these cases, self-perceptions would result in less than complete self-inference information. It stands to reason that individuals may turn to others to answer questions such as "How am I doing?" when the answer cannot be directly determined through some score or through observations of one's behavior. It is this kind of comparison to others, then, that serves as the focus for the following chapter of the text.

CODA

This review of the implications of self-perception theory should be concluded by bringing the discussion back to Bem's final suggestion in his original writing on self-perception theory. Is it the case that social psychology should adopt the philosophy of science that nothing is interrelated until it is proved otherwise? Although I'm not sure how Bem would answer that question, I think the years of self research have moved the literature beyond the question. Certainly much of the self research being done in the years since Bem proposed his theory in 1972 seem to have adopted the stance that nothing is interrelated. This, of course, is not being leveled against the literature as a complaint as much as a point of fact. Some monumental efforts have been made to bridge the gap between various self theorists and their theoretical positions (e.g., Wylie, 1974, 1979), but the bulk of research has centered on very specific questions within very specific self domains.

As research on self has flourished, smaller efforts have been made to convince individuals working in the area to try to bridge the gaps between their theoretical frames of mind. Such is the main purpose of this text. The research seems to have proved that things in self are interrelated, and the time is right for an eclectic approach designed to tie up many of the loose ends. As the rest of the text unfolds, the reader is encouraged to reflect back on the interrelatedness of the material that is being presented and ask "What does this tell me about the other issues that have already been raised?" Everything we learn about self-esteem, for example, should tell us a little bit more about self-concept in general than we already know. Each piece of information gathered about how individuals acquire self-relevant information tells us more about how individuals use self to structure and make sense of their worlds. Together these pieces of information clarify the picture of what self is and delineate for us the impact that this entity called "self" has for the structure and functioning of the whole person.

Given the wealth of information that has been collected about self and all of its many facets, it should come as no surprise to the reader that many of the differently shaped pieces can be put together to solve many puzzles. Individuals with differing levels of self-esteem, differing self-images, differing expectations for self, and so on, have dramatically different views of the world. These views motivate them to do things differently, to have different priorities, and to expect different things from the other individuals who make up their social worlds. Part of these differences are a reflection of the individuality of the person based on the uniqueness of his or her self, and part of these differences are based on cultural expectations and assumptions. Certainly it is the case that the uniqueness of the individual influences his or her perceptions of the social world. It must also, therefore, be the case that the individual is determined in part by the social context in which he or she is developing. This social context is made up of both the other individuals within it (perhaps being used by the individual for making social comparisons) and the more global context labeled as culture. We have discussed a variety of issues related to individual differences in experiences and characteristics and the impact they have on self as a social construct. Let us now turn our attention to the potentially profound impact of the others within that context and then discuss the impact of culture on self.

Several authors (e.g., Filipp, 1979; Filipp, Aymanns, & Braukmann, 1986) have articulated a necessity for theories of self also to focus on the "boundaries" of self. Establishing an understanding of the parameters of self, indeed, is critical to an eclectic comprehension of self. Filipp, Aymanns, and Braukmann (1986) suggest that any theorizing about self inevitably would have to come around to issues about these self-related boundaries. According to these researchers, "These issues are centered around the following questions: How do individuals cognitively construe their experiences and what do they learn from these about themselves? What is the information like that is encoded as self-referent (versus not), thus entering the system of self-knowledge? How is the continuous flow of self-referent information organized and stored in memory (that part of the memory usually referred to as 'the self-concept')?" It is easy to see that these questions can best be answered by addressing issues related to self-knowledge. Related questions that will help to provide information relevant for addressing the issues raised by Filipp, Aymanns, and Braukmann (1986) would be: What sources of self-knowledge do individuals turn to? What individuals serve as self-knowledge sources for the individual? When will certain sources of self-knowledge information be preferred over others? These questions, then, will serve as the driving forces behind the chapters in this section.

CHAPTER FIVE

Social Comparison

INTRODUCTION TO SOCIAL COMPARISON THEORY

It has long been argued that self is a social construct (e.g., James, 1890; Mead, 1934) and individuals sometimes turn to others in the social environment to make judgments as to how they are doing. Given that social interactions are an important part of the self-development process, an eclectic theory of self would be incomplete without giving consideration to the active comparisons individuals make to others in attempts to understand their own self. Research has also suggested that attributes that make individuals seem unique often serve as the foundation through which individuals will describe self (e.g., McGuire, McGuire, & Winton, 1979; McGuire & McGuire, 1988). If an individual is the only one in his family to have blue eyes, he may see that characteristic as being important to his self-definition (McGuire & McGuire, 1988). This same individual's brown-eyed siblings, however, may not consider eye color important to their own self-definitions because their eye color matches the family norm. This suggests that an important part of the self-definition process is comparing self-attributes to those of the others who make up our social environment.

Leon Festinger (1954a) proposed social comparison theory to explain how and why individuals turn to others as standards for determining their own self-definitions. Festinger argued that people turn to others as comparison targets for self to the extent that other, more objective information is not available. A student, for example, might compare herself to other students in her math course to determine how good she is at math if the instructor has not provided her with more objective evaluative information (such as exam scores). At the outset, social comparison to others seems to be a very reasonable way to acquire self-evaluative information to the extent that other sources of information are lacking.

As Wheeler (1991) points out, the components and mechanics of social comparison theory were nicely summarized by Festinger (1954b, p. 217) when he proposed:

> We started out by assuming the existence of a motivation to know one's opinions are correct and to know precisely what one is and is not capable of doing. From this motivation, which is certainly non-social in character, we have made the following derivations about the conditions under which a social comparison process arises and about the nature of this social comparison process.
>
> 1. This social process arises when the evaluation of opinions or abilities is not feasible by testing directly in the environment.
>
> 2. Under such circumstances persons evaluate their opinions and abilities by comparison with others.
>
> 3. This comparison leads to pressures toward uniformity.
>
> 4. There is a tendency to stop comparing oneself with others who are very divergent. This tendency increases if others are perceived as different from oneself in relevant dimensions.
>
> 5. Factors such as importance, relevance, and attraction to a group which affect the strength of the original motivation will affect the strength of the pressure towards uniformity.

Wheeler (1991) suggests that social comparison theory has had a rocky road for multiple reasons. Although Festinger's summary of the theory's derivations provides an excellent foundation by which social comparison processes can be understood, the research clearly shows that many complex questions remain.

According to Wheeler (1991), social comparison theory seemed poised on the brink of launching a major research explosion. But, alas, the explosion never came. Several reasons have been cited by researchers to explain this lack of growth in the social comparison literature. Nissen (1954) disagrees that the drive that motivates social comparison necessarily would pressure the individual toward uniformity. Nissen argues that it is just as likely that individuals may find information about how they diverge from others to be just as, if not more, informative as comparisons of similarity. Singer (1966) explains that many studies published after social comparison theory was proposed use the theoretical idea as a point of reference (e.g., Schacter, 1959), but little theoretical work was done directly on the theory.

Why is it that social comparison theory was essentially abandoned in its infancy? Wheeler (1991) provides several answers to that question. According to Wheeler (1991) social comparison theory enjoyed little growth early on because Festinger himself abandoned it to work on dissonance theory. The social comparison theory seemed to be so tightly drawn that little other empirical work on the theory was needed, and the ambiguity of the theory left little room for drawing conclusions about what other questions needed to be asked or answered. This dry spell, however, slowly gave way to a steady progression of social comparison research. The bulk of the literature surrounding social comparison theory has centered on three crucial interrelated issues: when social comparisons will be made, toward whom these comparisons should be made, and what the implications of the social comparison process are. This is the foundation on which most refinements of and additions to social comparison theory have been built. These questions and the answers that have been discovered for them have served to clarify social comparison theory and lend important insights into the eclectic nature of self.

In order to tie these social comparison processes into an eclectic approach to self, it will be necessary to provide a summary of the implications of these questions for the individual who is making the comparison, as well as the implications for the individual toward whom the comparison is directed.

First, questions linger about when social comparisons will be made. Answers to these questions are important because self is affected by the comparisons that are made. If objective information is available, will such information always be preferred over the more subjective self-evaluative information that comes to self through social comparison? The second relevant question to ask is toward whom these comparisons should be made. When a decision has been made to make a social comparison, it follows quite logically that the next question involves toward whom one should make that comparison. The person one chooses to compare oneself to will have dramatic implications for the effect of that comparison on self. If a student compares his analytical skills to those of Albert Einstein, how is he likely to feel about his own analytical prowess? The third question centers on the implications of the social comparison process. As already suggested, whom the individual chooses to compare self to and the outcome of that comparison process can have a profound effect on the individual. Is social comparison always a good thing? Is it possible that social comparisons can lead to faulty information about self that may create or perpetuate self problems? It is reasonable to assume that answers to these questions can be quite important in terms of treating particular problems. If an individual is making comparisons to an inappropriate comparison other, it may lead to inappropriate interpretations of feedback, which in turn may foster or perpetuate low self-esteem.

This suggests that social comparisons need not be accurate to have a profound effect on the self of the person making the comparisons. This also suggests that comparisons can move in either an upward or a downward direction (as first suggested by Wills in 1981). Upward comparisons would usually result in fairly accurate impressions of one's ability ("I'm okay at tennis, but I won't win Wimbledon anytime soon"). If, however, the individual engages in comparisons directed downward, self-esteem may be enhanced ("Compared to this bozo, I'm an expert"). To maintain one's current conception of self, then, unilateral comparisons would need to be made. In this circumstance, the individual compares self to similar others, which leads to an "I'm okay, you're okay" frame of mind. Since these social comparison issues are so interrelated, the following discussion will cluster them into two overall questions: When and toward whom will comparisons be made? What are the implications of these comparison choices?

WHEN AND TOWARD WHOM WILL SOCIAL COMPARISONS BE MADE?

The most comprehensive summary on social comparison theory and research seems to be an edited volume by Suls and Wills (1991). In it, contributors provide a comprehensive coverage of social comparison theory and research. A few of the topics discussed include a history of social comparison theory (Wheeler, 1991), social comparison and self-relevant goals (e.g., Wood & Taylor, 1991), the impact of downward comparisons (e.g., Luhtanen & Crocker, 1991; Major, Testa, & Bylsma, 1991; Wills, 1991), and applied models of social comparison (e.g., Gibbons & Gerrard, 1991; Nagata & Crosby, 1991). Many of these topics relate directly to the three questions or issues previously raised. As such, an understanding of some of the main points these authors provide about social comparison will add to our understanding of how social comparison processes relate to an eclectic theory of self.

Luhtanen and Crocker (1991) provide a useful summary of research and theories focusing on intergroup comparisons and their subsequent effect on self-esteem. Part of the reason an individual may have for making social comparisons would be to protect an already fragile sense of self-esteem or to enhance self-esteem. From a diverse group of sources such as Erlich (1973) or noted philosopher Milton Mayeroff (1971), the literature has suggested that self-acceptance and acceptance for others may be interrelated processes. This means that acceptance of self may be a necessary precursor for acceptance of others (Erlich, 1973) and that acceptance of self may be impossible without first caring for and accepting others (Mayeroff, 1971). This becomes a complicated issue because an individual who does not like self may very well project that dislike onto others (e.g., Erlich,1973; Freud, 1938).

Not all research agrees with what has been referred to earlier in this text as an "I'm okay, you're okay" frame of mind. It may also be the case that individuals who have questions about their self-worth can use the tragedies of others as a method for bolstering self-esteem. If individuals have uncertain self-esteem or low self-esteem and wish to enhance those feelings, one method by which this can be accomplished is through derogation of others (e.g., Luhtanen & Crocker, 1991; Wills, 1991). In this manner, individuals may specifically choose a less fortunate comparison other in an attempt to make themselves feel better.

But what if a less fortunate comparison other is not directly available? At these times, individuals may engage in self-esteem enhancement by belittling, derogating, or discriminating against others (e.g., Wills, 1981). Wills suggests that individuals will be most likely to make downward comparisons (comparing self to less fortunate others) when they feel their well-being has been threatened or their self-esteem is low. Luhtanen and Crocker (1991) suggest that in the case of failure experiences or if negative failure feedback is directed toward self from others, individuals will be likely to attempt to restore self-esteem through downward comparison. "Biased intergroup comparisons may therefore be motivated by the need to restore self-esteem following threat" (Luhtanen & Crocker, 1991, p. 213).

These researchers further suggest that individuals with chronically low self-esteem may be most likely to engage in downward social comparisons due to the chronic threat to their self-concept. They also suggest that "chronically low self-esteem individuals who have further received a situational threat to their self-esteem should be the most in need of self-enhancement, and thus the most likely to compare downward by, for example, derogating members of outgroups" (Luhtanen & Crocker, 1991, p. 214). In this manner, self-esteem threats may not only motivate the individual to engage in social comparisons but may also motivate a particular style of social comparison toward a particular type of comparison other that is meant to bolster self-esteem through derogation of those less fortunate than self.

The previous paragraphs provide four different answers to the question of "when" social comparisons will be made. Although these are not the only answers to be provided, a quick summary of them might be beneficial before going on to the rest of the review.

First, social comparisons will be made as a self-protection strategy (e.g., Luhtanen & Crocker, 1991). If self is viewed as fragile, individuals may engage in social comparisons in an attempt to "shore up the defenses." Second, social comparisons can be made in an attempt to provide the information to be used in self-acceptance (e.g., Erlich, 1973; Mayeroff, 1971). In this manner, individuals may simply want to reconfirm to themselves that an attribute is, indeed, a part of their self-definition. Third, individuals may use particular kinds of social comparisons in an attempt to recover from self-esteem threats (e.g., Luhtanen & Crocker, 1991). This is not the same as protecting a self-esteem level that is fragile. This would be attempting to reestablish a self-esteem level that has been knocked about by some self-esteem threat. Fourth, individuals may use social comparisons as methods for engaging in self-enhancement (e.g., Luhtanen & Crocker, 1991; Wills, 1981, 1991). Whether the individuals' self-esteem level is low or high, certain kinds of social comparisons can reflect positively back on the self and, therefore, enhance self-esteem beyond its current level.

Further review of the literature suggests that numerous remaining factors seem to determine when and toward whom social comparisons will be made. Of these, the most important factors seem to be evaluation of possible selves, maintaining self-congruency, as a strategy of self-defense, providing accurate sources of self-information, and serving self goals. Markus and Nurius (1986), for example, have suggested that possible selves play a role in the comparisons that an individual will make. Markus and Nurius argue that possible selves can develop in either of two ways. First, prior social comparisons may help to indicate to individuals what may be possible for their self in current and future situations. Second, past selves may serve as guidelines by which individuals can reasonably determine what else may be possible for the self. This strongly suggests that social comparisons play an ongoing role in helping individuals to establish parameters for what is possible for the self (Markus & Nurius, 1986).

It is a well-established point that individuals value congruency in terms of self, behaviors, and interpretations and perceptions of those behaviors (e.g., Backman, 1988). According to Backman (1988), this congruency can be established in three forms: by implication, by validation, and by comparison. Congruency by implication is established when someone perceives individuals as having a characteristic the individuals believe applies to their self. Congruency by validation is established when others behave toward the individual in ways that are consistent with the individual's self-concept. Last, congruency by comparison occurs when the individual compares self to others and discovers that these others possess characteristics that are consistent with self characteristics (Brackman, 1988).

These points suggest that social comparisons also will be made when an individual experiences some threat to self-congruency (e.g., Luhtanen & Crocker, 1991; Swann, 1987). This is similar to the discussion of self-esteem threats presented earlier, but congruency threats need not involve a threat to self-esteem as well. These threats can come in the form of direct challenges (someone claims that a person who views his self as honest is actually dishonest), or indirect challenges (an individual through self-perception believes that she has behaved in a manner that is inconsistent with self). In this manner, social comparison processes can serve an important role that has been suggested several times throughout this work. Individuals value congruency between self, their behaviors, and the manner in which those behaviors are interpreted and/or perceived by others. Although social comparisons are typically made in an effort to draw conclusions about self, they can also be used as a method by which existing self beliefs can be verified.

Mettee and Smith (1977) argued that dissimilar others may sometimes be preferred as comparison others. These researchers suggested that dissimilar others may be preferred for two reasons. First, they serve as a method of self-defense because affective consequences may be blunted when comparing to dissimilar others. Second, dissimilar others may serve as better sources of information. Although this seems perfectly reasonable, is it always the case that affect is blunted when comparing to dissimilar others? It seems just as likely that negative affect can be activated if the comparison other is dissimilar because he or she is so much better than the one doing the comparing. But Taylor and Mettee (1971) found that dissimilar others may sometimes be liked more because, if the comparison that is being made comes out unfavorable, this comparison other can simply be dismissed as irrelevant. Such an out of hand dismissal is difficult if the comparison other is similar to self. But what if the dissimilar other is dissimilar only on the characteristic that is of importance to the individual making the comparisons?

If a student in a course in which nontraditional grades are given wants to know how she is doing, she may compare herself to another student similar to herself in most respects. But if the point of departure in similarity between her self and the comparison other is the ability being called for in the classroom, comparisons will lead to a negative affective state for the individual. All of this is tempered by the degree to which the comparing individual is familiar with the attribute in question (e.g., Friend & Gilbert, 1973). If individuals receive some sort of score but do not know what that score means, they will be motivated to compare to others because an objective standard for evaluating how they are doing is absent. Because the individuals are unfamiliar with the scoring system, however, the most informative comparison others would be those individuals whose scores are most dissimilar. In this manner, the comparing individuals could discover the grade for the lowest and highest scorers and then gain some sense of how their own score stands in comparison (Suls & Wills, 1991).

Brickman and Bulman (1977) suggest that social comparison may initiate a tug-of-war within the self. By this they mean that individuals may be motivated to compare socially and also may be motivated to avoid comparisons. If social comparisons are made between two persons, it is usually inevitable that one person will wind up being labeled as "better." This creates a sense of discomfort in the situation that both individuals are motivated to alleviate. The easiest way to eliminate this discomfort, of course, is to avoid it in the first place.

Wood and Taylor (1991) summarize some of the relevant social comparison literature in concluding that people will compare themselves to others for varied reasons. In this regard, individuals may be trying to fulfill a variety of goals (or satisfy a variety of self-motives) by making social comparisons, and the goal the individual is attempting to fulfill may have a dramatic impact on how the comparison ultimately effects self. The individuals, for example, may be comparing to others in an attempt to discover some global information about self (Singer, 1966) or even to evaluate their emotions (Schacter, 1959). But the literature seems to be coming full circle. In Festinger's (1954) original formulation of social comparison, he suggested that individuals socially compare in order to gather accurate information about self that eventually may be used to better the self. Theorists began to suggest that individuals may be motivated to compare socially in an effort to enhance the self (e.g., Taylor & Brown, 1988) rather than always gather accurate feedback. This suggests that an additional motive of social comparison is enhancing self-esteem. At the same time, however, other researchers are providing evidence that suggests that social comparisons may be made in such a manner as to perpetuate whatever level of self is currently in place (e.g., Swann, 1987).

This quick summary of issues related to when and toward whom social comparisons will be made suggests that understanding social comparison processes is complicated at best. Multiple factors are involved in determining if, when, and toward whom such comparisons will be made. Individuals have multiple reasons for initiating social comparisons. The reasons include efforts to establish an understanding of what is possible for the self, to maintain self-congruency, to initiate patterns of self-defense, to garner accurate information about one's current self, and to satisfy self-relevant goals. Cross-cutting all of this, however, is an understanding that social comparisons may sometimes be avoided for the very reasons that sometimes they are preferred. If an individual feels that self may be threatened by making social comparisons, such situations are likely to be avoided. Likewise, an individual may not be motivated to make social comparisons when well-established objective standards for performance are in existence.

As Wood and Taylor (1991) suggest, the issues involved in determining when and what type of social comparison will be made center around the goals or reasons that may be motivating the comparison. If individuals simply want to address the issue of "How am I doing?" comparisons should be made to a similar other if the attribute is familiar to the comparing individuals and to dissimilar others if the attribute is unfamiliar to the comparing individuals. This provides the individuals with the most diagnostic information because the similar other tells how he or she is doing on an attribute that is understood, and the dissimilar other gives valuable feedback in establishing performance guidelines on an attribute that is unfamiliar.

If individuals wish to self-improve, the comparison other that is chosen will be obviously superior to the comparing individuals. In this manner, individuals get the most critical feedback about their attribute, which can provide a point of reference from which improvement strategies can be devised. If, on the other hand, the individuals wish to feel better about self, downward comparisons (Hakmiller, 1966; Wills, 1981) are the best strategy. In this manner, individuals compare self to others who are inferior on a dimension that is self-relevant to the comparing individuals.

When such downward comparisons are made, the comparing individuals can feel better about their own level on an attribute because they can find at least one person who is significantly worse off. If dissimilar others are not available for comparison, Wood and Taylor (1991) suggest that the second preference would be for others who are similar. This provides the individual with the opportunity to say, "At least I'm as good as Bob." Finally, if the dimension of interest in the comparison is one that the individuals feel is out of their control (being unemployed, an illness), social comparisons may be avoided completely (Major, Testa, & Bylsma, 1991). Social comparisons on uncontrollable attributes may be avoided because there seems to be very little to be gained by making them. Comparing oneself to others who are better off (upward comparisons) on attributes that seem uncontrollable just points out that others are better off, whereas comparing oneself to others who are worse off (downward comparisons) may simply serve as an indicator of what is in the future.

Festinger's (1954) original assumption that individuals will compare themselves with similar others because these individuals provide the most accurate information about self abilities has been systematically revised. Goethals and Darley (1977) suggest that "similarity" is not necessarily of a global type. If a student wants to know how she is doing on mechanical aptitude, it makes little sense to compare herself randomly to a nineteen-year-old with brown hair. The individual, instead, will seek out comparison others who are similar on the attribute in question. In this manner, the student may compare herself with another student in the course, rather than a similar other taking a watercolor course.

Miller, Turnball, and McFarland (1990) and Turner, Miller, and McFarland (1988) refer to an individual's "universalistic standing." This involves the individual's standing on an attribute in relation to other individuals, not just similar others. This suggests that persons wanting to know how they are doing may have two different reasons for making the comparisons. First, the individuals making the comparison may compare to others in an attempt to analyze their attributes in relation to a particular reference group. This may suggest to the individuals whether an increase in effort is required in order to live up to some explicit standard for performance (Frank, 1985).

If an individual wishes to know exactly how good she is in biology, simply comparing to similar others in terms of age, gender, grade level, and intelligence will not give her a very clear picture of her universal standing. At these times, when individuals truly want to know "just how good they really are," comparing to someone who is dissimilar in many unrelated respects but truly similar on the attribute in question will provide the most accurate answer. All of these issues further complicate the social comparison picture and strongly suggest that no simple answers will be found for the questions of when and toward whom comparisons will be made. But it does seem plausible that providing answers to those questions will also be related to questions of what implications such social comparisons have for the individual doing the comparing and the person toward whom the comparison is directed. As these issues are further clarified, a working model of social comparison processes can be created to address the interconnections among these issues. Before presenting such a working model, however, let us quickly address the remaining issue. What are the implications, for both self and other, of the comparison choices the individual makes?

IMPLICATIONS OF COMPARISON CHOICES

It has already been suggested that comparison choices impact self-esteem (Luhtanen & Crocker, 1991; Major, Testa, & Bylsma, 1991; Will, 1991). But are there other implications for the choices individuals make about when and toward whom they make their comparisons? A quick perusal of the contributed chapters in Suls and Wills (1991) shows that social comparison has been implicated in envy and jealousy (Salovey, 1991), coping with threat (Gibbons & Gerrard, 1991), perceptions of justice (Nagata & Crosby, 1991), and coping with major medical problems (Affleck & Tennen, 1991).

As Salovey (1991) succinctly states, "although social comparison theory has inspired social psychological research for nearly four decades, until recently very little attention has been paid to the emotional consequences of social comparison processes" (Salovey, 1991, p. 261). Though Salovey's summary of envy and jealousy and social comparison processes is enlightening, the information most relevant to this eclectic presentation of self deals with the social consequences (implications) of these "resentment emotions." According to Salovey (1991), social comparisons that result in envy and jealousy must be resolved in some way, and five resolutions are suggested, each of which results in different implications for self. The individual can resolve these resentment emotions by (1) changing self-definitions, (2) reducing the relevance of the comparison person by minimizing contact with the comparison other, (3) derogation of rivals, (4) re-attributing the reasons for the other's success, and (5) violence (Salovey, 1991). Which of these strategies the individual chooses depends on a variety of factors, including what strategies have been successful in the past, whether other strategies have been tried but failed to resolve the current resentment emotions, the magnitude of the resentment emotions that are activated, and the degree to which contact with the offending comparison other can be avoided.

Gibbons and Gerrard (1991) start their discussion of "Downward Comparison and Coping with Threat" by stating that, "People engage in social comparison for one reason, and that is to gain information. While that motive remains constant, the desire to obtain information as well as the type of information that is sought vary considerably depending on the person and the circumstances in which the comparison occurs" (Gibbons & Gerrard, 1991, p. 317). This quote reinforces several points that have already been addressed in this discussion of social comparison processes. It seems quite clear that individuals may have a variety of reasons for making comparisons, and different comparison others may be chosen as a result of what type of information is sought by the person making the comparison. These authors argue that when an individual is threatened in some way (whether that threat is psychological or physical in nature), the threat impacts the social comparison process. In particular, they suggest that threat "steers that comparison in a downward direction."

In this way, downward social comparisons can serve as coping strategies that individuals can use to deal with psychological and physical threats. According to Gibbons and Gerrard (1991), there are two benefits to downward comparisons: positive effects on subjective well-being, and positive effects on coping. Downward comparisons enhance subjective well-being because (1) the understanding that things can always be worse leads to an enhancement of mood, (2) understanding that others have survived worse leads to feelings of optimism that the individuals can get through this, (3) self-esteem can be enhanced through downward comparisons, and (4) the individuals' sense of personal deviance is reduced if they realize that they are not alone in suffering whatever the problem happens to be. These researchers mention that many of these subjective benefits to downward comparisons may be involved in group therapy strategies, and this makes a great deal of sense. Individuals may garner many benefits from interacting with others who are suffering or have suffered through the same ordeal. The benefits accrued through enhancing subjective well-being may cycle back and lead the individuals to engage in more effective coping.

This summary of the main points made by Gibbons and Gerrard (1991) suggests that downward comparisons can have profound implications for the well-being of the individuals making the comparisons. The more information the individuals can gather about what realistically to expect with a particular problem, the better prepared they can be in facing the problem. Knowing that others are worse off or have been worse off and survived serves to keep the individuals grounded realistically in dealing with the problem. Such comparisons put the individuals in a better frame of mind than upward comparisons would. Comparing self to better off others in order to evaluate how self is doing can be a painful experience that actually provides less information than a downward comparison. This suggests that downward comparisons do not always lead to inaccurate information about self. If the individuals' sense of self is threatened by some problem or perceived problem, downward comparisons may provide the most realistic information for judging the severity of the problem and the prognosis they can expect.

Downward comparisons, however, need not always be active. Baumeister, Tice, and Hutton (1989) found that low self-esteem subjects were less likely to engage in self-enhancement, and Gibbons and McCoy (1991) found that low self-esteem persons are less likely to derogate others in response to self threats than their high self-esteem counterparts. This is not meant to suggest that individuals with low self-esteem do not use self-enhancement and downward comparisons. Tice (1991, 1993) already has suggested that low and high self-esteem persons may be motivated by different self-related goals. Low self-esteem persons were noted to be motivated to protect self or minimize the potential damage of threat. These individuals may use less active methods than high self-esteem persons. Indeed Brown, Collins, and Schmidt (1988) found that individuals with low self-esteem experiencing self threats rated a group of similar others more favorably than a group of dissimilar others. Brown et al. (1988) referred to this as "indirect enhancement." Likewise, Gibbons and McCoy (1991) found that persons with low self-esteem do not tend to derogate a less fortunate other when their own self is threatened, but they do feel better when exposed to that less fortunate other. This was referred to as "passive downward comparisons" (Gibbons & McCoy, 1991).

Nagata and Crosby (1991) remind the reader that social comparisons are not always made in attempts to evaluate the self. Social comparisons also can be made to evaluate the social system. Such comparisons may impact one's sense of justice. The most important part of Nagata and Crosby's (1991) enlightening work is the connection they discuss between the expectations one has about a social system, the social comparisons that therefore are made, and the resulting sense of justice (or injustice) that is experienced. When individuals make comparisons to the norms for a given social system, they may feel relatively successful if they performed at or above the level of the norms, or relatively deprived if they succeeded below the norms (Stouffer, Suchman, DeVinney, Star, & Williams, 1949). This concept suggests that the individuals' perception of how well they are doing is partially determined by their standing relative to the group norm. If everyone else in your social group goes to college, then doing so yourself will not impact your self feelings very much. Being the first one in the family or neighborhood to go to college, however, may be interpreted as a relatively big deal. Merton and Rossi (1957) argue that people's feelings of dissatisfaction depend on both objective and subjective reality. In this manner, an individual can be satisfied with a level of accomplishment or success that others may see as less than adequate. Likewise, an individual who has achieved what others would consider to be a high degree of accomplishment could be quite dissatisfied.

In summary, the points made by Nagata and Crosby (1991) provide a balance between social comparisons that are made in an attempt to evaluate self and social comparisons that are made in an attempt to evaluate a more global entity like a social system. If individuals feel that their levels of success or accomplishment are deprived compared to the group norm, feelings of injustice can result. These feelings of deprivation, which are created through a combination of the individual's objective accomplishments and subjective expectations, can motivate social comparisons in an attempt to alleviate the injustice. Individuals are motivated to believe that they function as well as or better than their comparison others. If social comparisons illuminate injustices that may threaten this assumption, the individuals may become motivated to choose different comparison others, perhaps downward comparing as suggested by Gibbons and Gerrard (1991), or to avoid further comparisons in a sort of "ignorance is bliss" mentality as suggested by Brickman and Bulman (1977).

Affleck and Tennen (1991) summarize the literature surrounding social comparison processes and coping with serious medical problems. This summary provides a good look at the far-reaching implications of social comparison processes. Although a complete review of these findings is beyond the scope of this text, several key points should be mentioned. Affleck and Tennen (1991) argue that individuals with major medical problems are particularly likely to use social comparisons because (1) they are often unable to obtain clear, objective information about the illness or prognosis, (2) they experience threats to their self-esteem because they and others may perceive them as victims, and (3) they experience times of extreme emotional distress. Information from a variety of sources suggests that social comparisons to others who are worse off than self not only can be beneficial in terms of emotional well-being, but also that such downward comparisons may provide the most accurate information by which the individuals can learn exactly how they are doing (e.g., Taylor, 1983; Osborne, Karlin, Baumann, Osborne, & Nelms, 1993).

Affleck and Tennen (1991) discovered that downward social comparisons are made by individuals suffering from major medical problems for multiple reasons, as has been suggested by the other findings in this chapter. Social comparison choices have profound implications for both the individual making the comparisons and the individual toward whom the comparisons are directed. Downward comparisons provide the individual with a sense of "It can always be worse," which may provide a bit of hope that, therefore, it could get better in the future. Such comparisons, as Gibbons and Gerrard (1991) suggest, also may help the individual deal with the threats to self-esteem and subjective well-being that accompany the discovery of a major medical problem. It also may be the case that downward comparisons in these circumstances provide the afflicted with more realistic information about both the best and worst they can expect. If the individuals made comparisons only to others who were better off (making upward comparisons only), the picture might seem particularly bleak. In such ambiguous circumstances, only making both upward and downward comparisons will provide the individuals with the parameters that may set their expectations for prognosis, allowing them to gain some sense of how much they can control the progression of the illness, and determining the possibilities for how much they can improve their circumstances. This of course is similar to the discussion of Markus and Nurius (1986) of possible selves.

WRAPPING IT UP: WHAT DOES ALL THIS MEAN?

The previous pages of this chapter have summarized many of the more important findings in the area of social comparison processes. Questions of when and toward whom social comparisons will be made are tempered by an understanding of the implications that such comparisons have for the individuals making the comparisons and the person toward whom the comparisons are directed. An eclectic understanding of social comparison, then, must provide information about the effect that such comparisons have for the self of the individual. The information provided in this chapter has suggested that several self benefits accrue from making certain types of social comparisons to particular social comparison targets. A quick summary of these findings will lead directly to a working model of social comparison processes that will combine the research discussed in this chapter.

Seven basic issues are involved in understanding social comparison as it relates to theories of self:

1. Social comparison processes may be used in an attempt to protect an individual's sense of self or to insulate it against possible threat. In this manner, social comparisons may be initiated and certain comparison targets utilized in an effort to shield self from information that might call self into question.

2. Social comparisons also can be used to gather information that can be used to promote self-acceptance. If individuals are unsure as to the acceptability of their self, social comparison to similar or slightly dissimilar others may provide them with the information needed to accept self. This may promote what has been referred to in this chapter as an "I'm okay, you're okay" mentality.

3. When self-esteem has been directly threatened (which is different from item one above, in which the individual fears that self might be threatened), certain social comparisons may be prompted as the individual attempts to recover from such threats. The most likely comparison choice when self-esteem has been threatened is a downward comparison. The individual chooses the downward comparison in an attempt to make self feel bet-

ter by focusing on others who are worse off (e.g., Osborne, Karlin, Baumann, Osborne, & Nelms, 1993).

4. Individuals with uncertain or low self-esteem may be in what Luhtanen and Crocker (1991) refer to as a chronic state of low self-esteem. This state of perpetual threat may motivate the individual to choose comparison others in an attempt to self-enhance. Here the goal is not self-protection, self-acceptance, or recovery from threat. The goal is to seek constantly self-enhancement in an effort to counter the chronic feelings of threat that low self-esteem engenders in its sufferers.

5. Markus and Nurius (1986) suggest that social comparisons may be used by the individual in an attempt to delineate the parameters of what is possible for the self. Affleck and Tennen (1991) suggest that such comparison processes may be used as a method for delineating the parameters of what to expect from a major illness in terms of prognosis. In this way, social comparisons that are both upward and downward in nature may tell self the best and worst it can expect. In some cases, then, downward comparisons may be made to less fortunate others not just to make self feel better but also to provide more accurate feedback about self than would be possible from other self-knowledge sources (e.g., reflected appraisals or self-perceptions).

6. Social comparisons may be made in a unilateral manner designed to maintain self-congruency. Backman (1988) suggests that congruency between self, behaviors, and others' interpretations of those behaviors can be maximized through the appropriate use of social comparisons. Here the individual avoids self-enhancement or self-esteem threat by making comparisons that perpetuate congruency. This is slightly different from self-protection because here the individuals choose comparison targets in an effort to maintain a balance between self, behavior, and interpretations, not just a balance of thoughts or feelings directed toward self.

7. Finally, many social comparison choices will be made in attempts to satisfy a host of self-relevant goals. If individuals want to wallow in pity, this is possible through upward comparisons. If they want to know truly how they are doing, such information can be obtained through upward comparisons. Personality characteristics (such as need for cognition, self-monitoring, and competitiveness) also can be supported through social comparison choices. Individuals who are highly competitive may bolster their self feelings through downward comparisons or derogation of others. High self-monitors who wish to know what is expected in a given situation may turn to others as sources of feedback about what is or is not expected in the situation. Persons who enjoy thinking about things (those who are high in need for cognition) may be more likely to use social comparisons in situations as sources of information than their low need for cognition counterparts, who find such thought work significantly less enjoyable.

A WORKING MODEL OF SOCIAL COMPARISON CHOICES AND IMPLICATIONS

As can be seen in Table 5.1, the previous discussions of social comparison choices can be summarized in a working model. This model provides insights into when and toward whom social comparison choices will be made, and what the implications are of these choices.

TABLE 5.1 Social Comparison Choices and Implications

When	Toward Whom	Implications
1. Self-Protection	Ingroup Comparisons or Unilateral Comparisons	Maintenance of Current Self-Views
2. Self-Acceptance	Unilateral or Slightly Upward Comparisons	"I'm Okay, You're Okay"
3. Self-Esteem Threat	Downward Comparisons to Less-Fortunate Others	"Compared to This Guy, I'm Not So Bad Off"
4. Chronic Low Self-Esteem	Chronic Downward Comparisons	Chronic State of Self-Esteem Threat
5. Possible Selves	Both Upward and Downward Comparisons	Establishing Upper and Lower Limits on Expectations
6. Self-Congruency	Unilateral Comparisons	No Real Information Acquired About Self
7. Self-Relevant Goals	Upward, Downward, Unilateral, and Derogatory Comparisons	Potentially Satisfying the Self-Goal That Motivated the Comparison

If an individual is self-satisfied, social comparisons may not be activated. If, however, something has caused the self to be called into question or questions of performance have in some fashion been initiated, social comparisons will be made. Once the individual has decided to make a social comparison, choices must be made about toward whom that comparison should be directed. As can be seen in Table 5.1, comparison target choices will be based upon what aspect of self has been called into question, the severity of the self-threat, the degree to which more objective information is available, the extent to which the individual wishes the comparison information to yield accurate versus self-enhancing information, and the other self-goals the individual may be hoping to satisfy by using social comparison processes.

CHAPTER SIX

Self and Culture

BACKGROUND ON SELF AND CULTURE

Few texts on self devote much attention to self as a cultural entity, and this seems to leave a void in our understanding. Certainly self is, at least in part, a cultural phenomenon. Can researchers really speak of self-understanding without paying attention to the cultural influences that shape the person? Is it truly possible to discuss self as a research topic devoid of any concerns for the implications of the culture in which that self is developing? The answer to both of these questions is "No." Self is partially determined by the dominant culture in which the individual is developing. It is also the case that different cultures place differing expectations on individuals that ultimately influence the self that is developing. Not all cultures value the same things, not all cultures allow their citizens the same freedoms for becoming who they wish to become, and not all cultures clearly articulate the role of self within the society.

Cross-cultural research is not something new to the research enterprise. Initial attempts to understand cultural influences on self were made by comparing individuals within the same dominant culture but raised within different socioeconomic status cultures (e.g., Wylie, 1961, 1979). In a comprehensive review of the self literature at the time, Wylie suggests that "various aspects of self-concept, such as sense of self-identity, components of ideal self (self values), views of one's particular personality attributes, and over-all self-regard" may be a function of socioeconomic differences (Wylie, 1979, p. 59).

It is reasonable to assume that individuals raised within different dominant cultures may also experience self-related differences as a function of culture. Certainly different cultures value different personality traits within their members. But articulating an awareness of this diversity does not guarantee that this awareness will find its way into the theoretical underpinnings of a science. In an eye-opening text on the subject of self in culture, De Vos (1990) discusses the resistance on the part of some social scientists to open their eyes to the fact that many social theories may be based on culturally specific assumptions. "Even today," De Vos reminds the reader, "anthropology, psychology, and sociology are not sufficiently free from egocentric and ethnocentric biases" (De Vos, 1990, p. 17). At the very heart of this discussion is the fact that our methods of data collection and analysis cannot be completely removed from the influence of human consciousness, and consciousness is, in part, culturally determined. According to Lutz (1992), "culture is the sum total of our experience in the world including those explicit and implicit interpretations that have been created by our cultural forbears. Culture, then, is inextricable from consciousness—in part, it is consciousness" (Lutz, 1992, p. 67).

De Vos (1990), however, does not advocate breaking down the influence of culture on self to such a level that the discussion ends up focusing on the functioning of self in social roles. There are two extremes in studying the self in culture. One would be to ignore the cultural influences on self and assume that differences in self that are discovered are consistent across cultures. The other extreme would be to assume that self is entirely a cultural construct that can be explained away simply as a given individual fulfilling a given role at a given time. The goal of our brief foray into the self in culture, then, will be to walk the fine line between these two extremes and discuss some of the more obvious connections between the construct called "self" and culture.

DESCRIBING CULTURE

One of the simplest methods for distinguishing cultures is to refer to cultures as either collectivist or individualistic (e.g., Hofstede, 1980; Parson & Shils, 1951). The basic difference between collectivist and individualistic cultures is the center of emphasis. Collectivist cultures emphasize greater commitment to family or the clan. Cross and Markus (1991) suggest that this type of cultural emphasis leads to a state of "we" consciousness. Individuals within these cultures see themselves within the framework of the bigger picture. Self is determined, in part, by the family or clan in which the individual resides. It is common in collectivist cultures for assumptions to be clearly made about individuals based on the family or clan to which they belong. One's sense of self takes second place to a sense of family, and individual interests are expected to be placed lower on the hierarchy of needs than familial interests. It stands to reason, then, that individuals developing within collectivist cultures would describe self mostly in collectivist terms.

In contrast, other cultures emphasize a cultural ideology that is significantly more individualistic. Bellah, Madsen, Sullivan, Swidler, and Tipton (1985) suggest that American culture stresses self-reliance and a freedom to make choices based on an individualistic hierarchy of needs. The self that develops within an individualistic culture will have some dramatic differences from the self that develops within a collectivist culture. An important part of describing culture and self is to emphasize the fact that neither self nor culture develop in a vacuum. This means that individuals do impact the culture as certainly as culture impacts the individual. It doesn't matter whether the ideology of the culture is more collectivist or more individualistic in orientation; self and culture mutually influence each other.

THE SELF–CULTURE CONNECTION

Contemporary self theories make differing assumptions about the role of the individual in the self-development process. Some theories emphasize the individual nature of self (e.g., Bem, 1972; Markus, 1983), whereas other theories focus on the social nature of self (e.g., Festinger, 1954). If self develops within a social context, then, which of these approaches is correct? As can easily be deduced from previous discussions of the eclectic nature of self within this text, they are both right. Trying to emphasize self as individual in nature or as social in nature misses the point. Self is simultaneously an individual and a social entity. The reason so many different self theories have been proposed is that different theorists focus on different aspects of the self–culture connection. An eclectic theory of self allows for the individual to influence the culture and for culture to influence the individual. Questions about how much of self is determined by one or the other, however, only serve to minimize the importance of both.

Individuals are given roles to play by their culture, and role-expectations even dictate some of the behaviors one would expect given the role. But individuals still differ in the manner in which they act out their roles. Individuals labeled "American" carry with them a set of expectations that others place there based on interpretations of American culture. American culture suggests (sometimes quite strongly) that the individual should be self-driven and motivated to satisfy personal goals. But certainly not all individuals find this emphasis to their liking. Others may devote most of their energies to a selfless attention to others, with seemingly little concern for more individualistic pursuits. Summary descriptions such as these, however, can often mask more important points. Individuals who choose to engage in selfless caring for others, for example, are still making choices that define their self. So cultural expectations do not entirely dictate who the individual will or will not become.

Markus and Kitayama (1991) discuss the difference between individuals with an "independent construal of self" and individuals with an "interdependent construal of self." Individuals who have an independent construal or focus to self represent and think about self in relation to the individual. When asked to describe themselves or answer questions such as "Who am I?" these individuals would focus on individual abilities, characteristics, ambitions, and so forth. The interdependent individual, on the other hand, would tend to think about and describe self in more situational terms. The self as it is seen by the individual is determined, at least in part, by the demands and expectations being placed on the individual by the situation and the other individuals within that situation. Although these points seem perfectly valid, one must not assume that all individuals within a collectivist culture will have an interdependent construal of self nor that all individuals within an individualistic culture will have an independent construal of self.

Findings by Osborne and Young (1994) suggest that individuals within the same culture can differ to the extent that they think about and define self in more interdependent or independent terms. Personality characteristics, such as self-monitoring, have been shown to be related to how the individual describes self or categorizes information about others. Personality characteristics that foster a more internal focus on self (e.g., low self-monitoring) promote self-descriptions that are more individualistic in nature. Likewise, personality characteristics that foster a more outward oriented focusing on self (e.g., high self-monitoring) promote self-descriptions that are more collectivist in orientation. This, again, shows the interconnectedness between self and culture. Culture does not completely override self, and self does not completely ignore the culture. Individuals, however, vary to the extent to which they balance the two.

It stands to reason that the dominant nature of the culture (whether it can be categorized as a collectivist or individualistic culture) has ramifications for the structure of the self-development system. Figure 6.1 illustrates the different theoretical frameworks possible for self based on the dominant nature of the culture. As can be seen in Figure 6.1, individualistic cultures would tend to promote early independence for self and foster a reliance on different sources of self-knowledge than would collectivist cultures. Self develops only within a familial framework in collectivist cultures, and therefore the family unit would play a more enduring role in self-definition. Individualistic cultures, however, would stress direct action and responsibility for self, and therefore the family's role would have less impact.

The two diagrams depicted in Figure 6.1 show the differing degrees of emphasis that types of cultures place on the familial unit. In collectivist cultures, the influence of the family is more dramatic, more obvious, and longer lasting. The sense of self that develops is tied directly to the familial unit and the emphasis that the culture places on a sense of belonging and not violating familial norms. Individual needs are sacrificed for the greater good of the family unit. To a certain extent, the individual is lost within the true collectivist culture because trying to establish a sense of self can be interpreted as selfish and self-centered. In this sense, trying to negotiate an identity that stresses individual wants or needs (which is an important part of the entity we call "self") would run counter to cultural norms. Putting individual concerns before those of the familial unit would directly violate the expectations for cooperation and interdependence that collectivist cultures stress (Cross & Markus, 1991). The outcome of the self-development process within collectivist cultures, then, would be a sense of self that is "other-directed." When questions are raised about self, they center on whether individuals are fulfilling their roles within the familial unit, not whether they are being interpreted in a manner that is consistent with self-images.

Continued dependence and connectedness to the family would also be stressed within collectivist cultures. To a large degree, the ability of the family unit to continue to thrive is related to the degree to which the family members remain committed to the family base. Since the family helps define each of its members, the family is, in turn, defined by its members. If one of the individuals breaks from the unit, the cohesiveness of the entire unit can be threatened (Hofstede, 1980). Because of this vulnerability, great pressure would be placed on individuals to maintain the commitment to the family even when they are old enough to strike out on their own. It is quite common, in fact, for many collectivist cultures to have familial units in which several generations live within the same household structure (for example, the Jewish Kibbutz).

So far this description has focused on how the collectivist culture influences self definitions. But culture also influences the manner in which the individual perceives, evaluates, and presents self to others (Brehm & Kassin, 1993). When individuals from a collectivist culture think about self, they are likely to focus on self in relation to the others within the family unit. This can be of great advantage to the individuals because they can bask in the reflected glory if a family member is successful, but they also must wallow in the defeat

FIGURE 6.1 Theoretical Frameworks for Self

Collectivist Cultures

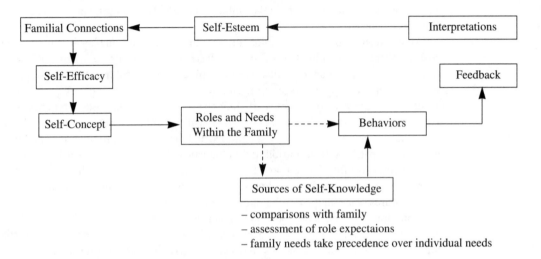

– comparisons with family
– assessment of role expectaions
– family needs take precedence over individual needs

Individualistic Cultures

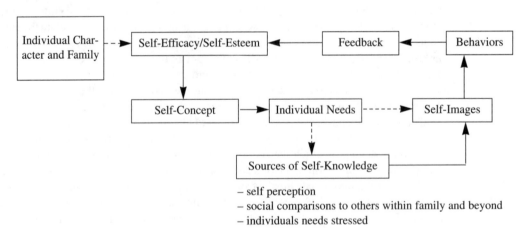

– self perception
– social comparisons to others within family and beyond
– individuals needs stressed

if a family member is unsuccessful (Cialdini et al., 1976). Cialdini and his colleagues discovered that sports fans often experience elevated self-esteem when their favorite team is winning. This reinforces the assumption that individuals gain a part of their self-esteem through association with others (Snyder, Lassegard, & Ford, 1986). The sports fans cheering the loudest, however, may be jeering the loudest when their team is losing (Cialdini et al., 1976). This may seem paradoxical but is understandable to the extent that the self-esteem of the fans is being threatened by the failure.

Within an individualistic culture, the influence of the family is more subtle and loses significance or power as self develops. Early independence is stressed, as can be noted by the importance placed on individual needs. Over time, this increasing emphasis on individual needs necessitates a break with the familial unit. As the influence of peers becomes more important and individuals seek to classify themselves, conflicts with the family seem almost inevitable. Perhaps more than anything else, this push for identity and the struggle to separate self from important others serves as the catalyst for the potential storms and stresses of adolescence (Osborne, 1993b, 1993d). As already suggested in Chapter One, many people are trying to influence the sense of self that is developing within the adolescent, and many of these demands can be in direct conflict with others. The real dilemma, however, is that at the same time that adolescents are being pushed to become more independent (a major emphasis of the individualistic culture), they also are being told who to become. This paradox between being pushed toward independence and pulled toward conformity establishes the storm and stress patterns that some adolescents experience, which must be resolved successfully for a firm identity to be put into place.

The "individually oriented" self-images that develop through this identity negotiation process guide or direct behaviors and feedback on feelings of competency or self-efficacy. As a further consequence of the more individualistic quality of these cultures, the sources of self-knowledge used to gather information about self will be more individually based as well. Questions about self, therefore, focus on such issues as, "How am I doing?" or "Who am I supposed to be?" The reader will note that both of these questions are self-centered in focus. Although other individuals may be used for reflected appraisal or social comparison purposes, the main emphasis is on self, self-desires, and establishing consistency in life that reconfirms the sense of self that is projected toward others.

The main question asked by individuals developing self within an individualistic culture when feedback is directed toward self is "Am I presenting the image of self I had intended?" If the answer to this question is "No," then several follow-up options are available. First, the individual could reject that information as coming from a source that is unacceptable or uninfluential. Second, the individual could seek out further feedback in an effort to either confirm or disconfirm the original feedback. Third, the individual could accept the feedback and engage in efforts to alter behavior to bring feedback in line with the image of self that is desired.

Markus and Kitayama (1991) found three main differences (in terms of self) between individuals from collectivist and individualistic cultures. First, individuals within individualistic cultures, like the United States, believe they are unique. When students were asked questions about their similarity to others, American students believed they were less similar to others than did Asian Indian students (Markus & Kitayama, 1991). Second, individuals from individualistic cultures gain a sense of self-esteem through personal accomplishment and individually oriented achievements. In contrast, individuals from collectivist cultures strive to fit in with the group and gain a sense of self-worth from success in becoming part of the group. It should be noted, of course, that individuals within individualistic cultures can be more or less collectivist in orientation, and vice versa. Certainly some individuals within the United States want nothing more than to fit in with the group, and some individuals within collectivist cultures like Japan are mostly motivated by individualistic needs. Third, Markus and Kitayama (1991) suggest that Americans are more likely to express self-focused emotions such as jealousy and pride, whereas individuals from collectivist cultures express other-focused emotions such as indebtedness and love.

IMPLICATIONS OF A CULTURAL INFLUENCE ON THE SELF

It has long been argued that societies perpetuate themselves by passing on their culture to their new members through teaching (Patterson, 1959). This is accomplished in part by indoctrinating children with the attitudes, ideas, and normative expectations for behaviors that are accepted by that culture. Likewise, it has long been accepted that no other institution within a culture exerts more impact over the self-concept of the child than the family (Combs & Snygg, 1959). But what impact does this cultural emphasis on self have for an eclectic approach to self? Perhaps more than anywhere else in this text, this look at culture and the self clearly portrays the powerful role that self plays in the individual's life. Self is not an entity that the individual is completely free to create and perpetuate. Other people have a vested interest in who an individual becomes, and therefore they will make continuous attempts to shape and mold the individual into becoming who they need him or her to be.

A cultural emphasis on self also has profound implications for Chapters Fourteen and Fifteen of this text, which are devoted to applications of an eclectic approach to self in daily life and educational settings. One of the primary responsibilities of the educational system (whether this responsibility is explicitly stated or implicitly assumed) is to indoctrinate children into the culture. Although the term "indoctrinate" may seem quite strong and may bring up horrible visions of dictators and torture, the word is appropriate. School systems use rules that reward children for what is deemed acceptable behavior and have patterns of punishment in place for children who violate those expectations. What expectations would be in place if not the expectations of the culture? There also is the possibility of conflict between the expectations for self being passed on to the child from the family and those being placed on the child from the culture. To a certain extent, if these expectations from family and culture are at odds with each other, the educational system may be expected to resolve the conflict. Although this may seem beyond the realm of the educational setting, sometimes the conflict may directly interfere with learning and must be resolved in some way before learning can take place successfully.

It is important to keep in mind that culture and self mutually influence each other. Culture is reflected in the laws that societies adopt and in the punishments that are established to deal with those who violate those laws. Collectivist societies may elect to use punishments that stress the interdependent nature of individuals within that society. An entire family, for example, may be disgraced by the transgressions of one of its members. Likewise, the selfless accomplishments of a family member may shine honor down upon the family name. Individualistic cultures, however, seem to stress more individually based punishments. Criminal justice systems like those in the United States, for example, stress the loss of individual freedoms when laws are broken. Individuals who drive while intoxicated may lose their right to operate a motor vehicle, and individuals who steal or commit violent crimes may lose the right to come and go as they please by being incarcerated.

Finally, it is crucial to remember that individuals within a culture set the limits of acceptable behavior by always pushing the parameters of what is considered acceptable. At the same time that some television viewers in 1993 were expressing delight over the realistic police drama *NYPD Blue*, other viewers were expressing moral outrage at the flashes of nudity and free and easy use of profanity by the main characters. Are we to assume that these groups of individuals come from drastically different cultures? No. This merely makes the point that individuals have something to say about cultural expectations, just as culture can place behavioral limits on the individual. If the viewers who are pleased with the realism of the show win out over those who are outraged by it, will the limits of acceptable television realism be forever changed? Probably. What seemed completely unacceptable yesterday may seem commonplace today. Although culture establishes limits, laws, and guidelines, the individuals who make up that culture ultimately determine what those rules will be and how long those rules will stand.

WRAPPING IT UP: WHAT DOES ALL THIS MEAN?

Certainly this chapter has not presented everything there is to know about the influence of culture on the self. It should be kept in mind, however, that such was not the goal. The research literature surrounding culture and the self is sometimes disparate and haphazard. Although attempts continue to be made to clarify the connection between self and the culture in which it is developing, much more work needs to be done. For the purposes of an eclectic approach to self, however, this summary of the research provides the foundation that is needed to establish the importance of culture in a theory of self. The main differences between individuals raised within collectivist versus individualistic cultures are points of reference. For the collectivist culture, the family unit and commitment to the family serve as the referent point by which self is constructed. A self developing within an individualistic culture, however, will be encouraged to use family as a point of stability from which explorations into self-definition can be made.

Once an individual has discovered her self, it expected that a break with family will be made and she will set off to make a name of her own. Although an individual can be pleased with the successes of other family members, cultures like that in the United States allow very little room for the individual to gain much in terms of self-definition from the successes of someone else. Individualistic cultures consider reflected glory no substitute for individual success. Collectivist cultures, on the other hand, would expect individuals to be as happy with a family member's success or accomplishment as they would be if the success or accomplishment had happened to themselves. The greater good must be placed above individual needs, and selfish behaviors are often interpreted as a direct slap to the family face. In individualistic cultures, however, independence is encouraged, and individual accomplishments are valued. Cultures like that in the United States find it perfectly acceptable for one individual to amass unimaginable wealth while others live barely above or substantially below the poverty line. This is not meant as an assessment of the fairness of the United States capitalistic system. Inequity is simply a consequence of individualistic orientations in culture.

Cultural expectations and influences also affect such diverse things as an individual's feelings of uniqueness and common emotions. Persons from individualistic cultures believe themselves to be more unique than persons from collectivist cultures, and their emotions are more self-focused. It seems perfectly reasonable, then, that persons from collectivist or individualistic cultures will choose dramatically different sources of self-knowledge, will incorporate success and failure feedback into self differently, will prefer different lifestyles, and will interpret the actions of self and others differently based on the independent or inter-dependent focus of the culture in which the self has developed.

CHAPTER SEVEN

Organismic Approaches to Self

BACKGROUND INFORMATION

As the reader is probably figuring out, the cement that bonds this section of material into a self theory is the eclectic nature of that theory itself. Sources of self-knowledge are quite diverse, yet each influences the complete self that is created. Whether that information comes from assessment of how one's image is perceived by others (via the process of reflected appraisals presented in Chapter Three), observations of one's own behavior (via self-perception as outlined in Chapter Four), by making comparison with a variety of comparison targets (via the social comparison processes outlined in Chapter Five), or through indoctrination and teaching in a social context (via self as a cultural entity detailed in Chapter Six), it is incorporated into a global construct better known as the "self." But our understanding of the eclectic nature of self would not be complete without making one last stop on our journey into the sources of self-knowledge. An eclectic approach to self would be remiss if it did not assess the impact of the organism on itself. This suggests that the organism to a certain extent dictates the self that is developing as surely as do the culture and the comparison standards that are present.

Although this certainly sounds reasonable, it is imperative that such a point be clearly articulated before the text moves on to a discussion of the consequences of self-knowledge in Section Three. Self is by its very nature a complicated organism. The behavior of any organism, human or otherwise, is determined in part by internal characteristics and values that motivate the being into action. To ignore the individuality of the person as it affects the self that is developing would be as inexcusable as ignoring the impact of culture on the developing person. An eclectic approach to self, then, assumes that individuals play a vital role in their own development and therefore individual characteristics influence the self that is created out of that developmental process. This was established toward the end of the previous chapter in Figure 6.1. The reader will recall that within collectivist cultures individuals are encouraged (if not required) to subdue their individual needs for familial concerns. Individualistic cultures, on the other hand, nurture a frame of orientation that places self above others and stresses the value of individual needs. Individual needs, in these cultures, drive self-images, which in turn drive behaviors, and so on.

The reader also will recall, however, that such "other" versus "self" focus demands are not written in stone. All individuals seem motivated to express their individuality. This is not frowned on in collectivist cultures as long as it serves the family. An artist would not be discouraged to paint if such painting brought wealth, fame, or honor for the family. Likewise, persons within individualistic cultures are not necessarily discouraged from putting others first. Cultures like those in the United States, however, frown on individuals who place others above self at all cost. Being selfish is not in and of itself a bad thing. It is clearly the case that an eclectic theory of self must combine the outward oriented sources of self-knowledge (including reflected appraisals, self-perception, social comparison, and culture) as well as the internally oriented sources of self-knowledge (including aspects of reflected appraisals, social comparison, and organismic approaches to self). It may seem strange to consider social comparison as an internal source of self-knowledge, but clearly social comparison is not strictly a social phenomenon. Individuals must make choices about what characteristics within themselves are important enough to seek comparative information on, and these comparison processes may sometimes be determined by nothing more than an internally based need to know the self.

Organic theories in psychology are certainly not new (e.g., Blasi, 1976; Deci & Ryan, 1986). Such theories assume that individuals play an active role in their environment, and this activity leads to a more sophisticated internalization of the organism within that environment. Individuals are motivated to act on their environment in accordance with their own wishes, desires, goals, and motives. Playing an active role in the environment, then, provides the individual with self-related feedback that is internalized and used to define, refine, and redefine self.

Deci and Ryan (1990) attempt to integrate a motivational approach to self into personality. In summarizing the self literature, Deci and Ryan remind the reader that contemporary self theories assume either one of two basic features of self, that self is mostly cognitive in nature or mostly social. The assumption that self is mostly cognitive in nature means that self is an information processing construct that uses cognitive structures (schemas) to sort out and process information that is relevant to self. Theories based on the assumption that self is mostly social in nature point to contextual variables that impact the self-system. Clearly the social world in which the self is developing will play a vital role in the outcome of that developmental process (e.g., self in culture as described in Chapter Six). But as Deci and Ryan (1990) succinctly state, self may go deeper than that. These researchers suggest that a self theory must go beyond the information processing constructs such as schemas that influence the self. They note that underlying motivational processes may determine how the individual assimilates self-relevant information and regulates self. This assumption that motivational processes play a key role in self-concept development is at the very heart of what has been referred to as an organismic approach to self (Deci & Ryan, 1986, 1990).

The brief discussion of an organismic approach to self that follows, then, serves as the transition chapter into the second half of the text. Once internal motives and how they influence self-determination are discussed, the text will shift focus and move into the ramifications of this self-knowledge for the individual and the situations in which the individual must interact. When all is said and done, the eclectic approach to self will integrate the factors that impinge upon the person from the environment and the factors that drive the person from the inside. This integration, and the resulting combined self that results from it, then, is the true definition of an eclectic approach to self.

SELF-DETERMINATION IN HUMAN BEHAVIOR

The main suggestion being made by individuals who argue for an organismic approach to self is that self is, in part, individually determined (e.g., Deci, 1992). As Deci's (1992) review indicates, as early as 1932 researchers like Tolman were suggesting that motivation serves to both energize and direct human behavior. Certainly self-determination can be considered a part of motivation. But self-determination does not simply mean choosing who one would like to be. In order to fulfill wishes about self, certain behaviors are required. An organismic approach to self, then, suggests that individuals are motivated to acquire self-definition, and this is partially accomplished by self-determined behaviors. If Kevin wishes to become a star tennis player, he certainly must know that this wish will not be fulfilled without a concerted effort on his part. Self-determination means knowing who one is or would like to be and then engaging in behaviors specifically designed to maintain or attain that sense of self.

This point has been suggested several times throughout this text, including the self-concept, self-esteem, reflected appraisal, and social comparison chapters. Individuals are motivated to be perceived in a manner that is consistent with their own views of self. If individuals feel that they are not being perceived as they would like, one method for correcting that misperception is to engage in behaviors designed to reinforce the self-image that was meant to be portrayed. Rotter (1954) was one of the first to suggest that expectations about the future impact the behaviors of the present. Who an individual wishes to be will motivate behaviors in the present that are designed to make that future as likely to come to pass as possible. Individuals within this organismic framework, then, are goal-driven (Deci & Ryan, 1985), and self-determination can be seen in the fact that individuals are driven to attain self-related goals.

It can be argued that self as a construct cannot be so removed from the organism as to permit discussing the two separately. The self is often defined as "the sum total of who one believes oneself to be." Would it truly be possible, then, to discuss self as something separate from the individual? The eclectic approach to self being outlined in this text will follow the lead of Deci and Ryan (c.f., 1990) in suggesting that assumptions about self are intricately linked with the assumptions that individuals make about human nature. Organismic approaches to self assume that a key ingredient in human nature is an active tendency. This promotes within the human being a striving toward expression of abilities, values, attitudes, and so forth. This striving, however, is not simply something that is learned. Organismic approaches to self assume that the desire for competency and the tendency to incorporate new experiences into the self are intrinsic characteristics of human nature (Deci & Ryan, 1990).

Dorothy Lee (1976) draws a connection between self and culture that suggests human behavior can be motivated by some inner drive. Across cultures, Lee found consistent examples of individuals engaging in behaviors that served no useful survival function. Even within what might be called "primitive cultures," resources and energy were devoted to tasks that were not utilitarian in nature. Lee argues that such behaviors merely reflect the natural tendency for the human being to be "propelled by some inner drive." Such an inner drive motivates behaviors that are designed to satisfy some function that may be important only to the individual who has decided to engage in them. Despite the fact that cultural differences exist in terms of acceptable behaviors, goals, or needs, cross-cutting all cultures is this striving for self-determination. According to Lee, the Hopi Indians provide a perfect example of such an internalized sense of striving and autonomy. The Hopi follow the "Hopi Way." Their belief in a universal pre-destiny may seem antithetical to individuality or autonomy, but interestingly enough, they also believe that such a universal plan can only be fulfilled with the cooperation of the humans. In this sense, the plan for the universe can only be fulfilled with the self-determined behavior of the humans (Lee, 1976).

Certainly behaviors are not always determined by factors external to the individual. Individuals can choose to respond to external pressures to act in particular ways, but it is just as likely that they can choose not to act on those pressures (Deci & Ryan, 1991). Deci and Ryan refer to behaviors as self-determined versus controlled, and this distinction emphasizes the degree to which the individual is engaging in free choice. If the individual chooses to engage in certain kinds of behaviors (as has already been suggested in Chapter Four on self-perception theory), then those behaviors would be potentially much more informative about that person's self than behaviors that the individual felt compelled or obligated to perform. Deci (1992) suggests that this assessment of not only the quantitative aspect of motivation but also the qualitative aspect provides much more precise information about the impact of those behaviors. If two individuals are equally motivated to engage in a certain behavior, one might expect the outcome for self to be the same. But this simplistic approach ignores the impact of the nature of that motivation. If the motivation is self-determined (e.g., "I really want to do this because I believe in it") rather than controlled (e.g., "I really need to do this because the group is demanding it from me"), then the self-related consequences will be dramatically different.

Behaviors that individuals choose to engage in because of self-deterministic goals will impact self more dramatically than behaviors that are engaged in because of external demands or pressures (e.g., Deci & Ryan, 1980; Deci & Ryan, 1986). As will be discussed in Chapter Thirteen on self-esteem enhancement, however, this impact on self is not necessarily a good thing. If an individual chose to engage in a behavior because it was important to her self definition, and the feedback she receives about that behavior is negative, the resulting impact on self-esteem will be much more profound (and painful) than if the individual felt that she had little or no choice in the behavior. Being compelled to do something exonerates the individual to a certain extent if the behavior fails. The reverse is also true. If the behavior leads to feedback that is positive, it is difficult for the individual to own it as part of self if others had to poke and prod the individual into action. Freedom of choice (or the illusion of it) can play a powerful role in determining the impact that success and failure feedback will have on self-esteem.

But Jones (e.g., Jones, 1990; Jones & Gerard, 1967) would be the first to remind the reader that even constrained behaviors may sometimes alter the self-concept. Jones and Gerard (1967) distinguish between the definitions of self that assume that self is a relatively stable cognitive structure (e.g., Markus & Sentis, 1982) and that which Jones and Gerard label the "phenomenal self." The phenomenal self is "a loose appellation that refers to features of the self-concept that are available and readily tapped" (Jones, 1990, p. 70). This suggests, as has also been suggested throughout this text, that part of the individual's self-definition is determined by the context the individual is currently in. The experiences that the individual has gone through in the recent past may also influence the current self-definition that is in place. If Rachel has just suffered a humiliating divorce, certainly her self-esteem and overall self-definition will reflect that negativity. But does this mean that Rachel's global self-esteem is truly low? The question is impossible to answer without taking the recent and current self experiences into account. Perhaps if we measure Rachel's self-esteem five months from now when she is in the early stages of a new and satisfying relationship, we will find her self-esteem score has changed dramatically.

An organismic approach to self for the most part would not concern itself with the "phenomenal self" because it is too transient and open to situational constraints. The aspect of self that is important in self-determination, then, is the more stable self-concept or identity (Baumeister, 1986). Individuals project this stable sense of self or identity into the situations in which they find themselves, and the manner in which others respond to those presentations can have an impact on self-esteem and further self-definition. Individuals of course have access to both the more reflexive (phenomenal) aspects of self as well as the more enduring aspects of their self-concepts. Jones and Nisbett (1971) argue that individuals have greater access to instances of the variability in their behavior than do observers. Certainly knowledge of this variability may lead the individual to see self as reactive or determined by situational parameters. Why, then, do individuals tend to feel that they have more traits than others do (e.g., Monson, Tanke, & Lund, 1980)?

Sande (1990) provide empirical replication of the Nisbett, Caputo, Legant, and Maracek (1973) proposition that individuals believe they possess more traits than other individuals. Sande's (1990) findings also suggest that an increase in the variability of behavior may result from possession of many traits. Certainly the more traits one possesses, the more options are available for interpreting situations and choosing appropriate behaviors. All of this ties directly into an organismic approach to self because it suggests that individuals understand that their traits allow for flexibility in their behavioral repertoire. Being able to choose behaviors that are appropriate for a given situation (or inappropriate if that is the choice that one prefers to make) is the epitome of self-determination. The feedback that comes back to self from such behaviors, then, can be used to integrate further those traits into the self-concept.

According to Deci and Ryan, "the development of self entails integrating new experiences and regulatory processes with one's intrinsic self" (Deci & Ryan, 1990, p. 239). This is of profound importance to understanding the full ramifications of an organismic approach to self. Such approaches assume that there is an innate aspect of self that develops as individuals experience the world around them. As already suggested in Chapter One, part of the difficulty of self-concept development is integrating the multiple aspects of self into a synthesized whole that everyone can live with. This process (which takes on monumental importance for the individual during adolescence) is called identity negotiation. Part of the conflict during identity negotiation comes from within the individual. First, the individual tries to decide who he or she would like to be out of all that seems possible. Second, the individual struggles to reconcile the external demands being placed on self with the internal self-feelings he or she has. As Deci and Ryan (1990) suggest, if the individual integrates these new experiences and regulatory processes into the self, then the resulting behaviors will be self-determined.

At first, this may sound a bit contradictory. It would seem that if the individual is integrating external regulations with something internal like the self, then the resulting behaviors would be less than self-determined. But Deci and Ryan (1990) are comparing such an integration with the opposite possibility. What if no integration takes place? In this case, the individual will probably still follow the regulation but will not incorporate such regulatory processes into the self. The resulting behaviors would be the same as for the individual in which integration has taken place, but the first individual will accept the regulatory process as a part of the self, whereas the second person will not.

Deci's (1992) summary of motivation theories suggests that self-determination has a profound effect on individuals and their behaviors. From greater creativity (Amabile, 1983) to better physical and psychological health (Langer & Rodin, 1976), self-determination enhances the individual in emotional, physical, and cognitive ways. For the purposes of this text, then, an organismic approach to self and self-determination will be used hand in hand. It is difficult, if not impossible, to discuss the implications of the internal characteristics of the organism on the self that develops without also including self-determination. It has been argued consistently through this work that self does not develop in a vacuum. It is also the case that internal and external forces do not impact the self in a uni-directional manner. As surely as the individual's motivations influence the developing self, the developing self will influence the individual's motivations.

Perhaps the moral of an eclectic approach to self is simply to remember that most self processes are cyclical in nature. As one aspect influences another, so it is influenced by it. An organismic approach to self, therefore, is included to remind the reader that individuals are not completely at the mercy of external forces in terms of developing a sense of self. In the end, one of the main reasons why identity negotiation can be so difficult is because both the individual (the organism) and the other individuals within that person's social context have a lot to say about who that person becomes.

SELF-DETERMINATION AS AN ENERGIZING FORCE

Deci (1992) suggests that individuals have a need to take action designed to sustain life. This echoes a similar sentiment expressed in previous chapters of this text where it has been argued that individuals are driven to maintain a particular view of self. When others do not agree with the images of self that were intended, the individuals projecting their self may feel threatened because the inconsistency threatens the self-stability that is needed. In this regard, the energy that results from this motivation drives the individuals toward particular goals, choices, and consequences. The anticipated outcome of these choices, then, is self-determination (Deci, 1992). Deci and Ryan (1990) suggest that motivation theories assume that individuals are motivated by a need for autonomy. Such a concept has been incorporated into organismic approaches to self because such a concept is the fundamental component of self-determination. As suggested previously in this chapter, self-determined behaviors can have a positive influence on self. Individuals can be motivated to engage in behaviors for no other reason than they find them internally rewarding. But as much research has shown, this internal pleasure can be easily extinguished if external reinforcements are introduced (Deci, 1971).

The fact that extrinsic reward can reduce intrinsic motivation is important to understanding the energizing nature of self-determination. Individuals derive pleasure from doing things simply because they enjoy doing them. This is, in fact, the epitome of self-determination. Individuals who are self-determined set their own agendas, make their own behavioral choices, accept the consequences of their actions, and reap the self-esteem rewards for a job well done. If that ability is undermined by external reinforcements, though, not only is some of the pleasure lost but other self benefits are lost as well. Individual cannot take complete credit for a job well done and receive positive self-esteem if they receive a paycheck for doing that job.

Snyder (1992) suggests that individuals attempting to get acquainted may do so for different motivations. Certainly the motive that underlies the attempt to get acquainted may profoundly influence whether self-determination will be attempted or whether the individual will give in to control attempts. Individuals, according to Snyder (1992), may initiate the acquaintance process to get to know each other or to get along. If the motive is knowledge, then it would make sense for both individuals to engage in self-determination and express their autonomy. Getting along, on the other hand, may be more easily accomplished if one puts autonomy on hold and tries a certain degree of give and take with the interaction partner. In this manner, the motives that underlie the decision to enter an interaction may directly influence the degree of self-determination or autonomy that is expressed. Then, in patterns previously discussed, the behaviors that are chosen may influence the responses one receives from the interaction partner. These responses, then, may further refine the future of the interaction.

It also must be the case that self-esteem plays a role in determining the impact that self-determination will have on self. If an individual has high self-esteem, she may feel more self-determined and may trust more in her ability to make things happen. The low self-esteem individual, however, may question her ability to control actions and outcomes. As data by Osborne and Stites (1994) suggest, low self-esteem individuals will willingly interpret failure as being due to self-determining factors, but these same individuals interpret successes as being due to factors beyond their control. High self-esteem persons, on the other hand, prefer self-determining interpretations for their successes and externally controlled interpretations for their failures. Perhaps the low self-esteem individuals have learned a pattern of behaviors and choices that calls into question their ability to self-regulate (or self-determine) their behaviors (e.g., Osborne, 1993d).

This discussion suggests that individuals can sometimes engage in behaviors that purposely thwart their ability to take credit for success. If individuals have learned to take credit for success (which can enhance self-determination and, therefore, further perpetuate self-esteem), self-determination becomes more likely in the future. If, however, the individuals have learned to take self-determining credit for failure but not success, it directly diminishes their ability to gain self-determining benefits from any successes in the future. The implications of this organismic approach to self-esteem are profound and rigid. Once individuals have learned that they can determine self, it makes sense that they would be very unwilling to give up that self-regulation. Individuals who have learned to take credit for failure but not success, however, are just as likely to hold onto that pattern at all costs.

Deci and Ryan (1985) propose a self-determination theory that suggests individuals have three basic fundamental needs: the need for competence, the need for relatedness, and the need for self-determination. Each of these needs results in different implications for the individual and would motivate different types of behaviors. Competency needs would certainly lead individuals to engage in behaviors that put their best foot forward. Such needs also would motivate individuals to put forth the kind of effort that successful accomplishment of tasks requires. This is not to say that individuals must always "succeed," but that they would be interested in achieving some level of mastery over the task. The need for relatedness suggests that individuals are fundamentally social creatures. Human beings desire the company of others (there are, of course, always exceptions), and a certain degree of self-definition comes from the associations and relationships one has with others. This concept seems to play a role in basking in reflected glory (e.g., Cialdini et al., 1976) and trying to avoid basking in the reflected failure of others (e.g., Snyder, Lassegard, & Ford, 1986). The need for self-determination motivates the individual to be autonomous. This suggests that individuals prefer to make their own behavioral choices. An understanding of the role of these three needs provides substance to motivation theories that may have been lacking in the past.

Deci and Ryan (1990) refer to what is known as organismic integration, the concept that certain fundamental strivings serve as the developmental catalysts for the self. Two such strivings are suggested: toward unity of self, and toward meaningful personal relationships. The first is what Deci and Ryan (1990) refer to as a striving "toward coherence in one's regulatory activity and experience." This point is fundamental to an eclectic approach to self. Such an eclectic view of self-concept and self-esteem assumes that individuals strive toward unity of self. Individuals so motivated seek to clarify the more important aspects of self and bring them into harmony with the other aspects of self. The resulting self, however, is not merely some conglomerate melting of all aspects of self. Unity in self means reconciling the more important characteristics of self with other perhaps less important but still vital aspects of self. This has been referred to earlier in this text as self-understanding.

Occurring hand in hand with self-understanding, however, is identity negotiation. This concept suggests the second basic striving articulated by Deci and Ryan (1990) toward meaningful interpersonal relationships. Although it is known that human beings are social creatures, it must be kept in mind that part of the implications of a person's social nature is an impact on the person's individuality. This means that individuals are striving to satisfy both a need to have a unified sense of self (individuality) and a need for that self to be integrated in an interpersonal context. What results from this analysis of these strivings, then, is an understanding that self plays an active role in its own development. Individuals, therefore, are motivated to seek unity and integration both within self and with others. This integration prompts behaviors that are self-deterministic and dynamic. This means that individuals sometimes must modify self because of environmental demands and the results of the integration process. But it also means that individuals acts on and influences the nature of the environment (Deci & Ryan, 1990).

SELF-DETERMINATION AS A SOURCE OF CONFLICT AND STRIFE

Perhaps in a perfect world the integration within self and with others would be conflict free. But cultural expectations or environmental demands sometimes can be at odds with the needs of the individual. Deci and Ryan (1987) and Ryan (1992) suggest that the autonomous nature of the individual sometimes can be in direct conflict with environmental demands (such as those toward conformity). Chapter Two of this text already suggested that society can sometimes demand mutually exclusive things from the individual. American society, for example, seems to demand simultaneously "You must be unique, but don't you dare be different." These demands, of course, are in direct conflict, and the individual will either have to choose one or the other or try to walk the tightrope between them. Such tightrope walking, however, involves a relinquishing of some autonomy and a giving in to some control.

Individuals do such relinquishing and giving in on a daily basis. Some, however, find such loss of autonomy more disconcerting than others. Individuals sometimes wear their self-determination proudly on their sleeves and may experience attempts by others to regulate their behavioral choices as a threat to personal autonomy. Deci and Ryan (1987) suggest that individuals may differ to the extent that certain person factors (ego involvement and other personality traits) may also influence the extent to which the individual will engage in self-determination of behavior. It makes sense that personality constructs that focus the individual's attention inward (such as private self-consciousness as suggested by Fenigstein, Scheier, & Buss, 1975) may impact self-determination (Plant & Ryan, 1985). These researchers also summarize research evidence that supports the contention that individuals may orient themselves toward environmental events that are "autonomy supportive" or "controlling." This, again, suggests the importance of self-determination.

Even those individuals who make specific choices to orient their behaviors toward controlling situations (situations in which their behavioral choices will be limited or dictated) are engaging in a certain degree of autonomous self-regulation. Not all situations allow the individual the freedom to choose between autonomy and control. Those situations that do offer such choice, however, offer the individual a certain degree of autonomy regardless of which choice is made. If Tom decides to go along with the group even though it isn't necessary, he has clearly made a choice. Tom has given up a certain degree of subsequent autonomy and self-determination by making that choice, but initially anyway, it was a fairly autonomous decision. All of this must be tempered, of course, by the realization that Tom may have felt that he had very little choice but to give in to the controlling attempts. There would seem to be, yet again, another cycle at work here. Individuals who feel more self-determined may perceive less pressure to give in to control attempts. This choice to be self-determined, then, further perpetuates their impression that they are autonomous. Individuals who feel less self-determined, however, may perceive themselves as having little choice but to give in to the control. Upon giving in, however, they are faced with yet one more bit of evidence to suggest that they have little autonomy.

The eclectic nature of self clearly seems to be at play here. Individuals tend to engage in behaviors (whether they are aware of it or not) that perpetuate their current perceptions of self. But these behaviors, once chosen, can further limit the options that will be open to them the next time around. Sometimes, however, individuals can manage to succeed in giving in to the control attempt and at the same time exercise self-determination. This at first may seem impossible. How can an individual relinquish control and simultaneously exert autonomy? An eye-opening experiment by Nyquist and Spence (1986) shows that it is possible to have simultaneous adherence to control (in this case adhering to gender-role expectations) and exertion of self-determination (in this case acting in a manner that is consistent with one's personality characteristics that are in direct conflict with the gender-role expectations).

In this study, Nyquist and Spence (1986) paired male and female subjects based on dominance scores on a previously administered questionnaire. Four subject pairings were used: a high dominant male with a low dominant male, a high dominant male with a low dominant female, a high dominant female with a low dominant female, and a high dominant female with a low dominant male. These subject pairs were then told that they were going to be performing a task and to take a few moments to decide who was going to be the leader. In this manner, Nyquist and Spence were able to establish situations in which internal motives (the need for dominance) could be in direct conflict with gender-role expectations (males should be leader). In both pair types in which the high dominant individual was male, that individual overwhelmingly became leader. In the condition in which the high dominant female was paired with a low dominant male, however, the low dominant male usually became the leader. This may seem to suggest that when personality (level of dominance) is pitted against control variables (gender-role expectations), control comes out on top. But Nyquist and Spence audiotaped the conversations between subject pairs to gather more information on how the decision about who would become leader was made. In eighty percent of the pairs with a high dominant female and a low dominant male in which the low dominant male was made leader, it was a direct result of a decision made by the high dominant female. Such statements as "You be the leader" were quite common.

Nyquist and Spence suggest that such dominant actions were used by the high dominant females in order to adhere to the gender-role expectation that the male should be the leader, but not at the expense of the woman's need for dominance. In such scenarios, surface behaviors may seem to give in to the attempts by others to control the actions of the self. Only digging deeper allows a look at the interplay of autonomy and control. Finally, only such exhaustive, deep-level analyses of an individual's behavioral choices and the reasons behind them will shed light on the issue of conflict between the individuals' need for autonomy and self-determination and society's demands that individuals "tow the line," "go with the flow," and avoid "rocking the boat."

WRAPPING IT UP: WHAT DOES ALL THIS MEAN?

Such detailed analyses of behaviors (as suggested above) play a vital role in an eclectic approach to self. Surface behaviors are rarely as simple as they seem. Even when individuals are asked to adhere to some control attempt and they agree, more questions need to be asked. How does the individual feel about the decision to give in? What are the implications of such choices for future behavior? What ramifications do such choices have for the perceptions the individual holds toward self? How does the individual maintain a balance between the internal need for autonomy, suggested by Deci and others, and the overwhelming desire to fit in? These questions (many of which already have been addressed in this text) reinforce the fundamental nature of the self system.

Individuals are concerned with not only their individuality but their collectivity as well. Although cultures and cultural subgroups can be labeled as either individualistic or collectivist, any given person within such groups must struggle with the need to be both. An eclectic theory of self must be able to explain when individuals will choose to express their self-determination through autonomous behaviors and when that same person will choose to adhere to the demands or control attempts of others. Being successful as an individual is not possible without being able to be both autonomous and controlled as the situations and circumstances dictate.

As can be seen in the flow chart in Figure 7.1, the eclectic theory being developed in this text has been expanded once again. The flow chart illustrates not only the main com-

FIGURE 7.1 Expanded Flow Chart of the Self System

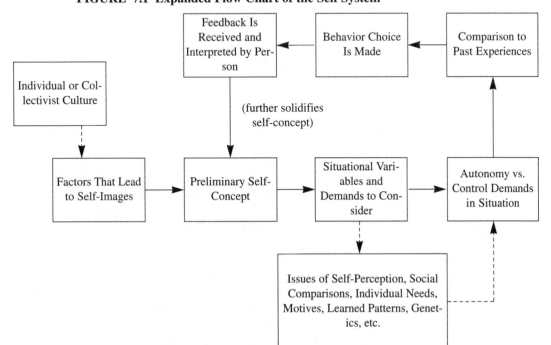

ponents important to the development of self-concept and self-esteem, but also the variables that are used by the individual in deciding when to be autonomous and when to go with external constraints on behaviors. Issues of social comparison, self-perception, cultural expectations, individual needs and motives, learned patterns of interpreting success and failure, and genetic tendencies all must be reconciled if the behavioral choices of individuals are to be understood. Likewise, the ramifications for self of those behavioral choices can only be completely understood if the individuals' subjective reality can be understood. No two individuals will perceive the same series of events in the same manner. Issues of subjective reality play a pivotal role in discussions of personality disorders, for example, Adler's (1969) use of the term "individual psychology." Even Adler's use of the concept "style of life" suggests that individuals have unique ways in which they pursue their goals (Adler, 1927). The concepts of autonomy and self-determination, according to Adler and other social psychoanalysts, such as Karen Horney, play crucial roles in the development and maintenance of a healthy personality.

Erich Fromm uses the term "need for relatedness" (Fromm, 1955) to stress that human beings at times can feel overwhelmingly isolated because of our unique capacity for pondering our own existence and making a fundamental choice in life. This choice, Fromm argues, is between leading a healthy and productive life by striving to develop our potentials (a concept closely related to self-determination as discussed in this chapter) or submitting to others (a concept very much like submitting to control). The need for relatedness is reflected in the human being's need to unite self with others, but such a union can have both positive and negative implications for the individual. In order to experience mature love, the individual must relate to others in a productive manner. Such productivity, however, must come at the expense of some of the individual's self-determination. Mature love involves care and concern for others, meaning that others' needs must sometimes take precedence over the individual's (Fromm, 1955).

This point reinforces the previous discussion centering on the assumption that all individuals are more or less autonomous or controlled given the situational parameters that are present. Jake may be very unwilling to give in to the control demands of others, but he may ask "How high?" when his wife asks him to jump. Having a healthy personality does not mean always looking out for number one. On the other hand, it doesn't mean totally subjugating self to the needs of others either. The relationship between internal needs and external demands is an important one, and one that serves as the driving force behind organismic approaches to self. The eclectic theory can incorporate both the internal drives that push the individual's behavior and the external demands that pull it. Individuals must make the best behavioral choices they can given the circumstances at the time. Healthy individuals (as depicted in Figure 7.1) can promote their own self-esteem by being realistic about why they made the behavioral choices they made. If individuals believe they have made a decision for all of the wrong reasons, self will suffer.

An organismic approach to self accurately reflects the nature of an eclectic theory. No theory of self could be complete that ignores the internal characteristics and past experiences that individuals bring into any situation. Individuals who are trying to understand the complex entity called "self" will only be successful if they keep from assuming that self develops or behaves in a vacuum. A person's prior history not only plays a role in determining the situations in which the person may be found but also may influence the behavioral choices that the person makes or even the behavioral options that the person sees as being viable. This is not to say that we must always get inside the head of the person in order to understand why certain behavioral choices were made. Sometimes situations are so powerful that any semblance of freedom of choice is lost. The opposite, however, also must be considered. Unless it is possible to clarify and understand both the internal factors that may be driving behaviors and the external pressures or demands that may be striving to limit them, our ability to completely understand the "self" of another will be imperfect at best.

WRAPPING IT UP: INTEGRATION OF SECTION TWO

Fundamental to an understanding of the dynamic nature of self is an understanding of the methods by which individuals acquire self-related knowledge. Clearly the source of self-relevant information will play a pivotal role in how that information affects self-concept and self-esteem. This section has focused on a variety of paths by which individuals gather information that can be used to define, clarify, refine, alter, or maintain self. Several relevant questions guided the formation of this section of material, and the answers provided for them further refined the eclectic theory that is being built. First, why do individuals seek self-knowledge? The summary of self-related literature presented throughout this section suggests that individuals have a fundamental need to know who they are. Although this certainly is not surprising, it can be problematic. When individuals seek information and ask questions designed to help them come to know who they are, they have a vested interest in the answers that are acquired. Self is defined in part by both the questions the individual is asking and the answers that are being provided. If the answers are in direct conflict with the images of self the individual had hoped to portray, self may be directly challenged.

Several options are open to individuals as they struggle to determine the best course of action for dealing with the self-related discrepancy. If possible, individuals may choose to ignore the discrepancy, avoid that information source in the future, or attempt actively to change the image that is being projected so that the feedback that is received is closer to the original image that had been intended. Despite the individuals' best efforts, however, they may fail to bring others' perceptions of self in line with the self-images they had intended to project. In such cases, the individuals may be forced to re-evaluate self and ask the painful question "Am I really who I thought I was?" The manner in which the individuals attempt to answer that question may serve as the foundation on which positive or negative self-esteem will be built.

Another question is "How much can individuals learn about self from observing their own actions?" This question can only be answered if the connection between sources of self-knowledge and organismic approaches to self is understood. Certainly individuals can look at their own actions and draw inferences about self. Those inferences, however, may be further influenced by the degree to which the individuals felt autonomous in choosing the action. If Rachel observes herself acting honestly, wouldn't it make sense for her to draw the conclusion that she is an honest person? The answer depends on the environmental circumstances in which the behavior occurred. If she chooses not to steal a pair of gloves because she is standing right in front of the security camera, can she really use that behavior as evidence of her honesty? If, however, she chooses not to cheat on an exam even though the instructor is not in the room and the exam key falls off the desk right in front of her, such autonomous honesty can allow her to conclude that she is an honest person.

Situations carry with them some degree of control that is exerted on the individuals interacting within them. Individuals vary in the degree to which they value autonomy. Self-determined persons value making their own choices. They take more responsibility for their actions and may have a more clearly articulated idea of who they are. Other situations, however, seem less clear cut. Sometimes individuals don't know how they are doing because no objective standard of correctness exists. In such cases, individuals may have to draw inferences about self by making comparisons to other persons and then making connections back to their self. The comparison target that is chosen, however, can have a profound impact on the self-concept and self-esteem of the person making the comparison. Chapter Five summarized the implications of comparison choices and suggested that individuals may choose certain comparison targets for very specific reasons. Table 5.1 summarized the motives that may be behind comparison choices and discussed the implications that those comparison choices would have for the self of the person making them.

Raskin, Novacek, and Hogan (1991) suggest that the variability in individuals' self-esteem levels is due to three sources: self-evaluations, reflections of self coming back from others, and ideal selves. An understanding of these influences on self-esteem ties directly into this section on the sources of self-knowledge. First, self-esteem is influenced by self-evaluations. When individuals' self-esteem is influenced by self-evaluation, the individuals are making decisions for themselves about self-regard and the positivity and negativity of their attributes. Such self-evaluations are similar to the processes of self-perception as discussed in Chapter Four of this text. Second, individuals may gather self-esteem from others. This relates directly to the discussion of reflected appraisals in Chapter Three. The individual's self-esteem is determined in part from the reflections of self that the individual perceives as coming back from others. If the reflections seem positive, high self-esteem should be the result. If, however, the individual believes the reflections to be negative, low self-esteem is the likely result. Third, individuals establish ideals for self and make efforts to live up to those ideal expectations. Discussions of self-esteem presented earlier in this text suggested that discrepancies between individuals' actual and ideal selves can have dramatic implications for self-esteem. To a certain extent, the formation of ideal selves can relate back to Chapter Five and discussions of social comparison theory. Ideal selves are created partly as a matter of comparison to others, including societal norms of who individuals should or should not be.

Individuals do not always have total freedom of choice in terms of who they become. Chapter Six presented an overview of the potential relationship between self and culture. Certainly individuals are influenced by the cultural expectations that are placed upon them. The goal for the individual, then, is to reconcile such external demands on behavior with individual needs for autonomy and self-determination. Organismic approaches to self remind the reader that self is both internally and externally shaped. Perhaps more than anything else, the reader should now understand that individuals do not truly know themselves until all of these sources of self-knowledge are considered. Life experiences teach individuals a lot about who they are, what their limits are, how much they can be bounced around and pushed and pulled by life events and still bounce back, who they are not, who they would like to be, and who they would like not to be. It makes sense, therefore, that no single source of self-knowledge can possibly give the individual all the information needed to develop a conception of self that is both accurate and complete.

Consequences of Self-Knowledge

INTRODUCTION TO SECTION THREE

Now that the reader understands some of the major methods by which individuals come to know who they are, the logical next step would be a discussion of the implications of this self-knowledge. Once the individual has gathered self-relevant information, how is that information used (or abused)? The theory of self that has been presented so far suggests that self may serve as a guiding principle in the individual's life. Indeed, it has already been suggested that self and consciousness cannot be completely separated. Where does the individual stop and consciousness start? Individuals spend a great deal of time and energy gathering self-relevant information and feedback. It therefore seems perfectly reasonable to assume that the self would serve as the foundation upon which other kinds of information are processed. Rubin (1986) reminds the reader that memories of things that have impacted an individual's life form the basis of the self-concept. Indeed, it is hard to imagine self-concept even being possible without such memories. This suggests that memories influence self-concept, but surely it works both ways. Is it possible that self influences memory as well?

Research by Rogers, Kuiper, and Kirker (1977) provides evidence to support the contention that individuals have a better memory for items when they think about those items in reference to themselves. Brehm and Kassin (1993) suggest that self guides recollections in three ways: by virtue of the self-reference effect, egocentric bias, and the hindsight bias. The self-reference effect, as already suggested by Rogers et al., suggests that individuals are more likely to remember things when they are processed in relation to self than in relation to other contexts. Egocentric bias is based on the notion that individuals remember themselves as having a larger role in past events than actually occurred. Hindsight bias seems to be based on a similar principle. With this bias, individuals look at events (after the fact) and assume that they should have been able to anticipate them. In this manner, self guides the recollection of the past by tainting events to be more in line with self. When individuals are asked to recall how a game or event went, they tend to focus on their actions in the situation. If we were to listen to all of the members of a basketball team describe their performance, it wouldn't be unusual to discover that the combined recollected contribution based on the players' memories far exceeds the actual score.

Such self-biased memories, however, bring up a further point. Self-schemas (Markus, 1977) are constructed as individuals gather information about self. These constructs then may serve as information processing modules that cause self-relevant information to be processed in ways that are consistent with those schemas. Schemas can be defined as generalized organizations of knowledge, based on past experience, that organize past experience and guide the processing of future experiences. When such cognitive constructs are considered in relation to the self, they suggest that past self-relevant experiences lead to the formation of mental representations of self. These self-schemas then guide the processing of self-relevant information that comes to the self in the future. If through her experiences Jessica has come to believe herself to be a sensitive person, then such thoughts about self may dictate future actions. Jessica may be more likely to empathize with others or help them in a time of need. But self-schemas also may lead the individual to reject certain kinds of information if that information is not consistent with the cognitive representations the individual holds for self.

Finally, Lewicki (1983) suggests that individuals may use their own self-schemas to process information about other individuals as well. This suggests that Jessica (who considers herself sensitive) may be more likely to notice sensitive or insensitive behaviors on the part of others. Thus self-knowledge can be used by persons in a variety of ways, and certainly the manner in which this self-knowledge is used can profoundly impact further refinements to the self.

Section Three addresses the question of how self-knowledge is used by looking at three major issues. The self-reference effect discussed in Chapter Eight examines the extent to which individuals use self and self-knowledge as a referent point for making sense of their social worlds. Chapter Nine discusses the continuing controversy between self-enhancement and self-verification theories. These theories make dramatically different assumptions about the guiding principle behind self-related behaviors. Self-enhancement theories assume that individuals are primarily motivated to seek out self-relevant information that will enhance their self-esteem, whereas self-verification theories assume that individuals are primarily motivated to maintain their current sense of self. Finally, Chapter Ten looks at the concept of self-fulfilling prophecies. A self-fulfilling prophecy suggests that individuals' expectations of others may shape their behavior in such a way as to prompt behavior from the others that confirms the expectation.

CHAPTER EIGHT

The Self-Reference Effect

BASIC QUESTIONS

Numerous lines of research converge on what has come to be known as the self-reference effect. Since the early writings of James (1890), theorists have suggested that the self is central in the processing of information about others. It makes sense, given how much energy is expended to know the self, that individuals may consider such a construct useful in defining others as well. Discussions of self-schemata (Markus, 1977), self-image bias (Lewicki, 1983), and egocentric bias (Greenwald, 1980) all suggest that self serves as an important information processing strategy. Several questions, however, need to be discussed. First, given the intuitive appeal of such a concept, why has there been difficulty verifying the effect? Second, what are the implications of this self-referent processing of information? Third, what cognitive strategies underlie the self-reference process? As this chapter proceeds, each of these questions will be considered both separately and in connection with each other.

Kihlstrom et al. (1988) provide an excellent summary of issues related to information processing and the self. According to this review, one of the major implications of self and information processing is the self-reference effect. Findings on the self-reference effect, of course, make perfect sense in light of depth of processing principles in memory. The more an individual is able to process and elaborate the information, the more accurate memory for that information should be (e.g., Craik & Lockhart, 1972). Kihlstrom et al. (1988) suggest that self can be considered one of the most complex and elaborate knowledge bases in memory. If this is true, then it makes sense to conclude that information that can be connected with this elaborate memory structure would be easier to remember. Markus (1977) reminds the reader that the opposite is just as true. If the individual is asked to process information that is contrary to self-schemata, such conflict may hinder memory for that information.

PROBLEMS WITH VERIFYING THE SELF-REFERENCE EFFECT

Despite the intuitive appeal of the self-reference effect, it has enjoyed only limited empirical support. Klein, Loftus, and Burton (1989) summarize several dual problems that may have kept the self-reference paradigm from being as successful as might have been expected. First, empirical attempts to verify and replicate the seminal findings of Rogers, Kuiper, and Kirker (1977) have led to conflicting results. Some studies have yielded results that overwhelmingly support the self-reference effect paradigm (e.g., Erdelyi, 1984), but others have been nonsupportive (e.g., Bower & Gilligan, 1979, experiment two). Second, the self-reference effect has enjoyed limited success as a paradigm because few can agree on the mechanisms that might underlie the effect. Though everyone seems to agree that self-reference is mediated by some underlying cognitive process, everything from elaboration to cuing has been suggested as the underlying mediating mechanism.

Klein, Loftus, and Burton (1989) also suggest that many of the discrepancies can be explained if one takes a closer look at the memory task the subject is being asked to carry out. These researchers distinguish between "descriptive" memory tasks and "autobiographical" memory tasks. Asking individuals simply to note some word and answer the question "Does this describe you?" is a much different task from asking individuals to think of some event in their past that is related to the word. The level of processing required to relate the word to an autobiographical memory is much deeper than a simple yes/no comparison of the target word to the self. Clearly the self-reference effect would be much stronger with autobiographical tasks than simple descriptive ones.

IMPLICATIONS OF THE SELF-REFERENCE EFFECT

It seems somewhat strange that few connections have been made between the self-reference effect and how individuals may process information about others in their social worlds. Certainly a case can be made for self serving as a global information processing strategy (e.g., Kihlstrom et al., 1988). Certainly the information processing nature of the self system is not limited to processing information that is directly self-relevant. Individuals tend to use self as a means for processing information about others (Carpenter, 1988; Lewicki, 1983, 1984). Though this has not been specifically labeled as an extension of the self-reference effect, Osborne and Young (1994) provide evidence to support the contention that the strength of individuals' personality characteristics may determine the extent to which they will use the same characteristics to process information about others. Numerous studies have addressed the issue of whether the self-reference effect is due to some favored status of information that is processed in connection with the self or whether the effect is due primarily to the depth at which the information is processed (e.g., Higgins & Bargh, 1987). Again the findings have been contradictory at best. Some experiments yielded results that support the favored status view of self-relevant information, but others have yielded findings that draw this conclusion directly into question. Again, however, the true differences between the conditions may be masked by the manner in which the data are being analyzed. Just looking at the number of items correctly recalled as a function of self-referent versus other-referent processing may be too simplistic an approach. Indeed, Kuiper and Rogers

(1979) looked at the response latencies for subjects' responses in the self-referent versus other-referent conditions and discovered that significantly less time was needed to recall information in the self-referent than the other-referent conditions.

It may be the case that some of the ramifications of the self-reference effect are being obscured by assuming that self-reference is strictly a memory-based phenomenon. The findings by Lewicki (1983) and others provide support for the contention that important characteristics of self may be used to process information about others in the individual's social world. Such an idea is of critical importance in outlining the implications of the self-reference effect because it suggests that individuals may access self as an information processing strategy even when not specifically asked to do so. In a sense, this would be a more global example of the self-reference effect than simply showing that asking subjects to process memory information in relation to the self enhances recall. Asking questions about the generalizability of the self-reference effect not only is important for understanding the implications of the effect. The answers also may provide insights into the nature of the cognitive processes that may underlie the effect.

Sedikides and Skowronski (1993) argue that the greater the centrality of a given trait for the individual, the more likely that trait is to be used in impression formation. After pretesting to determine if the traits of intelligence and honesty were central or peripheral to subjects, Sedikides and Skowronski (1993) engaged subjects in an impression formation task. Results support the suggestion that central traits play a more influential role in impression formation than peripheral traits. Subjects for whom intelligence was a central trait were more influenced by intelligent behaviors than subjects for whom intelligence was a peripheral trait. The same pattern, of course, held true for the centrality of honesty. In further discussions of the results, Sedikides and Skowronski (1993) also suggest that the resulting effect on impression formation was caused by the influence centrality had on negative cues. This means that central traits caused subjects to rate negative examples of the trait more negatively than subjects for whom the trait was peripheral. In other words, a person who values honesty (one for whom honesty is a central trait) would perceive dishonest behaviors as significantly more dishonest than a person for whom honesty is peripheral.

This, of course, further supports the notion that characteristics that individuals value (including those that persons believe define who they are) strongly influence the manner in which other individuals are perceived. These findings also suggest that characteristics (traits such as honesty, intelligence, self-monitoring) that are a central part of the individual's personality may play an especially pivotal role in the impression formation process. If an individual holds a particular trait as central to his or her personality, then it stands to reason that the same trait would be relied upon in extracting, encoding, storing, and perhaps retrieving information about others. If Sara feels that her self-monitoring tendency is an important part of who she is ("It's important to me to be situationally successful"), then it may be reasonable to conclude that Sara will be likely to pay attention to the same characteristic in others.

Osborne and Young (1994) suggest that traits on which an individual scores particularly high may serve as a heuristic by which the individual processes other types of information in the social world. To address this possibility, subjects were scored on Snyder's eighteen-item, self-monitoring scale. Subjects scoring in either the upper or lower third of the distribution of scores were selected for participation. In experiment two, subjects were asked to do the "Who Am I?" task (e.g., Gordon, 1968; McGuire & Padawer-Singer, 1976), fill out a demographic questionnaire meant to serve as a filler task, and fill out an open-ended questionnaire describing their best friend. This questionnaire was identical to the "Who Am I?" but the subjects were asked to respond by listing the words and phrases that first came to their minds when they were asked to describe their best friend.

In analyses of the data, Osborne and Young (1994) discovered that high self-monitors use significantly more physical and social relationship descriptors to describe themselves than do low self-monitors. Low self-monitors, on the other hand, use significantly more trait descriptors to describe themselves than do high self-monitors. These findings provide empirical validation of long-standing assumptions about the manner in which high and low self-monitors view themselves. Analyses of the descriptions of best friends also suggest a strong connection between the way in which individuals process information about self and the manner in which they process information about others. Did high and low self-monitors show the same differential use of descriptive categories when describing their friends that they did when describing themselves? Yes. Low self-monitors used significantly more trait descriptors to describe their best friends than did high self-monitors, and high self-monitors used significantly more physical and social relationship descriptors to describe their best friends than did low self-monitors.

What are the implications of these findings for explaining the generalizability of the self-reference effect? Osborne and Young (1994) argue that such findings may simply reflect the individuals' tendency to use the same information processing strategies to encode and retrieve information about others that they do to encode and retrieve information about self. It must be kept in mind, however, that Osborne and Young's (1994) data provide no direct method by which information about encoding and retrieval strategies can be studied. The consistency in descriptive category choices for self and friend, however, does suggest that the self may be serving as a referent point by which other social information is processed. But the findings could also be explained in a variety of alternative ways. Perhaps the most important alternative explanation was suggested by Osborne and Young (1994). The authors suggest that individuals may rely on the same descriptive categories for self and friend because they tend to like persons who are similar to them. In this manner, then, the similarity in use of descriptive categories for self and friend may simply reflect the actual closeness in similarity between self and friend.

To determine the validity of such an alternative explanation, Osborne and Young (1994, experiment three) attempted to replicate the findings by using an unknown other. In this experiment, high and low self-monitors were asked during a pretesting to complete a "Who Am I?" questionnaire. Several weeks later, those subjects scoring in the upper and lower thirds of self-monitoring scores were eligible to participate in another (supposedly unrelated) experiment. In this experiment, subjects were shown a videotape of an unknown target other who had been asked to describe himself. Following a script, the target described himself in terms of ten physical descriptors, ten trait descriptors, and ten social relationship descriptors, in jumbled order. Subjects were then given an unexpected recall test. Subjects were called one week after the videotape experiment and asked to recall over the phone everything they could about the individual they had seen on the videotape.

Analyses of initial recall for the target's descriptors showed no significant differences for high and low self-monitors. Analyses of the follow-up data, however, yielded the predicted patterns. High self-monitors recalled significantly more physical and social role descriptors for the target than did low self-monitors, and low self-monitors recalled significantly more trait descriptors for the target than did high self-monitors. Analyses of the subjects' "Who Am I?" descriptors also replicated the original finding that high self-monitors used categorically more physical and social relationship descriptors, whereas low self-monitors used categorically more trait descriptors. Osborne and Young (1994, experiment three) found no significant differences in category recall immediately after subjects viewed the target tape. Although this is interesting, not enough data are available to speculate as to why it occurred. The presence of the predicted differential use of categories of information at time two, however, suggests that the high and low self-monitors either encoded the information differently or were using fundamentally different categories for retrieval. Further research should be directed toward delineating the cause of these effects with specific attention paid to encoding and retrieval processes.

Although these findings taken alone are not enough to determine if the high and low self-monitors use differential categories to encode, store, or retrieve social information, they do have a profound impact for understanding the nature of the self-reference effect. In other self-monitoring studies, Young, Osborne, and Snyder (1994) discovered that high and low self-monitors rely on different characteristics in making their political choices. High self-monitors tend to choose political candidates that match their perception of who "looks presidential," whereas low self-monitors rely on data about the candidates' stance on issues when making their choices.

It could be that these findings also represent an analysis of social information in a manner that is relevant to self. High self-monitors value being situationally successful (e.g., Snyder, 1987) and, as such, they are more cognizant of situational constraint information than their low self-monitoring counterparts (e.g., Snyder, Berscheid, & Matwychuk, 1988). Low self-monitors, on the other hand, value congruence between who they are and what they do (Snyder, 1987) and therefore are more likely to be thinking in trait terms (Snyder & Cantor, 1980). In this manner, high and low self-monitoring individuals may be very likely to process information about others in a manner that is relevant to self because they believe these categories to be important. Sedikides and Skowronski (1993) suggest that the centrality of traits may be especially important to impression formation when negative cues are present. High self-monitors, then, may be more aware of the low self-monitoring behaviors of others because it goes against what they consider a central (and, therefore, important) part of their personality. Low self-monitors, on the other hand, may be particularly aware of the high self-monitoring behaviors of others in their social worlds.

These two lines of research (Sedikides & Skowronski, 1993; Osborne & Young, 1994) suggest that individuals may be more likely to notice behaviors or characteristics in others that are consistent with their own. If, however, the characteristics or behaviors of the other individual are negative in relation to the self trait in question (e.g., a person for whom intelligence is a central trait witnesses someone acting particularly stupid), those negative cues may be even more likely to be used in forming an impression of that individual than other characteristics the self and target might share. This means that when all other things are equal, individuals may use self as a referent point from which others in the social world can be categorized. In these cases, the high self-monitor will notice the outward oriented aspects of the other person, whereas the low self-monitor will notice more internal characteristics. If the behaviors emanating from the other person, however, are in stark contrast to the characteristics that individuals feel are a central part of who they are, then the behaviors are especially likely to be noticed and, therefore, used by the individuals in forming an impression of that target person.

In both of these cases, the individual is using self as a heuristic for sifting through the myriad of information in the social world. It makes a certain degree of sense for individuals to believe that categories that are relevant to their self might be beneficial for understanding others as well. Lewicki (1983, 1984) refers to this as the "self-image bias" in person perception.

The processing of self-relevant information may have broad-based implications for other types of information processing. McGuire and Padawer-Singer (1976) suggest that the more distinctive one's traits in a given situation, the more likely such traits would spontaneously be a part of the self-concept. Extending this finding even further, McGuire and Padawer-Singer (1976) further suggest that the distinctiveness of one's traits also may have an effect on one's perceptions of external stimuli, including other persons in one's social world. Frankel and Prentice-Dunn (1990) report results supporting their contention that the self-schemata of lonely individuals would lead to them to process self-relevant information differently than do non-lonely individuals. The results support a selective-attention bias in that lonely persons made fewer errors in identifying negative information, whereas non-lonely individuals made fewer errors in identifying positive information. Frankel and Prentice-Dunn conclude their discussion by suggesting that lonely individuals may get caught in a self-derogatory cycle because the self-schemata they develop may cause them to pay particular attention to negative feedback. In this manner, self has become a referent point from which other information is processed. If self is viewed negatively, then incoming self-relevant information is likely to be processed according to those same schemata.

PROCESSES THAT MIGHT UNDERLIE THE SELF-REFERENCE EFFECT

Klein, Loftus, and Burton (1989) take on the admirable task of trying to articulate the processes that might be underlying the self-reference effect. As previously mentioned, these researchers argue that self-reference tasks can be either descriptive or autobiographical tasks. Answers for questions concerning the processes that underlie the self-reference effect may be extremely important in clarifying the role that self plays in memory. After a series of experiments, Klein, Loftus, and Burton (1989) conclude that the descriptive and autobiographical tasks that produce enhanced recall in self-reference experiments rely on different underlying processes. This contention is dramatically supported by results showing that memory is enhanced more by having subjects perform both a descriptive and an autobiographical task than either by itself. Though this finding is of great significance in understanding the implications of the self-reference effect, little is known about those underlying processes and what implications those processes might have for other aspects of memory. In their summary of the cognitive processes that individuals have suggested might underlie the self-reference effect, Klein, Loftus, and Burton (1989) mention elaboration, organization, evaluation, cognitive cuing, and distinctiveness. Future research should be directed at explicating and analyzing each of these cognitive processes and their implications for the self-reference effect.

CHAPTER NINE

Self-Enhancement Vs. Self-Verification

BACKGROUND INFORMATION

One of the biggest controversies in the self literature involves issues of self-esteem. Initially suggested in groundbreaking work by Deutsch and Solomon (1959), the literature has enjoyed healthy and spirited debate about the nature of self-esteem feedback individuals will prefer. Two schools of thought have developed surrounding the issue of what kind of self-esteem related information individuals will seek. The self-enhancement school of thought argues that individuals are motivated to gather self-related feedback that enhances their feelings of self-worth. This seems a perfectly reasonable assumption to make. Certainly most individuals would prefer self-relevant feedback that casts them in as positive light as possible. Numerous discussions throughout this text, however, directly challenge such an assumption. Although it certainly is true that individuals sometimes want, and therefore seek, self-enhancing feedback, individuals may not always want positive feedback. The self-verification school of thought suggests that individuals value self-consistency and therefore would be motivated to acquire information that confirms what they already know about self. This means that individuals with low self-esteem may actually seek out negative information because it confirms what they already know about who they are.

Individuals have a hard time swallowing an argument that seems so counterintuitive. Surely everyone wants to feel better about self. But one question needs to be asked to shed light on this assumption. Is it necessarily the case that positive feedback will always make the individual feel better? No. Individuals do not always find positive feedback pleasing. If a person feels worthless, then positive feedback coming in from others may put him or her in the uncomfortable position of questioning self. Sometimes, rather than re-evaluate self, the individual will simply reject or avoid the positive feedback and maintain a state of negative but predictable self-worth. Low self-esteem actually should be viewed as at the midpoint of self-esteem. Feelings of self-uncertainty are much more disquieting for the individual than any form of self-certainty. Although individuals with low self-esteem consider many of their attributes to be negative (or at least less than positive), they are at least certain of those things. When a low self-esteem individual is given positive feedback, it threatens that certainty, and therefore that information may be rejected.

The literature surrounding self-enhancement suggests that individuals rely on four major techniques for elevating self-esteem. Each of these techniques relies on a slightly different process, and each may be used at various times depending on situational circumstances. Brehm and Kassin (1993) summarize these four techniques as self-serving cognitions, self-handicapping, basking in reflected glory, and downward social comparisons. Several of these techniques have already been discussed in other contexts within this text. A quick summary of each of these techniques as they relate to self-esteem enhancement, however, will be beneficial before considering the literature supporting self-enhancement and self-verification.

Self-serving cognitions involve interpreting success and failure feedback in whatever manner is necessary to make self feel better. If a tennis player performs poorly and loses a tournament, self-esteem may be threatened. By adopting a protective pattern of interpreting that failure, however, the individual can minimize the negative impact that failure will have on self-esteem. In this case, then, the individual may lament the poor calls by the line judge, the poor weather and lighting conditions, and the noise of the crowd as explanations for his less than stellar performance. The opposite, of course, could be used to maximize the positive self-esteem benefits to be derived from a success. If this same individual wins the tournament, he can maximize the positive impact that success will have on his self-esteem by assuming that it was his responsibility. In this case, then, he should boast about his skill and his savvy. In this manner, the individual simply adopts an interpretive strategy that internalizes the responsibility for positive events and externalizes the responsibility for negative events. These interpretive patterns, in turn, maximize the positivity of self-esteem.

Individuals also can enhance their self-esteem by utilizing what is known as a self-handicapping strategy (e.g., Berglas & Jones, 1978; Snyder, 1990). If an individual feels that failure is probable or even just possible in a given situation, she may try to defuse the impact of that failure by providing excuses that others can use to understand why the failure occurred. In these situations, the individual "prepares" the audience for the performance by leading them to expect failure for a variety of reasons beyond the performer's control. The novice lecturer may plead with her students "Be patient with me because I've never done this before." In this situation, a bad performance will not be too damaging, and a good performance will seem excellent in comparison to what the students had been led to expect. Such a strategy minimizes the negative impact of a failure performance, and maximizes the positive benefits accrued from a successful performance. Research in this area suggests that individuals use self-handicapping not only to minimize failure and maximize success, but also to avoid having to face the possibility that they lack ability (e.g., Baumgardner, 1991; Brehm & Kassin, 1993; DeGree & Snyder, 1985). The literature seems to agree that self-handicapping is most likely to be used under conditions of self-uncertainty (e.g., Berglas & Jones, 1978; Snyder & Smith, 1982; Harris & Snyder, 1986).

Berglas, however, pointed out that little empirical evidence exists to support the assumption that self-handicapping would serve as an effective means of enhancing self-esteem, although he does suggest that theoretically such an assumption should prove to be quite valid (Berglas (1986). Tice (1991) was one of the first to break successfully the drought of support for Berglas' assumption. In a series of four studies, Tice was able to demonstrate successfully that high self-esteem persons self-handicap to enhance success, whereas low self-esteem persons self-handicap to protect or defend against the self-esteem threat of failure or to maintain current self-esteem levels (Tice, 1991). Perhaps the lack of empirical support has come from the inconsistency in the self-enhancement/self-verification literature. Part of the problem may arise from the manner in which self-esteem enhancement is defined.

When individuals refer to self-esteem enhancement, are they referring to positive gains in self-esteem beyond some current or former level? Or are these individuals referring to enhancing self-esteem following some self-esteem threat? In both cases, self-esteem is being enhanced. In one case, the outcome is self-esteem that is higher than it has been before (for example, a high self-esteem person feeling even greater because she just won a major award). In the other case, self-esteem is higher than after the self-esteem threat but not higher than before the threat (the person feels her self-esteem threatened because she failed a test but now feels better because she told the teacher ahead of time that she wasn't feeling well and she can use this as an explanation for her poor performance). It is easy to see how this subtle distinction in the definition could confuse the literature profoundly. In this text, "self-enhancement" will be used in either case. In order to be considered self-enhancing, the resultant effect on self-esteem must merely mean that self-esteem is higher now than it was just a short time ago.

It seems reasonable to conclude (given prior discussions in this text about the self-related information processing strategies used by individuals low or high in self-esteem) that self-esteem level may play a role in determining whether the individual will use self-handicapping to minimize the impact of failure or to maximize the impact of success (Tice, 1991). Low self-esteem persons should choose self-handicapping strategies designed to minimize the impact of anticipated failure, and high self-esteem persons should choose self-handicapping strategies that allow them to draw more positive benefits from their successes (Tice, 1991). These findings are consistent with other literature involving the differences in the kinds of feedback high and low self-esteem persons will seek (e.g., Swann & Ely, 1984) and the patterns of interpretation high and low self-esteem persons will adopt for interpreting success and failure (e.g., Berglas & Jones, 1978; Kolditz & Arkin, 1982; Osborne & Stites, 1994). These findings are also very relevant to the discussion of when individuals will self-enhance or self-verify that comes later in this chapter.

Individuals may also self-enhance by basking in reflected glory (Cialdini et al., 1976). It certainly is the case that individuals come to be known by the individuals they associate with. If a group we belong to is successful in some great endeavor, then we can reap the benefits of that relationship. Jake, an injured player of a high school basketball team, can consider himself to be a state champion even if he didn't play a single minute of the games that ultimately led to that title. Likewise, being related to an individual who is quite successful can have its benefits as well. Individuals are all too ready to say they "know a friend of a friend of a friend who is second cousin to a rock star." It may seem strange that such a tenuous relationship would reflect positively on the individual, but Cialdini and De Nicholas (1989) showed that individuals would attempt to bask in reflected glory following failure even when the association between themselves and the glorious person was completely coincidental ("But I have the same middle name as the President of the United States").

It stands to reason, however, that relationships with others can sometimes reflect poorly on the individual. Several types of associations may make the person look or feel bad. If William is closely associated with someone who performs quite well on an attribute that is particularly self-relevant for William, it may make William's performance seem particularly bad by comparison (this is a concept similar to that expressed by Tesser, 1988). Through associations with others, individuals can sometimes come to be suspects in crimes or even have their fidelity questioned. The point being made is that it is difficult for individuals only to claim the positive benefits of being associated with others who are having good things happen to them. Through association, individuals come to be seen in a variety of ways. Television and movies portray such situations when a friend of someone who is accused of something horrid states "I've never seen this person before in my life." In the same manner that individuals can use self-handicapping to self-esteem enhance in the face of potentially negative outcomes, individuals can bask in reflected glory when their friends or family members are up and attempt to eliminate those connections when those same persons are down. Basking in reflected glory has its advantages, but these same persons may be the first to sever an association if there is the threat that the failure may "rub off on them."

Finally, it has been suggested that self-enhancement can be accomplished through a careful choice of targets to use for social comparison purposes (e.g., Wood & Taylor, 1991). Individuals wanting to feel better about self may be able to accomplish that by comparing themselves to less fortunate others. This process, known as downward social comparison (e.g., Hakmiller, 1966), suggests that individuals may attempt to make themselves feel better by reminding themselves that it could always be worse. If Anne is questioning her intellectual capabilities because of less than superior performance on an exam, she can make herself feel better by comparing her grade to that of a student she knows has performed significantly worse than she has. In this manner, Anne, by comparison, can shield herself from having to make the attribution that she is lacking in ability. She can look to the other individual's performance and say "At least I passed the test." As discussed in Chapter Five, individuals can choose a variety of comparison targets to fulfill a myriad of purposes. One of the major goals of social comparison, then, would be self-enhancement in the face of otherwise threatening circumstances.

Proponents of self-verification theory, however, suggest that individuals will not always be motivated to cast themselves in as positive light as possible (e.g., Swann, Griffin, Predmore, & Gaines, 1987). Sometimes individuals might want to remain in the shadows or simply maintain the level of self-esteem they currently have. One important thing to bear in mind as self-verification is discussed is the point that individuals cannot assume that all other individuals view reality the same way that they do. Psychologists discuss the importance of subjective reality. Subjective reality suggests that no two persons can see the world in exactly the same fashion. Seeing the world through someone else's eyes is an imperfect process. The only way to truly see the world through someone else's eyes would be to have all of his or her experiences, and you would have to rid yourself of all prior experiences that were your own. Given this, it is understandable that individuals can never truly understand how and why other people think, feel, and act the way they do.

Individuals with high self-esteem could not truly put themselves in a low self-esteem frame of mind. Even individuals who have suffered low self-esteem and gotten through it cannot look back with an unbiased eye at what it was like to have low self-esteem. If the reader keeps this in mind then, perhaps it will be a bit easier to accept the fact that not all persons want to self-enhance. Being labeled as a worthy person can put certain demands and expectations on the person that were not there before. These expectations, in turn, may cause the person to worry about "living up" to the expectation (e.g., McFarlin & Blascovich, 1981; Shrauger, 1975; Tesser & Cornell, 1991; Tice, 1991). Low self-esteem persons probably doubted their ability to achieve in the first place. It makes sense, therefore, that those same individuals would be unwilling to let others place even higher expectations for achievement upon them. Self-verification theory is built upon the relatively simple idea that individuals are sometimes motivated to maintain their sense of self (e.g., Swann, 1983). This idea is consistent with the discussion of reflected appraisals in Chapter Three and certain social comparison choices as outlined in Chapter Five (and summarized in Table 5.1). The discussion that follows will focus on the evidence in support of self-enhancement and self-verification theories and then an analysis of the literature that provides evidence for how these two theories may be integrated. It is this integration that will be incorporated into an eclectic approach to self.

THE SELF-ENHANCEMENT LITERATURE

Berglas and Jones (1978) and Tice (1991) suggest that self-handicapping is a protective strategy specifically used to protect self-esteem. Tice (1991) reasons that individual differences in self-esteem would result in differential use of the self-handicapping strategy. Indeed, Harris and Snyder (1986) found that individuals who were low in self-esteem certainty would self-handicap more than individuals who were high in self-esteem certainty. This makes perfect sense. If self-esteem certainty is low, then to a certain extent the individual's self-esteem is fragile. The individual therefore should be highly motivated to protect what self-esteem he has. Self-handicapping provides a method by which a failure performance can have minimal impact on self-esteem and a success (especially in light of the great adversity the self-handicapper has set up for himself) will be seen as even more exceptional. Individuals with high self-esteem certainty, however, should be less threatened by temporary successes and failures and, thus, would need less self-handicapping to protect self-esteem.

Tice and her colleagues (e.g., Baumeister, Tice, & Hutton, 1989; Tice & Baumeister, 1990; Tice, 1991) argue that low and high self-esteem persons may choose differential amounts of self-enhancement because they are motivated by different self-esteem related goals. Low self-esteem persons (as also suggested by Harris & Snyder, 1986) may be motivated to protect self-esteem, whereas high self-esteem persons may be motivated to maximize self-esteem. In this case, low self-esteem persons should self-enhance on fewer occasions than high self-esteem persons. Tice (1991) reasoned that the differences in goals for the low and high self-esteem persons may also prompt different self-handicapping strategies for the individuals. The individual with low self-esteem may prefer self-handicapping strategies that allow the maximum protection for self-esteem, and the individual with high self-esteem may prefer to self-handicap in situations in which self-esteem is most likely to be enhanced. Consistent with these predictions, subjects low in self-esteem self-handicapped more (in this case by practicing a task less) when a failure was meaningful (thus allowing themselves to "explain" away the failure as due to a lack of practice). High self-esteem persons, on the other hand, self-handicapped more (again by practicing less) when a success was meaningful (thereby allowing themselves an "excuse" should they not succeed and the maximum boost to self-esteem should they succeed).

Social comparison research suggests that self-enhancement motives may play a role in determining the targets toward whom individuals will compare themselves (e.g., Taylor & Loebel, 1989; Wills, 1981). The goal with choosing particular social comparison targets (as suggested in the prior discussion of downward social comparisons) may be to provide evidence for self that things weren't as bad as they could have been. When individuals choose to make downward comparisons, the resulting impact on self-esteem may be the type of enhancement in which self-esteem is simply restored to the level it was before the threat occurred. If the individual has not received some self-esteem threat, social comparisons can still be used to make self feel even better. The individual publishing her first novel may compare herself to her successful friends (who haven't yet published their novels) and feel, by comparison, that she has really got it together. The important point being made is that upward, downward, and unilateral comparisons can be made, and depending on the situational circumstances, any of these comparisons can lead to self-esteem enhancement. The individual who feels threatened may prefer downward comparisons today, but may be just as likely to use upward or even unilateral comparisons when things have gone really well.

Swann and his colleagues (e.g., Pelham, 1989; Swann & Ely, 1984; Swann, Pelham, & Chidester, 1988) suggest that individuals are motivated to fulfill both self-enhancement and self-verification motives. Thus, individuals should strive to self-enhance their positive views and strive to self-verify negative self-views. Even individuals with low global self-esteem have been shown to have some aspects of self they feel positive about (e.g., Pelham & Swann, 1989). Given this assessment, it makes sense that the literature would be somewhat contradictory in relation to self-enhancement and self-verification. If it is simply assumed that individuals will either prefer self-enhancement or self-verification, the literature is inconsistent at best. If, however, one looks at the type of self-views subjects are being asked about, the literature is much more reconcilable.

Pelham (1990) argues that individuals will prefer information consistent with their self-views (thereby self-verifying) if those self-views are held with a high degree of certainty. Even if the self-view in question is negative, individuals prefer not to have that certainty called into question. This makes sense if it is assumed that individuals have an investment in their self-views. Presumably, self-views are created over time as a result of multiple experiences in a myriad of situations. Thus, individuals may believe they have good reason to hold the self-views they do, and they gain a certain degree of self-certainty and consistency from that (e.g, Pelham, 1991; Swann, Pelham, & Krull, 1989). Swann, Pelham, and Krull (1989) offer evidence in support of self-enhancement under certain conditions. These researchers discovered that, all other things being equal, individuals prefer feedback that is self-enhancing (e.g., Taylor & Brown, 1988) and prefer interaction partners that offer them self-enhancing feedback. This research also suggests, however, that individuals will not always choose to self-enhance.

Shrauger (1975) hypothesizes that low self-esteem persons may choose to self-enhance (either by preferring success feedback or choosing interaction partners who give them positive feedback) when affective reactions are being measured. In this case, the feedback individuals receive can enhance their affective state. When nothing else is at stake but the individuals' own mood, it makes perfect sense to assume that they would choose to be in as good a mood as possible. In fact, McFarlin and Blascovich (1981) show that low self-esteem persons desired success as much as their high self-esteem counterparts (thus confirming Shrauger's assumption that they prefer positive affective information). They still, however, anticipated failure. Tesser and his colleagues (e.g., Tesser, 1988; Tesser & Cornell, 1991) have elaborated the self-evaluation maintenance model that predicts that individuals may choose evaluative methods that result in self-verification when self is threatened by the performance of others, and self-enhancement when self can be augmented by the performance of others.

THE SELF-VERIFICATION LITERATURE

A perusal of the self-verification literature indicates that research on self-verification has centered on three crucial questions: "Why do individuals self-verify?" (e.g., Swann & Ely, 1984; Swann, Stein-Seroussi, & Giesler, 1992a); "When will individuals choose to self-verify?" (e.g., Swann & Hill, 1982; Swann, Hixon, & De La Ronde, 1992b); and "How do individuals go about self-verifying?" (e.g., Swann, 1983; Swann, Griffin, Predmore, & Gaines, 1987). Each of these questions must be addressed if we are to understand the relationship between self-enhancement and self-verification and to understand how self-verification processes relate to an eclectic approach to self. It is certainly true that these questions are interrelated. Questions of why individuals choose to self-verify provide insights into when they would choose to do so. Answers to questions of why and when self-verifications will take place will also shed light on how individuals carry out the self-verification process.

The "Why" Question

Swann, Pelham, and Chidester (1988) argue that individuals will seek feedback to verify their firmly held self-views. The motivation for this solicitation of self-verifying feedback comes from the individual's need for predictability and control. This assumption that individuals are sometimes motivated to maintain or satisfy their self at the expense of self-enhancement is certainly consistent with the existing literature (e.g., Simon, 1990; Tesser & Cornell, 1991). As already suggested, individuals with low self-esteem may prefer to garner self-verifying feedback because they doubt their ability to maintain a favorable identity should they acquire self-enhancing feedback (e.g., Brown, Collins, & Schmidt, 1988; Tice, 1991). Hattie (1992) summarizes the differences between high and low self-esteem persons in terms of the self-enhancement versus self-verification controversy. He suggests that high self-esteem persons have harmony between their self-enhancement and self-verification motives, whereas low self-esteem persons are driven to maintain their negative self-views (through self-verification) because of the doubt they have about their ability to maintain a positive self-concept (Swann, Griffin, Predmore, & Gaines, 1987).

Self-verification may also be a more complex cognitive process than self-enhancement. If this is the case, individuals may be motivated to self-enhance when possible simply because it requires less mental effort than self-verifying. Swann, Hixon, Stein-Seroussi, and Gilbert (1990) provide compelling evidence to suggest that self-verification strivings do require more complex cognitive computations than self-enhancement. Self-verification, therefore, would be a more difficult process to complete and would require some concerted effort on the part of the individual for its completion. This suggests that individuals may make relatively automatic self-enhancements but, when time and resources permit, may prefer to put forth the effort that self-verification requires. For the high self-esteem person, self-enhancement and self-verification are two means to the same end (e.g., Tice, 1991). Positive feedback confirms and reinforces the already favorable view of self held by the individual. Low self-esteem individuals, however, face the dilemma of wanting self-enhancing feedback but knowing that such feedback also violates their need for self-verifying information or puts them in a tenuous position because they may not believe that maintenance of that enhanced image is possible. Rather than attempt to reconcile this conflict then, it may simply be easier for low self-esteem persons to seek confirmatory feedback in the first place.

Berglas (1988) suggests that the self-handicapping literature has used "self-handicapping" to mean two dramatically different things. Some studies use the term to refer to strategies that individuals use to protect their self-esteem, whereas other studies use the term to refer to strategies individuals use to enhance their self-esteem. The literature now seems to support the contention that individuals can adopt self-handicapping strategies that allow for either benefit to accrue. As suggested by Tice (1991), low self-esteem individuals may be more strongly motivated by the goal of self-protection and, as such, should be more likely to seek out self-verifying information. If, however, the individuals have an attribute of self that they believe is positive, they may be likely to seek out self-enhancing information for that attribute and self-verifying information for all other attributes (e.g., Swann, Pelham, & Krull, 1989).

Strube, Lott, Le-Xuan-Hy, Oxenberg, and Deichmann (1986) discuss the differences between self-assessment and self-enhancement. Self-assessment involves individuals seeking information that provides maximum evaluation of their abilities. This is, of course, somewhat similar to self-verification although the underlying motive might be quite different. The individual choosing to self-verify may actually be doing so with the specific goal of avoiding any information that may call self into question. The individual engaging in self-assessment, however, is opening self up to confirmation or disconfirmation. Although these researchers did not specifically address self-esteem, it might have been quite fruitful to measure individual differences in the tendency to engage in self-assessment as a function of self-esteem. The literature already summarized allows one to speculate that the choice of engaging in self-assessment ("How do I really stack up on this attribute?") or self-verification ("Tell me what I already know about my ability on this attribute") would be a function of self-esteem, the certainty with which the self-view is held, and the positivity or negativity of the attribute in question.

The "When" Question

Low self-esteem persons overall would tend to shy away from self-assessment for the very reason that they would shy away from self-enhancement. Both of these processes might challenge what the individual knows about self. Possibly doubting their ability to alter self to be in line with the new expectation, low self-esteem persons would be motivated to avoid the discrepancy in the first place (e.g., Tice, 1991). The easiest way to avoid the controversy, then, is to seek self-verifying information. Individuals who are certain of a given attribute would not seem to need to engage in self-assessment because they already know all they need to know. In this case, then, the individuals would be likely to self-verify or self-enhance depending on whether they perceive themselves to be positive or negative on the attribute in question (Swann, Pelham, & Krull, 1989).

Pelham (1991) argues that an important ingredient of self is certainty. In order to have certainty about self, the individual must have acquired enough consistent information about self to be convinced that self is, indeed, predictable. This also suggests however, that each and every time individuals seek diagnostic information about self (either through self-assessment efforts or self-enhancement strivings), they are opening up self to disconfirmation. Confidence in self comes from the very sources of self-knowledge described in Section Two of this text, including reflected appraisals, self-perception, social comparison, culture, and organismic approaches to self (Pelham, 1991). A small number of instances of negative feedback may create a kernel of self-doubt within individuals, but certainly many more cases of negative feedback are necessary before the individuals will abandon their previously positive impressions of self (Pelham, 1991). Only a few instances of negative feedback, however, may initiate self-protection strategies on the individuals' part. The effort here is to throw the shields up and protect self before enough damning evidence comes in and "forces" a revision of self.

One of the easiest strategies for protecting self is adopting a self-verifying strategy. This maintains self at its current levels because no truly diagnostic information is being sought. This, of course, means that the individual cannot come to feel better about self but he can't come to feel any worse, either. This becomes a "status quo" approach to self. In this manner, self-esteem threats (whether negative feedback directed toward individuals with positive self-esteem, or positive feedback directed toward individuals with low self-esteem about an attribute of which they are certain of their negativity) will initiate the self-verification process (e.g., Swann, Hixon, Stein-Seroussi, & Gilbert, 1990).

If, however, the individuals are not certain about the attribute in question, a "wait and see attitude" may be adopted. In this case, the individuals may test the water by seeking self-assessment or even self-enhancement feedback. If the information coming into self, though, is either too positive or too negative, the information gathering process may be turned off and self-verification will be initiated. Chapter Two in this text suggests that individuals who are uncertain of how they rate on a given attribute may be unwilling to accept either extremely positive or extremely negative feedback because it may prove to be too much to handle at one time. In this manner, self-verification can be used by the individual in an effort to control the type and flow of information about self that is acquired.

Swann, Stein-Seroussi, and Giesler (1992) collected data specifically designed to address the "why" question in self-verification. Across several studies using multiple report methodologies, Swann et al. (1992) discovered that individuals self-verify in an effort to retain perceived predictability and control. Their findings also show, however, that such predictability can be achieved in either of two ways. First, individuals can use what the researchers referred to as "epistemic" considerations. With this type of consideration, the individuals state that they would be reassured by an interaction partner who verifies (or confirms) their self-views. This epistemic consideration centers on the individuals' desire to have accurate knowledge about self. If the interaction partner sees them in a dramatically different vein than they see themselves, it may cause them to question just how well they truly knows their "self." Second, individuals are motivated by pragmatic considerations. These considerations focus on more "practical" considerations. In particular, the subjects in Swann, Stein-Seroussi, and Giesler's (1992) experiments believed that they would have more harmonious (fruitful, smooth) interactions with interaction partners who viewed them the same way they viewed themselves.

The "How" Question

Swann and Read (1981) remind the reader that it is important not only to ask "when" individuals will self-verify, but also "how" individuals self-verify. In summarizing their findings, Swann and Read (1981) suggest that at least three different self-verification techniques will be used, depending on when in the interaction the individual seeks feedback. As the interaction gets started, individuals may engage in self-verification by adopting an information seeking strategy that is specifically targeted toward self-verifying feedback. During the interaction, however, individuals may continue the self-verification process by engaging in behaviors that are specifically directed toward eliciting confirmatory feedback from the interaction partner. This is different from seeking specific types of information because, in the second case, the individuals are engaging in behaviors specifically designed to elicit particular self-verifying responses from the interaction partner. After the interaction is over, the individuals may engage in a biased recall strategy that allows them to recall more self-verifying feedback from the interaction. It is quite clear that an understanding of these three processes is important to understanding the total picture of self-verification and the impact such a process has for an eclectic approach to self.

Swann (1983) stated that the issue of how individuals can accomplish self-verification converges on three basic strategies. Each of these strategies is used with the specific intention of creating self-verifying opportunities. This, of course, suggests that individuals are aware of their self-verification strivings. Given the literature already summarized, such an assertion appears to have considerable validity. Certainly, individuals are aware of their desire to have predictability and control in their lives. It is also likely to be the case that these same individuals are aware of the uneasiness they experience when others do not perceive them the way they would prefer. It is reasonable to assume, therefore, that individuals are aware of their self-verification efforts and will willingly expend that energy to "bring social reality into harmony with the self" (Swann, 1983). Swann suggested that individuals engage in the process of self-verification by (1) displaying signs and symbols of who they are, (2) using selective affiliation, (3) and adopting interpersonal prompts.

To adopt a particular identity successfully, individuals will often wear the trappings of that identity. The cowboy wears the cowboy hat and boots; the sex symbol wears the tight dress and high heels. Swann (1983) states that signs and symbols can only be effective in clearly articulating self to others if the signs or symbols contain three characteristics. Specifically, these signs and symbols must be noticeable, evoke predictable reactions from others, and be controllable by the individual wishing to lay claim to the identity. The individual wishing to be seen as cool would carefully select a "look" that tells one and all who she is. This is important because individuals surround themselves with trinkets and objects that tell the world who they are. Sometimes, these symbols can have a profound impact on the perceptions others have of the individual even before any interaction is initiated. Society's belief in the cliché that you "never get a second chance to make a good first impression" certainly holds true in terms of claiming a particular identity. The teacher wishing to be considered "organized" may have his work cut out for him if he trips and throws fifty syllabi across the front of the room as he walks in on the first day of class.

Individuals also may self-verify by carefully choosing the individuals they affiliate with. The individual wishing to be seen as cool, then, would avoid the school nerds at all cost. This, of course, also brings up the concept of basking in reflected glory, mentioned several times earlier in this text. Individuals are judged by the company they keep. In this manner, the individual hanging out with the debate team may be instantly labeled as "intelligent." Individuals may choose their acquaintances with the express purpose of the labeling that may come with them. The student wishing to be seen as smart may specifically choose to do a group project with the students setting the curve in the class. This, of course, can backfire. Comparisons play an important role in this process. If individuals don't come close enough to fitting in with those they wish to be affiliated with, the contrast can make the differences between them seem even greater by comparison.

Finally, individuals can rely on the use of interpersonal prompts or interaction strategies to engage in successful self-verification. This relates back to the concept of self-fulfilling prophecies mentioned in Chapter One (and discussed in greater detail in Chapter Ten). If Jana wishes to be seen as a leader, she may portray herself in an assertive fashion. The goal here is to get the interaction partners to see her as having leadership qualities. Rather than leaving those perceptions to chance, however, Jana adopts behavioral strategies that transmit the very qualities she wishes the group to have of her. Swann (1983) reminds the reader that these interpersonal prompts are not always successful, and therefore it may be necessary for the individual to adopt new strategies or attempt one or more of the other methods already described for carrying out successful self-verification.

WRAPPING IT UP: WHAT DOES ALL THIS MEAN?

Overall, the factors that influence the individual's decision to gather either self-enhancing or self-verifying information are not as complex as the literature might seem to suggest. Given the wealth of research in this area since Swann and Read's (1981) summary of self-verification processes, the literature has started to converge on a compromise. Psychology can be described as a science of pendulum swings, and certainly the self literature is no exception. Researchers follow trends in the literature that sometimes can create the illusion of controversy. Once this illusion is in place, however, true controversy may follow. Surely this is one of the fundamental paths by which a science advances itself. Science progresses when individuals publish findings that capture the empirical interest of other scientist. Invariably, somewhere along the way, another researcher will publish findings that are completely counter to the original findings. Some of the scientists will move to the other side, but others will remain steadfast, grind in their heels, and refuse to accept the controversial findings. In this manner, two schools of thought are created, the illusion of controversy is fostered, and research explodes in two opposite directions as each side tries to discover the finding that will be the empirical nail in the other side's coffin.

The same type of controversy permeated the self-perception, social comparison literature. This in-fighting, however, began to come to an end with Fazio, Zanna, and Cooper's (1977) seminal paper establishing the proper domain for each theory. Given this tendency for controversy to give way to integration and compromise, the reader will readily note that what has been labeled as a controversy in the literature has not been treated as such in this chapter. Research findings in the literature support a newer way of thinking about self-enhancement and self-verification. Swann, Pelham, and Chidester (1988) argue that individuals are motivated to fulfill both self-enhancement and self-verification strivings. The apparent battle being waged in the literature, then, seems more a matter of emphasis than an insurmountable divide. Questions now center on the relative importance of self-enhancement versus self-verification motives rather than each side arguing that one exists and the other does not.

Swann (1983) suggests that attention be turned toward understanding how self-verification strivings are achieved. This movement away from controversy has been both beneficial for the literature and perhaps overdue. Without individuals taking sides and doing research in their perspective, however, it seems certain that the self literature would not have gained as complete an understanding of the issues involved in self-enhancement and self-verification as it has. Given the state of the literature, it is now possible to ask questions about when and under what conditions individuals will choose to self-enhance or self-verify rather than arguing about whether individuals self-enhance or self-verify.

The key to understanding the extent to which the individual will seek self-enhancing and/or self-verifying information is at the same time simple and complex. Because multiple factors play a role in this decision process, the literature seemed to be providing many competing answers to the same question. Now that the interplay of these factors can be understood, however, understanding the connections between self-enhancement and self-verification becomes much simpler. As can be seen in Table 9.1, the multiple factors that influence self-enhancement and self-verification processes can be clarified, and behavioral choices and the implications those choices have for self can be predicted. Factors that influence the individual's decision to self-enhance or self-verify include the certainty of the self-view being called into question (e.g., Pelham, 1991; Swann, 1983), self-esteem level (e.g., Arkin, 1981; Tice, 1991, 1993), how well the individual knows the individual providing the feedback (e.g., Swann & Read, 1981), the positivity or negativity of the particular attribute being called into question (e.g., Pelham & Swann, 1989), whether affective preferences or cognitive preferences are being measured (e.g., Shrauger, 1975; McFarlin & Blascovich, 1981), and if self-esteem has been threatened (e.g., Hakmiller, 1966; Wills, 1981).

FIGURE 9.1 Self-Enhancement and Self-Verification Processes

Individual or Situational Characteristic	Usual Behavior Choice	Implication for Self
1. Low Self-Esteem Certainty (Fragile Self-Esteem)	Self-Verification via Self-Handicapping	Self-Esteem Protection
2. Self-Esteem Level	Self-Verification for Low vs. Self-Enhancement for High	Self-Consistency for Both Low and High (Plus Potential Enhancement for High)
3. Type of Relationship Between Individual and Interaction Partner (Close vs. Acquaintance)	Self-Enhancement and Self-Verification for Close	Maximizing Mood with Acquaintance and Desire for Close Individuals to Know Us Truly
4. Positivity or Negativity of the Attribute Being Considered	Self-Enhancement If Positive and Self Verification If Negative	Self-Esteem Elevation with Positive but Self-Protection with Negative
5. Affective vs. Cognitive Feedback	Self-Enhancement for Affective and Self-Verify for Cognitive Feedback	Maximizing Mood with Affective and Desire to Know and Portray True Self with Cognitive Feedback
6. Self-Esteem Threat	Downward Social Comparison	Self-Esteem Restoration

To help explain the impact of the self-enhancement and self-verification processes on an eclectic approach to self, a summary of the main factors in those processes is given below.

1. Individuals who have low self-esteem certainty are in a significant bind. Chapter Three presented evidence that suggests that self-esteem uncertainty is more traumatic for the individual than certain low self-esteem. Low self-esteem persons, in fact, often resist self-esteem enhancement efforts directed toward them by others because such positive feedback calls into question the certainty about self they have established. Rather than allowing the positive feedback to threaten the predictability they value, then, the individuals will engage in self-verification attempts. One successful strategy that can be employed in this case is self-handicapping. This allows persons with uncertain self-esteem to guarantee that any feedback received can only maintain or benefit the self. If, despite the self-handicapping, individuals succeed, then they can accept that enhancing information. It is important to note, however, that in this case the enhancement effect is a welcome, but accidental, consequence of the self-verification attempt. If the individuals fail, as their self-handicapping led others to expect, then the fragility of self is protected because the individuals absolved self of any responsibility for that failure. Individuals with high self-esteem certainty, however, will self-verify if that self-esteem is negative (because too much is at stake to risk by self-enhancing) and self-enhance if that self-esteem is positive (they have nothing to lose by trying to feel even better).

2. Self-esteem level (which refers to the direction and level of the affect associated with self-esteem, and not self-esteem certainty as outlined above) also influences the individual's choice to self-verify or self-enhance. Low self-esteem persons choose to self-verify because their goal is self-consistency or protection, whereas high self-esteem individuals can feel free to self-enhance. The low self-esteem persons may want to self-enhance (e.g., Shrauger, 1975) but doubt their ability to achieve that enhanced state (e.g., McFarlin & Blascovich, 1981), and therefore the safe alternative is to self-verify. High self-esteem persons, on the other hand, trust in their ability to achieve that new higher level of self. After all, these individuals have a history of successful goal attainment they can point to as evidence to support their faith that they can attain the next step up as well.

3. Decisions to self-enhance or self-verify are also influenced by how well the individuals know the interaction partner or the individual who will be providing the chosen feedback (Swann & Read, 1981). In this case, even low self-esteem persons may feel they have "nothing to lose" by allowing an acquaintance to give them positive feedback. If, however, that positive feedback comes from someone who should know them quite well, it can be disquieting for two reasons. First, the fact that an individual who knows them well views them differently than they view themselves may call their self-certainty into question. Individuals are uncomfortable when the images they meant to portray are not perceived in the intended fashion. Second, it is troubling to the individuals receiving the discrepant feedback because it suggests that the other person does not know them as well as he or she should. In this case, the individuals receiving the inconsistent feedback may wonder why this person has not gotten to know them as well as he or she should have. This of course can cast doubt and trouble on the relationship.

4. Self-enhancement and self-verification choices are also made with respect to the positivity or negativity of the attribute being considered (Pelham & Swann, 1989). If the attribute is positive (and the individuals are certain of this), then self-enhancement will be the choice. If, however, the attribute is negative (and, again, the individuals are certain of this), then they will feel no alternative but to self-verify rather than attempt self-enhancement and possibly threaten self-consistency and predictability. The reader will note that this brings together both the positivity or negativity of the attribute and the previous discussion of the impact of certainty and the role it plays in understanding the self-enhancement and self-verification choices individuals will make.

5. It is also crucial to examine the type of feedback individuals are being asked to consider. If the information is strictly affective in nature, then the overwhelming preference of individuals is to self-enhance. If, however, the feedback is more cognitive in nature, the individuals are being asked not just to accept temporary mood information, but possibly to revise or alter the self. In this case, the low self-esteem person will choose to self-verify in order to maintain self-predictability and avoid self-uncertainty (McFarlin & Blascovich, 1981).

6. Individuals sometimes experience direct threats to their self-esteem. In such cases, the individuals may be motivated to engage in quick maneuvers designed to restore self-esteem to its pre-threat level. Perhaps the simplest and most common method by which self-esteem can be restored following a threat is to make downward social comparisons. In this manner, the individuals can make self feel better as a matter of comparison. This does not elevate self-esteem higher than it was before the threat, but it can restore self-esteem to a reasonable level.

It should be obvious that an understanding of these processes relates directly to an eclectic approach to self. Part of understanding the complexity of the self system involves understanding the behavioral choices that individuals make. Figure 1.1 and Figure 7.1 both display a self system that is influenced dramatically by individuals' behavioral choices. The factors that lead to these choices also are an important part of understanding the complexity of the self system. Once individuals have decided to behave in a particular way, they inevitably will receive feedback even if that feedback is not wanted. This feedback then is interpreted, and the individuals will draw certain conclusions about self. These conclusions, of course, have profound implications for the self-esteem of the individuals, and the whole process continues to cycle on.

CHAPTER TEN

Self-Fulfilling Prophecies

BACKGROUND INFORMATION

Most individuals would agree with the cliché "To see is to believe." It should be pointed out, however, that the opposite statement is just as true. The expectations that an individual holds for others can elicit behaviors from them that confirm the original expectations, which suggests that "To believe is to see." This is the fundamental point underlying the concept of self-fulfilling prophecy. The power of self-fulfilling prophecies can be seen in individuals' lives on a daily basis. Terry's first grade teacher mentions something to his new teacher about his tendency to mouth off. Can Terry's new teacher, then, walk into the classroom without that prior knowledge impacting her perceptions of and behaviors toward Terry? Teachers who expect a child to be a problem can elicit those very behaviors from the child simply in response to the manner in which they interact with the child. The new teacher may refuse to acknowledge Terry's raised hand in response to a question or treat him in a curt manner. Surely this sounds tragic. The true tragedy, however, is that this pattern of self-fulfilling prophecy can be initiated without the teacher realizing that she is doing it.

Self-fulfilling prophecy is traditionally defined as, "a process by which the individual's expectations about another person eventually come to elicit behaviors from that person that confirm those expectations." Possibly without our being aware of it, the expectations we hold toward other persons may cause us to engage in behaviors that promote the very kinds of behaviors we expected from those persons in the first place. A father, for example, might believe that his son is a sissy. Because of this expectation, he believes that his son probably will cry a lot. He then proceeds to play rough with his son to the point that the child gets hurt and starts to cry. At this point, the father throws up his hands, hollers "See, I told you you're a sissy," and walks away. Sound like something out of a made for television movie? Anyone who has spent any time watching individuals interact will notice these patterns occurring. The wife who believes her husband would rather be "out with the boys" than spending time with her can, without realizing, elicit those very behaviors from him. The boss who believes that a certain employee will always make mistakes can put enough demanding work on that person that mistakes are guaranteed to follow.

All of this makes perfect sense given what has already been stated innumerable times throughout this text. People value consistency and predictability in their lives, even if that predictability has to come at the expense of someone else. It is comforting to know that other persons are who we expected them to be. Our subtle (and sometimes not so subtle) behaviors can be used in such a way as to confirm those expectations. Self-fulfilling prophecies, as you might have guessed, are quite powerful and pervasive. Once the cycle has been started, it is extremely difficult to get individuals to realize that their behaviors may be the cause of the other person's behaviors. The father may be all too quick to yell "I didn't make my son a sissy; I'm just trying to toughen him up." Although on the surface this sounds fairly reasonable, it may have just the opposite effect. The "toughening up" may cause the child to appear weaker than he really is. This apparent weakness then is interpreted by the father as an indication that his son is indeed a sissy.

Not all theorists use the term self-fulfilling prophecy for this effect. Snyder (1984) coined the term behavioral confirmation to describe the effect. Snyder states that he prefers this terminology because it emphasizes the role that the target's behavior plays in confirming the perceiver's expectations (e.g., Snyder, 1992). This is important because it clarifies the fact that self-fulfilling prophecies are a two-way street. If individuals did not engage in behaviors consistent with the perceiver's expectations, the effect would not be validated and the cycle would, perhaps, stop. Such a term is also important because it illuminates some of the other related constructs that might strengthen the impact of self-fulfilling prophecies for an eclectic approach to self. If individuals engage in behaviors that are consistent with a perceiver's expectations, those behaviors to some degree will influence their perceptions of themselves. The processes of self-perception described in detail in Chapter Five suggest that individuals come to know themselves partly from watching what they do. Even if those behaviors are motivated by the expectations others hold for them, the behaviors can come to be incorporated by the individuals into their perceptions of self.

THE CYCLICAL NATURE OF SELF-FULFILLING PROPHECIES

As mentioned in Chapter One, the concept of a self-fulfilling prophecy was first reported by Rosenthal and Jacobson (1968) in *Pygmalion in the Classroom*. In this groundbreaking report, Rosenthal and Jacobson discovered that a student's performance is consistent with a teacher's expectations for that student's performance. A crucial question to come from this line of research is how does the teacher's expectations get translated into the student's performance. Jussim (1986) suggested that self-fulfilling prophecies (what Rosenthal and Jacobson referred to as the Pygmalion Effect) actually involve a three-stage model: (1) teachers develop expectations about students; (2) teachers treat students differently, based on those expectations; (3) students perceive this differential treatment and react to it by behaving in ways that confirm those expectations.

Certainly this three-stage model of self-fulfilling prophecies makes sense. Missing in the picture, however, is an assessment of this model as it applies to individuals outside the educational setting. Surely the same three-stage model would hold for interactions between parent and child, boss and employee, teacher and student, or coach and athlete. Individuals who are in an authority position and therefore can establish expectations for other individuals can be in a position also to initiate self-fulfilling prophecies. Individuals who are looked up to are in a position to take advantage of that power. That is not to say that all individuals in positions of power would take advantage, but the possibility is there. Even if the individual tries very hard not to initiate a self-fulfilling prophecy, avoiding one can be extremely difficult. Children often look to their parents to gauge the worth of their accomplishments. Parents must be good actors to avoid subtly behaving in ways that express disappointment over less than successful endeavors by their children. It is also the case that children often ask their parents to explain the expectations they hold for them. A child's anguished "What do you want from me?" is not just an expression of exasperation; it is a direct attempt to get the parent to articulate an expectation that the child can then try to live up to.

If this cycle strikes you as potentially devastating, it can be. It should be noted, however, that self-fulfilling prophecies are not necessarily negative. Parents who set reasonably high standards and expectations for their children often have children who reach those levels of success. The key to using self-fulfilling prophecies effectively as a parent is to establish standards or expectations that indeed are reasonable. Setting expectations that are too high can result in disappointment for both the child and the parent and creates the danger for negative self-fulfilling prophecies to be initiated. Jussim (1986) reminds the reader that there is a difference between a biased action and an expectation. This is meant to illustrate the point that expectations are not, in and of themselves, the culprit in the self-fulfilling prophecy. Once the individual with the expectation engages in an action biased by that expectation, however, the potential for a self-fulfilling prophecy is in place. Although this is certainly a fair distinction to make, we might ask the following question: "Is it possible to have an expectation for someone and not act in a manner that is biased by that expectation?" The answer is probably "No."

A mother who believes her daughter would make a great nurse may innocently bring nursing school literature home for her to read. The mother is not intentionally forcing such a career path on her child (although this certainly does happen). Part of the complexity of separating expectations from biased actions is that the individual who holds the expectation may have a hard time separating where her expectation stops and the other individual's preferences begin. When the daughter asserts "I want to be an accountant," the mother may register shock, replying "But I thought you wanted to be a nurse. You've always wanted to be a nurse." In this case, the mother has allowed her expectations not only to bias her actions toward her daughter, but also to influence the memories she held about her daughter's prior statements on career preferences. This goes hand in hand with the self-image bias in person perception that was described in Chapter Nine. In these cases, individuals assume that the characteristics that define them apply to others as well. Similarly, individuals could assume that the expectations they hold for others surely must be the same expectations those individuals hold for themselves.

In a succinct review of Jussim's (1986) three-stage model of self-fulfilling prophecies, Chow (1988) reminds the reader that certain characteristics of the teacher may influence the self-fulfilling prophecy process. In particular, a teacher's assumptions about the nature of intelligence may play a role in determining if a self-fulfilling prophecy will be initiated. Teachers who believe intelligence is cumulative (that is, intelligence is an ongoing process of accumulating knowledge across time) would be considered more flexible in their assumptions about intelligence than teachers who believe intelligence is fixed (you either have it or you don't). Which of these individuals would be the most likely to engage in a self-fulfilling prophecy? Jussim (1986) suggests that the teacher who believes intelligence is fixed would be more likely to succumb to the self-fulfilling prophecy. Teachers who believe intelligence is fixed also may be likely to assume that there isn't a whole lot that can be done to change it. This resignation may permeate the behaviors they engage in with the labeled child and, in return, the child may come to engage in behaviors that confirm that original expectation.

Crucial to an understanding of the complexity of the self-fulfilling prophecy, however, is an awareness that even teachers who believe intelligence is cumulative can initiate self-fulfilling prophecies. It is important to remember that self-fulfilling prophecies are not, in and of themselves, bad. Teachers and parents who set high expectations for children can often elicit those levels of success from the children. Having expectations for others need not lead to negative consequences for the individuals toward whom the expectations are held, but expectations for success can be damaging if children are not also shown the pathways by which such success can be attained. Understanding the cyclical nature of self-fulfilling prophecies, however, does not explain the processes that might underlie such effects.

THE MECHANISMS OF SELF-FULFILLING PROPHECIES

Although some disagreements exist in the literature about the underlying nature of self-fulfilling prophecies, most theorists seem to agree that there is a motivational foundation for such an effect. Jones (1986) suggests that enough experimental evidence exists for theorists to stop questioning the existence of the self-fulfilling prophecy. Implicit within these statements seems to be a call by Jones for researchers to get on with the business of extrapolating the processes that underlie the effect. Snyder (1992) suggests a fourth step in the self-fulfilling prophecy model. Although this step is not fundamentally different from those articulated by Jussim (1986), it is important because it emphasizes the behavioral roles that both the perceiver and the target assume in the process. Snyder (1992) states that behavioral confirmation involves these steps: (1) the perceiver makes assumptions about the target; (2) the perceiver then acts toward the target as if these assumptions were true; (3) the target alters behavior to match the perceiver's actions; (4) the perceiver interprets the target's actions as confirming the expectations.

As is readily apparent from this summary, both the perceiver and the target are engaging in behaviors that keep the process going. If the target were to stop at some point and say, "Wait a minute. Why are you acting like this toward me?" the cycle of behavioral confirmation might be broken. As long as the target simply adapts behavior to be in line with those of the perceiver, however, the process of behavioral confirmation will continue.

Snyder (1992) recommends that it would be useful to ask questions about the motivational foundations of behavioral confirmation. Researchers, he suggests, should focus more on the "why" question. Why do individuals behave the way they do to initiate the behavioral confirmation sequence? This question is of fundamental importance to an eclectic approach to self because it addresses one of the fundamental issues of this approach. Much of the information already presented in this text deals with the issue of why individuals choose to act the way they do. More often than not, the answer involves the self-related needs the individual is trying to fulfill. One of the most fundamental of those needs is a need for predictability and control in one's life. Such feelings of predictability would be difficult to acquire without a fairly high degree of self-consistency. How does this, however, tie into the concept of self-fulfilling prophecies? The answer is amazingly simple. One of the easiest paths toward obtaining predictability and control in one's life is to ensure predictability in others.

Snyder (1992) discusses the importance of using a functional analysis in approaching the cycle of behavioral confirmation. In essence, this concept has been at the heart of this text. A functional analysis involves considering the reasons underlying psychological phenomenon. Such an analysis has been at the heart of psychology since its beginnings. Functionalists such as Titchener argue that psychology should concern itself with understanding the functions of the brain and mind. Structuralists such as Wundt, on the other hand, concern themselves with breaking down consciousness into its component parts. The same dichotomy seems to permeate the self literature. Is it more important to explain how self-concept develops or why it develops the way it does? As is usually the case, there is no one answer. Chapter One argued that understanding the eclectic nature of self involves an understanding of how self-concept develops but also an understanding of the implications of that developmental process.

Individuals may develop and utilize self-fulfilling prophecies because they allow them to maintain a much needed level of predictability in their social worlds. The implications of this process, however, go beyond the individual. Once individuals initiate behaviors that are consistent with the expectations they hold toward targets, the targets themselves become involved. The victims of a self-fulfilling prophecy, in effect, have been labeled. The power of labels resides in the fact that they tend to perpetuate themselves. Understanding self-fulfilling prophecies or behavioral confirmation, then, involves an awareness that individuals have motives or needs that they are trying to fulfill in social interactions. To this end, they may make assumptions about other individuals within the interaction. Once these assumptions are made, individuals are motivated to validate them because if they do not, then the motives or needs that led to the expectations would not be fulfilled.

Snyder's (1992) functional analysis of behavioral confirmation suggests that two motivational foundations may underlie the self-fulfilling prophecy cycle, whereas two other motivational foundations may keep behavioral confirmation from taking place. For cases in which individuals may react against behavioral confirmation attempts, Snyder uses the term behavioral disconfirmation. First, individuals are motivated to acquire social knowledge. Part of the task in social interactions is "getting to know" the other person. Assumptions will be made and tested in an effort to figure the person out. Research has consistently shown that individuals draw multiple conclusions about other persons once they have decided one trait they think the other persons possess (e.g., Bruner & Tagiuri, 1954). Once a trait label has been applied to the targets, implicit personality theories (Bruner & Tagiuri, 1954; Cantor & Mischel, 1979) are put into motion. Implicit personality theories are defined as "assumptions individuals make about the relationships between traits and behaviors." More simply put, individuals assume that certain traits and behaviors go together; thus, if the individual is labeled "sneaky," it might also be assumed that he is a conniving, dishonest, suspicious cheat. In this manner, the assumptions that individuals make activate a whole host of related information that they assume must go along with the original impression of the person.

Second, Snyder (1992) suggests that individuals are motivated to "get along" with the individuals with whom they are interacting. The fewer potential conflicts in the interaction, the better. If the perceivers make an assumption about the target individual, it may seem perfectly reasonable for the perceivers to act on that assumption. After all, the perceivers would not make the assumption if they did not think it was valid. If we think we know someone, the simplest way to interact with him or her is to act on those assumptions. But what about the target of these assumptions. For the sake of the success of the interaction, the target may be motivated not to rock the boat by pointing out that the perceivers have made an erroneous assumption. Besides adding to the stability of the interaction, allowing the perceivers to have their assumptions also increases the chances that the perceivers will approve of the target. In the interest of maintaining a smooth interaction, then, both the perceivers and the target may be motivated to maintain balance by allowing expectations to be confirmed.

In contrast to these motives for engaging in behavioral confirmation (or attempting to initiate self-fulfilling prophecies), Snyder (1992) suggests that individuals may resist behavioral confirmation attempts in an effort to express personal attributes. Whether individuals are aware of it or not, they tend to assume that others see the world the way they do (e.g., Greenwald, 1980). Several different processes may actually be working in unison to motivate individuals to engage in patterns of behavior destined to confirm the expectations they hold toward the target person. To the extent that individuals believe their characteristics are good ones, they might be motivated to assume that others should possess these characteristics as well. In this manner, the assumptions the perceivers make of the target may be based in part on the self-reference effect (e.g., Rubin, 1986). Self-presentation also may play a role in this process (e.g., Tedeschi, 1981). Self-presentation involves the processes by which individuals attempt to shape the way others think about them. If the perceivers are concerned about self-presentation, they as a consequence will be thinking about self. Once self is activated in this manner, the self-reference effect may be initiated, whereby individuals try to imbue their attributes onto the targets of the interaction. It is entirely possible, however, that the behavioral confirmation sequence could be thwarted if the targets in the interaction realize that the perceivers may be trying to imbue a certain "impression" on them (Snyder, 1992; Snyder, Campbell, & Preston, 1982). At these times, individuals may engage in behavioral disconfirmation by refusing to go along with the impression the perceiver is trying to force on them.

It could be the case that individuals will engage in behavioral disconfirmation in an attempt to defend threatened identities (Snyder, 1992). In these scenarios, the perceiver may attempt to force an identity onto the target that directly threatens the target's identity. The perceiver, for example, may decide that the individual is a "liberal." If the target is in fact a staunch "right-winger," an attempt by the perceiver to label her as a liberal may be seen as a threat to self. Because individuals are so highly motivated to maintain consistency of self, such identity threats should promote clear efforts by the individual to disconfirm that behavioral expectation.

Snyder's (1992) analysis of the theoretical implications of this functional analysis suggests that perceivers and targets may be motivated by different goals within the interaction. Although the perceiver and the target both share the goal of getting acquainted, the definition of what "getting acquainted" means may be different for perceivers than for targets. Since the perceivers typically assume a more active role in the interaction, they may be actively trying to acquire knowledge, whereas the targets may assume that it is their job to facilitate the interaction. If targets and perceivers accept these roles within the interaction, then it makes sense that the perceivers will make assumptions about the targets. Once these assumptions are made, the targets may be put into the uncomfortable position of not wanting to accept an erroneous assumption. If they reject that assumption, however, it could be perceived as a violation of their role in the interaction. Thus, for the sake of facilitating the interaction, the targets may work to confirm the expectations being passed onto them by the perceivers.

Certainly the concept of self-fulfilling prophecy becomes crucial when discussions focus on educational settings. Tracking systems are sometimes utilized in academic institutions. Although the goals of tracking systems may be admirable, the outcome may not be. Tracking systems are used in an attempt to place students in classes and classrooms appropriate to their interests and skill levels. It is assumed that these students will perform better when the coursework fits their interests and skill level than when they are all clumped together in the traditional classroom. Many high schools, for instance, have vocational tracks in which students focus on acquiring skills (e.g., auto mechanics, shop, home economics) rather than on the more academic course content. There is nothing wrong with allowing students to choose the track that will best prepare them for what they wish to do beyond high school, but tracking, however well it is done, has problems. Guidance counselors sometimes make assumptions about what is best for the students and place them in the college track or the vocational track based on what they think the students are capable of. What if a student really wants to go to college? Shouldn't he be encouraged to try it?

The main problem with tracking systems is that they initiate a sequence of events that can easily lead to a self-fulfilling prophecy. A student decides to take the vocational track because the counselor advised him he is probably not college material. Once the student starts taking vocational courses and not college-oriented courses like Senior English and Senior Math, the cycle might already be in place. The student may look at the classes he is taking and decide that because so many are vocational courses, the counselor must have been right all along. The power of labels also comes into play. If the student decides to take Senior English, he already may be labeled in the teacher's eyes as a vocational student. This label then may serve as the basis for a self-fulfilling prophecy or the cycle of behavioral confirmation Snyder (1992) described. The influence of teacher expectations for the academic achievement of students will be discussed in more detail in Chapter Fifteen where applications for the eclectic theory in educational settings are discussed (e.g., Jussim & Eccles, 1992).

WHEN WILL PERCEIVER BIASES NOT BE CONFIRMED?

The impact of self-fulfilling prophecies can be profound. Fortunately, however, the target is not always destined to become the pawn in the perceiver's self-fulfilling game. Research suggests that, left to their own devices, perceivers will tend to confirm the negative expectancies they have for target persons (e.g., Neuberg, 1989). If, however, perceivers are motivated to form not only an impression but an accurate impression, will perceivers be able to look beyond the expectation? Neuberg (1989) suggest that accuracy could be enhanced by specifying the goal for the perceiver within the interaction. If no goals are set prior to the interaction, it might be assumed that perceivers would be motivated simply to acquire knowledge and form an impression (Snyder, 1992). If this is the case, the perceivers would be free to make whatever snap judgments they wished because, after all, there are no consequences for being wrong. If, however, the perceiver is instructed to form as accurate an impression as possible, would the goal override the tendency to attempt to fulfill the negative expectation?

In reviewing the self-fulfilling prophecy literature, Neuberg (1989) noted that perceivers tend to adopt information-gathering behaviors that may mediate the process. It could also be the case that individuals with expectations of the target may ask biased questions that either perpetuate the bias or make it difficult for the target to disconfirm (e.g., Neuberg, 1989; Snyder & Gangestad, 1981). Given what has already been stated about the prescribed role of the target within these interactions, the target may have little recourse but to behave in an expectancy confirming fashion. Thus, if no other guidelines or goals are given to the perceivers, they may be perfectly free to seek expectancy confirming feedback rather than truly testing the assumptions being made about the target.

Neuberg (1989) postulated that asking perceivers to form accurate impressions of targets could result in increased accuracy for a variety of reasons. First, the perceivers may approach the interaction with a hypothesis testing frame of mind rather than an expectancy confirming one. Second, the perceivers may gather more information before drawing conclusions about the targets, thereby providing the targets with more opportunities to provide the perceivers with expectancy disconfirming information. Third, the perceivers may ask less biased questions of the targets, thereby allowing the targets more input into the process. Half of the interviewers in Neuberg's (1989) experiment were given a negative expectancy of the targets. The interviewers were led to believe that the interviewees had scored poorly on ratings of sociability, goal directedness, and general problem-solving skills. The other half of the interviewers were not given this negative information. Half of the interviewers were also given the goal of forming the most accurate impression possible, whereas the other half were not given these additional instructions.

As predicted, Neuberg's findings replicated the traditional self-fulfilling prophecy effect. When interviewers were given a negative expectancy, their impressions of the targets were significantly more negative than those of perceivers who had no expectancy. The finding of most interest, however, is the effect of the goal manipulation. Neuberg discovered that perceivers who were given the goal of forming accurate impressions were significantly more favorable in their ratings of the targets than those perceivers who were not given the accuracy goal. These findings suggest that the goal of impression accuracy can sometimes override the impact of negative expectancy. Why would this be the case? If the findings of Snyder (1992) and those of Neuberg (1989) are combined, the answer seems to be apparent. If the goal of impression accuracy is introduced into the interaction scenario, it changes the perceiver's motivation. Rather than being motivated simply to acquire knowledge and form an impression, the perceiver now has been motivated to acquire accurate information and form an accurate impression. The goal for the target, however, remains pretty much the same. The target is still expected to facilitate the interaction. In the case of the accuracy motivated perceiver, however, the target gets the added advantage of having the perceiver seeking information in such a way that the target can facilitate the interaction by disconfirming the negative expectancy. This, then, is one of the rare cases in which both the perceiver and the target get something positive out of the interaction.

It seems quite reasonable to conclude from Neuberg's (1989) findings that interaction goals, to the extent that they alter the perceiver and/or target's motivation within the interaction, may dramatically change the face of the interaction. If perceivers are motivated to be accurate, their willingness to let their negative expectancies be disconfirmed by the targets goes up. In such scenarios, behavioral consistency for the targets is being enhanced because they can spend fruitful effort portraying self accurately to the perceiver and still fulfill the motivation of facilitating the interaction. What other interaction goals might lead perceivers to disconfirm the negative expectancies they hold toward the target? Neuberg, Judice, Virdin, and Carrillo (1993) suggest that the goal of ingratiation may be enough to motivate the perceiver to disconfirm negative expectancies.

In an interview setting, these researchers led perceivers to hold a negative expectancy toward a target. Half of the subjects then were given the additional goal of getting the target to like them. As predicted, those perceivers who were motivated to ingratiate the target person engaged in more warm and non-threatening behaviors toward the target. The targets in this condition, as one might expect, performed more favorably than those targets being interviewed by a perceiver holding a negative expectancy and no ingratiation goal. These findings are important for several reasons. First, these findings shed further light on the issue of when perceivers will engage in behaviors that will confirm their negative expectancies of targets and when they will attempt to disconfirm. When perceivers are given the goal of ingratiation, it makes perfect sense that their ability to do this would be seriously thwarted if they attempted to confirm a negative expectancy of the same target toward whom the ingratiation is supposed to be directed. It stands to reason that other interaction goals could be discovered that also motivate the perceiver to engage in behaviors toward the target designed to disconfirm a negative expectancy held toward that target. Goals such as cooperating to achieve some desired level of performance could certainly alter the perceiver's motivation in such a way as to prompt behavioral disconfirmation. Further research, of course, must address such variables.

It also makes sense to consider other categorical variables that might determine whether the perceiver is motivated to confirm a negative expectancy (thus initiating a self-fulfilling prophecy cycle) or disconfirm a negative expectancy. Research suggests that properties of persons, situations, and behaviors all determine the behavioral consistency subjects will display (e.g., Funder & Colvin, 1991). It seems reasonable to conclude from this, therefore, that aspects of these same variables would influence the behavioral confirmation/disconfirmation process. Osborne and his colleagues have already suggested that aspects of situations, perceivers, and targets all influence the extent to which a perceiver will form a biased impression of a target and the extent to which recovery from biased impressions is possible (e.g., Osborne & Gilbert, 1992; Osborne, 1990). Further research should explore the relationship of these same variables to the confirmation/disconfirmation process.

WRAPPING IT UP: WHAT DOES ALL THIS MEAN?

This quick perusal of the behavioral confirmation, behavioral disconfirmation, and self-fulfilling prophecy literature suggests that the variables underlying these processes are more complicated than might first have been thought. Certainly it is not the case that individuals will always work to fulfill the expectancies they hold toward targets. Some individuals may be more likely than others to give other people the benefit of the doubt. Osborne, Samborsky, and Marsh (1994) discovered that perceivers scoring high on the need for cognition scale are more likely to recover from biased first impressions than individuals scoring low. It stands to reason that other characteristics of perceivers would also influence the extent to which they feel compelled to confirm or disconfirm negative expectancies held toward targets.

When the goals for both perceiver and target within the interaction are fairly standard, behavioral confirmation (or self-fulfilling prophecy) is likely. In such standard interactions, perceivers operate with the goal of acquiring information and targets operate with the goal of facilitating interaction (Snyder, 1992). When alternative motivations or goals are introduced, perceivers may become motivated to disconfirm the negative expectancies they hold toward the target. Likewise, it seems reasonable to believe that targets may sometimes be motivated to engage in behaviors designed to force the perceivers into disconfirming a negative expectancy. If the characteristic of the targets that is perceived to be negative is important to the targets, they may become highly motivated to force the perceivers into disconfirming that negative expectancy. In the end, only a complete analysis of the characteristics of the perceiver, the target, and the interaction situation will allow comprehensive understanding of self-fulfilling prophecies.

Understanding the nature of the self-fulfilling prophecy cycle is of great importance to an eclectic approach to self. Perceivers and targets may be motivated by fundamentally different goals within an interaction. At the same time that these individuals are trying to negotiate the sometimes turbulent waters of successful interactions, they are also motivated by self-related goals. Both individuals in the interaction may desire to be perceived positively by the other. At the same time, both individuals are motivated to maintain self-consistency. Thus, both individuals are trying to reflect a portrayal of self that establishes who they are and, at the same time, may be attempting to confirm expectancies held toward the other because such confirmation makes the interaction more predictable. If these goals do not conflict, the interaction will be relatively smooth, and behavioral confirmation will take place. If, however, portraying self conflicts with the other individual's attempt to maintain self-consistency, the interaction will not be smooth, and behavioral disconfirmation or negative self-fulfilling prophecies may be employed.

WRAPPING IT UP: INTEGRATION OF SECTION THREE

Section Three is built on the important premise that the sources of self-knowledge an individual uses will have profound implications for that individual. An eclectic approach to self must consider, at the most fundamental level, questions of what impact the self-process has on the person. Self certainly does not develop in a vacuum. We are not shielded from the consequences of knowing who we are. Knowing who we are does not necessarily mean that we will be happy with the answer. Knowing who we are does not guarantee that others will perceive us in the same fashion. In order to understand truly the role that self plays in the daily life of the individual, then, the consequences of self-knowledge must be considered. Each individual within an interaction has goals he or she is trying to reach. Each individual also is aware at some level of the role he or she is being asked to play within that interaction. In order for interactions to be successful, both individuals must be willing to play the part and follow the rules.

Carpenter (1988), Lewicki (1983, 1984), and a host of others argue that self can become a referent point from which other social information is processed. If an individual sees herself as an honest person, then she may be particularly aware of honesty or dishonesty on the part of other individuals (e.g., Markus, Smith, & Moreland, 1985). This makes perfect sense. If an individual has a defining characteristic, it seems reasonable for that person to assign that characteristic importance. Perceiving the world, whether it is visual perception or person perception, is a matter of filtering out the unimportant and focusing on the important. Perception is said to have six defining features (Berstein, Roy, Srull, & Wickens, 1991) and each of these features adds to our understanding of why the self serves as a referent point for social information processing.

First, perception is knowledge based. Individuals are not born knowing how the world works. Their ability to perceive the world depends on what they are able to learn or already know. If Tom doesn't know what a snake is, how could he know that the particular species of snake he is looking at is dangerous? Where, though, does this knowledge come from? Knowledge is experience based. Two individuals with differing experiential backgrounds may perceive the same object in dramatically different ways. The experiences the individuals have incorporated into their sense of self, then, may very easily be used as a reference point for processing incoming perceptual information.

Second, perception is inferential. To make an inference means to make an assumption or take a best guess. The perceptual world usually provides the individual with imperfect information. Based on prior knowledge and experiences, however, the perceiver can usually fill in the gaps. Gestalt psychologists refer to this filling in of missing pieces of perceptual information as "closure." This term was used specifically for visual information, but it seems natural for individuals to use their prior knowledge to provide closure when other types of information are missing as well. This suggests, then, that different perceivers with different knowledge bases and prior experiences may make different inferences when some of the perceptual information is missing. It also suggests that perceivers will fill in the gaps based on what they know. Because self can be considered one of the most significant knowledge bases the individual has access to, it makes sense that self would be used to make inferences when perceptual information is otherwise missing.

Third, perception is categorical. Individuals strive to make sense of the world by assuming that similar objects belong together. This ability to establish categories makes the perceptual world a simpler place. It is important to note, however, that these categories can sometimes influence the manner in which that same world is perceived. Self as a category can influence other perceptions. The more clearly a category has been articulated, and the more elaborate the definitional rules are for that category, the more likely that category is to be used for the processing of new perceptual information. Perhaps more than any other schema, the self-schema influences information processing (and, therefore, perception) because it includes not only a conglomeration of past experiences but also an emotional investment (i.e., self-esteem) as well as a future-oriented component called "possible selves" (e.g., Markus & Nurius, 1986). This degree of articulation and elaboration makes the self a likely category to be activated when the individual is processing social information.

Fourth, perception is relational. The ability to understand the relationships between perceptual objects is critical if the individual is to understand completely the dynamics of the world. To notice that someone is particularly tall, for example, the perceiver must be able to relate that to something or someone else. By comparing that individual to other people, her tallness would then become obvious. Again it makes sense to consider self as the most obvious comparison point. This text has already suggested that individuals tend to assume that other individuals are more like them than they are in reality. Therefore, self is very likely to be used as the relational point against which the other individuals' characteristics will be compared.

Fifth, perception is adaptive. Survival depends, in part, on the individual's ability to adapt to the environment. If Jenny sees something coming at her from behind the trees, it is more important for her to ask "Is that a chihuahua or a bear?" than it is for her to ask "Is its fur brown or beige?" Although both questions are reasonable, only one allows for maximum adaptation. After noting that the animal is a bear and taking appropriate action, then and only then would it be wise for Jenny to spend the mental energy required to decide on the exact color of the animal's fur. This suggests that individuals tend to focus on what they think are the most important or relevant features of the perceptual target. Again, it makes sense that self will often be used as the referent point because self is so important to the individual.

Sixth, perception can be automatic. Just as an individual does not have to stop and ask himself "Is light hitting my eye?" he also probably does not have to stop and consider all the ways in which he is gathering and processing information about a target person. Patterns that have been used so extensively as to become second nature to the person often will be initiated automatically. If self is a common reference point, it may become an automatic reference point. This does not mean that self will always be used as a reference point for processing social information, but it does suggest that it will be likely to be used when other referent standards are not obvious.

Self-knowledge not only influences the manner in which the individual will process social information; it also impacts the type of self-related information the individual will seek. All other things being equal, it makes sense to assume that individuals will want to acquire as much positive self-related feedback as possible. All things, however, are not equal. Positivity is in the eye of the beholder. Individuals are also highly motivated to be perceived as consistently as possible (e.g., Swann, 1987). Feelings of self-consistency and predictability can be threatened if discrepant self-relevant information is acquired. This suggests that individuals may sometimes be motivated to verify their existing self-conceptions (self-verification) instead of seeking as much positive information as possible (self-enhancement). Individuals with low self-esteem must walk a tightrope between wanting to feel better about self (thereby wishing to self-enhance) and avoiding inconsistent information that could damage their already fragile selves. In these cases of self-esteem threats and fragile self-esteem, the individuals are more concerned with knowing who they are (thereby engaging in self-verification) than artificially inflating their feelings of self-worth.

Snyder (1992) and others suggest that perceivers and targets are motivated to fulfill different goals within an interaction. To this end, perceivers adopt the role of acquiring information about the targets while the targets assume the responsibility for facilitating the interaction. Self-knowledge (in this case meaning knowledge of the target's self) may lead perceivers to behave in ways that elicit behaviors from targets that confirm the perceivers' expectations. Because targets are motivated (if not expected) to facilitate the smoothness of the interaction, they may jeopardize that role if they act in a manner that is inconsistent with the perceivers' expectations. Targets, it appears, are sometimes put into the proverbial double bind because they may be considered at blame if the interaction does not go smoothly. Even if the perceivers hold negative expectancies toward the targets, the targets may behave in ways that confirm those expectations because the success of the interaction depends on it.

All in all, a little self-knowledge can be a dangerous thing. It is important for the reader to understand that an eclectic theory of self must not only predict when self information will help the individual but also when it will hinder the individual. Low self-esteem persons seem to perpetuate their own misery (e.g., Osborne & Stites, 1994; Tice, 1991, 1993), and mislabeled targets seem unwilling to behave in ways that will violate those misconceptions. On the surface, this seems appalling. The eclectic approach to self, however, reminds us that individuals have multiple roles they are trying to fill as well as multiple goals they are trying to achieve. Sometimes the goal of maintaining self-consistency (self-verification) is more important than achieving a temporary self-esteem boost (self-enhancement), and sometimes keeping the interaction running smoothly is more important than showing the perceivers that they are wrong about some expectation they hold toward the target. Only when we understand these roles and goals that motivate individuals to utilize self information the way they do will an eclectic theory of self be achieved.

Individual Differences

INTRODUCTION TO SECTION FOUR

Throughout this text, arguments have been presented, figures drawn, summary tables provided, and frequent references made to an "eclectic theory of self." Has this theory, however, been presented? The answer to this question is both yes and no. An eclectic theory is a dynamic entity that changes as more information about self-concept and self-esteem is acquired. Figures 1.1 and 7.1 move the reader closer and closer toward visualizing what this eclectic theory looks like. In the end, however, an eclectic theory is more fluid and open to change then these figures would suggest. As individuals gather new experiences and take on new roles in life, the self structure that has served as their guide in life will change as well. Self influences the situations in which individuals find themselves as surely as it influences the impressions individuals will form of the other individuals within those interactions. But the reader clearly understands at this point that self is also influenced by these interactions. Any factor that causes a dramatic change in an individual's life can cause his or her sense of self to be threatened.

An eclectic theory of self is not something that could ever be fully captured with boxes, words, and arrows. Visualizing this theory is more a euphemism for understanding than a reality. As the factors that play a significant role in the development, maintenance, and refinement of self are better understood, so too will the relationship between self and others become better understood. The ability to truly understand self in all its infinite permutations includes an awareness of the factors that influence the developmental cycle that helps self-concept and self-esteem to form (as outlined in Section One).

Also necessary for understanding the eclectic nature of self, however, is an awareness of the sources of self-knowledge that provide individuals with information about who they are (discussed in detail in Section Two), and an understanding of the consequences of self-knowledge (covered in depth in Section Three). Finally, before this analysis of the eclectic nature of self can be considered complete, we must turn our attention back to the individual. Given the importance of self for the individual, it makes sense that self may lead to characteristic differences between people. To the extent that individuals have differing characteristics that define who they are, they also will perceive both themselves and others in slightly different fashions as well.

Individuals differ on hundreds of trait dimensions—for example, honesty, intelligence, aggressiveness, sociability, dominance, or humor. Each of these characteristics can be considered a trait. A trait can be defined as "a relatively enduring characteristic or feature." The traits that define the individual are characteristic ways that individual has for interacting with the world. When traits are assigned to individuals, however, assumptions are made about the consistency we can expect in that person's behaviors. Honest people would tend to behave in honest ways. In this manner, we expect individuals who have been assigned a trait to behave in a manner that is consistent with that label. In fact, if people who have been labeled honest behave in a dishonest fashion, we are much more likely to notice that behavior than any number of honest things they have done.

Some of these characteristics have a profound impact on the individual because they can serve as a basic heuristic used in the processing of self-relevant information. Characteristic patterns in the individual's tendency to focus attention on the self (e.g., self-consciousness, as discussed in Chapter Eleven) or the focusing of attention on various aspects of self (e.g., self-monitoring, as discussed in Chapter Twelve) may play a key role in the general information processing the individual will engage in. Although these can be considered "trait" characteristics like honesty, these characteristics merit special consideration because they have been shown to have a profound impact on the social relationships individuals will have with others. These individual differences have global impact for the individual because they may completely color the manner in which the individual processes self-relevant information, makes choices about interaction partners, dates or mates, or decides on a career. Certainly aspects of self that can have such profound ramifications for individuals and their relationships merit inclusion in this eclectic approach to self.

CHAPTER ELEVEN

Self-Consciousness

BACKGROUND INFORMATION

When individuals turn attention toward self, what are they looking at? The answer to what might seem a facetious question is actually quite important. Certainly it is the case that different individuals focus on different aspects of self when self becomes the focus of attention. Perhaps some individuals turn to their appearance and concern themselves with how they appear to others. Other individuals may focus more on internal characteristics when self becomes relevant. Individuals may differ to the extent that they characteristically focus on internal or external aspects of self. Buss (1980) suggests that some individuals may characteristically attend to the internal aspects of self. These private self-conscious persons typically tune attention inward when self becomes the focus of attention. Other individuals, in contrast, may characteristically focus on external aspects of self when self becomes salient. These private self-conscious individuals are more likely to focus on their physical appearance, including hair, gestures, facial expressions, and mannerisms.

Buss (1980) suggests that understanding self-consciousness depends in part on one's understanding of self. Self can be differentiated along two main dimensions: sensory-cognitive and private-public (Buss, 1980, 1986). The distinction between sensory and cognitive self is certainly important. Individuals are aware of sensory events, and to a certain extent these events help the individuals to differentiate self from others. When an individual touches his own arm, the sensation is completely different than it is when someone else touches his arm. Why is this the case? Because, as Buss (1980) suggests, the individual touching his own arm receives two sets of stimulation. One set coming from his arm and the other coming from his fingertips. If, however, someone else touches his arm, the sensation is one dimensional and it feels somehow separate from the body. Buss claims that this awareness of the difference helps the individual to distinguish self from others. Compared with this sensory aspect, the cognitive self is considered much more advanced. The cognitive self is that side of self that includes thoughts, feelings, attitudes, and complex emotions. This aspect of self includes feelings of self-worth, private or covert thoughts and feelings, and a realization that other individuals have perspectives different from our own (Buss, 1980, 1986).

The second distinction that Buss makes centers on public versus private aspects of self. It should be apparent that the cognitive self can include both the public and private components of the individual, whereas the sensory self cannot. The sensory self is primitive and does not exist in the absence of sensory input. Self, however, continues to exist even in the absence of physical stimulation. This aspect of self that exists above and beyond the physical world sets higher primates apart from lower primates (Buss, 1980). The cognitive aspect of self exists not only within the mind of the individual but is visible in the world for others to see. It is this aspect of self that is of importance to this chapter. This, in essence, summarizes the distinction between the private and public sides of self. The sensory self stops when physical input stops; the cognitive self continues.

Research on public and private self-consciousness suggests that this distinction can be considered dispositional (e.g., Buss, 1980, 1986; Carver & Scheier, 1987; Fenigstein, 1987). That is, some individuals have the trait of private self-consciousness, whereas others have the trait of public self-consciousness. As with any trait, public and private self-consciousness is normally distributed (although researchers such as Wicklund & Gollwitzer, 1987, argue that private and public self-consciousness may not represent two distinct traits). Some individuals will score at the high end, some will score at the low end, and most will fall somewhere in the middle. Although the individuals scoring in the middle range on these dimensions are of interest, only extreme scorers will be discussed here. This makes theoretical sense. To relate issues of self-consciousness to an eclectic approach to self, extreme cases allow for the clearest connections. In order to understand the average, extreme scores must be analyzed. These extreme cases, then, establish the parameters by which the other individuals can be understood. Several issues are of importance as this chapter addresses self-consciousness. First, how do individuals come to be either private or public in their self-focus? Second, what are the implications of self-consciousness for the individual? Third, what are the implications of individuals' type of self-consciousness for their interactions with others? Finally, how does an understanding of self-consciousness enhance the eclectic approach to self? The remainder of this chapter will address these critical issues.

BECOMING PRIVATE OR PUBLIC IN SELF-CONSCIOUSNESS

Buss (1980) devoted an entire chapter of his book to the development of private and public self-consciousness. More than any other aspect of these traits, their development relates most directly to an eclectic approach to self. Buss mentions that an awareness of the difference between public and private aspects of self can be seen in older children as they play. Young children play entirely in the overt world, primarily because their sense of self is sensory in orientation (Buss, 1986). They manipulate and play very simple games. As children get older, however, they begin to use more covert forms of play, such as fantasy. Older children may pretend that a tricycle is a race car. Later still, children may engage in fantasy-oriented play together, with each individual fulfilling a different role within the elaborate scenario. To the extent that such play is encouraged, children may become quite successful at maintaining these complex but private adventures.

Numerous childhood characteristics seem to play a role in the development of private self-consciousness (Buss, 1980, 1986; Fenigstein, 1979). First, children who are frequently ill may become quite adept at focusing attention inward and paying close attention to internal bodily stimuli. Children with chronic stomach aches, asthma, or other frequent ailments are encouraged by parents, doctors, and nurses to "Describe how it feels." The ability to do this, of course, is related to the child's ability to attend to these internal states. Second, the degree of introversion in the child may be related to private self-consciousness. Buss (1980) suggests that introverts focus more on their own feelings, thoughts, perceptions, and imagination than do extroverted children. It also seems probable that shy children will spend more time involved in their own inner world because it is safe, predictable, and manageable. Third, children who have particularly vivid imaginations may spend a lot of time in their inner, private world because they find it inherently more interesting than the world outside. Buss (1980) reports that imagery (representing the imaginativeness of the person) is significantly correlated with private self-consciousness. Fourth, the tendency to reflect inward and engage in imagination may be intensified if the child is isolated. Children who are somehow socially isolated may develop intense private fantasy worlds, including but not limited to imaginary friends.

It seems perfectly reasonable that this list of factors would contribute significantly toward the child's level of self-consciousness. Parents also may play a role in this process. Encouraging children to speak their mind, explain themselves, tell us how they feel, and so forth, may all encourage children to focus on the private aspects of their inner self. But, according to Buss (1980), private self-consciousness seems mainly to be a manifestation of dispositions already present in the child. Certain environments, however, seem to nurture or encourage focusing on this internal, covert world, whereas other environments encourage a focusing on the overt world that all can see.

The ability to focus on the public aspects of self seems to be encouraged in modern society. Children are encouraged to get along with others, do what others expect of them, and be good children. Part of what is required to be labeled as a "good child" is an ability to monitor public behavior and engage in appropriate behaviors. This process is accomplished mainly through instrumental conditioning (Buss, 1980). Reward and punishment are used by parents to "teach" children almost from the moment the child is born. In this fashion, children are taught from an early age that other individuals are concerned with their public performances. Parents may reprimand children for poor table manners, sloppy dress, or inappropriate language. These continual reminders from parents that public appearances are important certainly suggest to children that they should, indeed, focus on their public self.

But parents teach children even without trying. Jim's father may constantly point out the public flaws of other individuals or make snap judgments about others based on appearances or outward characteristics. It stands to reason, then, that Jim may decide such public characteristics are important in judging others and therefore are also important for self. Other parents adopt strategies to keep their children from "judging the book by its cover" or making snap judgments. In this manner, parents may send signals to the child that "It's what's inside that counts," and the child may quickly adopt this emphasis on the more private, internal world of the individual. Buss (1980) suggests that a natural consequence of children learning to take the perspective of others is a gathering awareness of their own public self. Once this public self-consciousness develops, reinforcement and punishment may determine the extent to which the child develops a tendency to focus on the public self.

Environments that clearly reinforce or punish the child for public displays (e.g., piano recitals, beauty contests, school plays, band performances) all remind the child that the public self is important. Of course each of these displays also involves private characteristics (the knowledge required to learn music or memorize lines, for example), but these skills play a secondary role to the image or public self in the heat of the performance. If the child should make a mistake in playing the piano piece, not win the contest, forget a line, or hit a wrong note, the public self may be embarrassed. When individuals feel that they have failed in some public performance, in fact, they may start questioning whether they truly have the private skills they thought they had. Once again, then, the private self may be taking a back seat to the public self.

What situations focus attention on the private self? Children who are encouraged to "find something to do" may turn to imagination or fantasy to provide themselves with entertainment. Children who spend a great deal of time alone also may come to focus more on the private self because they have fewer reminders that the public self may be important. Some parents seem to adopt the philosophy that "Children should be seen and not heard." Certainly this suggests very clearly to the children that they should keep to themselves. Even with these environmental or parental differences, however, Buss (1980) argues that private self-consciousness appears to be largely due to dispositions already present in the child. Shy or socially isolated children may be more likely to be high in private self-consciousness than their more outgoing counterparts, but the direction of causality is unclear. Perhaps these children come to focus on their private selves because of their shyness or isolation, or their predisposition to focus on the private aspects of self may lead them to engage in behaviors that are interpreted as being indicative of shyness or isolation. Regardless of which of these two causal scenarios seems to be most accurate, there appears to be a fairly clear connection between shyness, isolation, and private self-consciousness.

IMPLICATIONS OF PRIVATE AND PUBLIC SELF-CONSCIOUSNESS

Several interesting lines of research have focused on the implications of self-consciousness for the individual and the potential differences between those individuals that are considered "true privates" or "true publics." These terms are meant to differentiate between those individuals who score high on the private or public domain but also score relatively high on the other dimension as well. In these cases, it is difficult to determine if the individual should be categorized as high in private or public self-consciousness. To a certain extent, the individual's tendency to be aware of private or public aspects of self may be situationally specific for the individual who scores high or relatively high on both dimensions. Some individuals, however, score high on one dimension and low on the other. As might be induced from this description, then, one might expect true publics to behave differently from those scoring high or moderately high on both dimensions (Carver & Scheier, 1985).

Doherty and Schlenker (1991) discovered that individuals they labeled as "pure publics" (those individuals who are high in public and low in private self-consciousness) adopt self-presentational strategies that confirm public information about their performance. If, for example, these individuals received reportedly valid feedback that they failed, they adopted a self-presentational strategy that was self-effacing. If, however, these individuals received feedback that they succeeded, they adopted a self-enhancing self-presentational style. These findings expand the understanding of the implications of self-consciousness for individuals and the interactions they have with others. Doherty and Schlenker (1991) also noted that pure publics do not always adopt a self-presentational style designed to minimize disapproval, as the research had suggested. These researchers report that pure publics will adopt such a self-protective strategy when a failure has occurred on a valid test, when evaluative feedback is readily available, or when a success has occurred. In these cases, the individuals have no need to self-protect and were shown by Doherty and Schlenker (1991) to attempt to create a positive social identity and seek approval.

Carver and Scheier (1985) provide evidence suggesting that individuals who can be described as pure publics alter their behaviors more to match the social norms and expectations of a given situation than do individuals low in public self-consciousness or high in private self-consciousness. Thus, the pure public individuals would appear to be more inconsistent over time. This appearance, however, is relative. Given that these individuals alter their self-presentational styles to match the situational expectations, within a given situation they would be perceived as being more consistent than their pure private counterparts. As already suggested, children are socialized to maintain consistency between their words and their deeds (e.g., Doherty & Schlenker, 1991). Pure publics, who are the most likely to be concerned about whether they appear to be consistent, therefore should be the most likely to adopt a self-presentational style that allows them to appear to match the evaluative feedback they are receiving.

Other lines of research in this area suggest that individuals who score high on private self-consciousness seem more likely to use self as a referent point when filling in missing pieces of information (such as in a sentence completion task), are very aware of changes in their internal states, and more quickly generate self-descriptive statements than their high public self-consciousness counterparts (e.g., Mueller, 1982; Scheier, Carver, & Gibbons, 1979). Individuals who are high in public self-consciousness are very aware of themselves as social objects. As such, these individuals are attuned to their self as seen from the observer's perspective (e.g., Hass, 1984).

These findings have direct implications for an eclectic approach to self because they further clarify the conditions under which individuals will adopt a self-verifying versus self-enhancing presentational style or seek self-verifying versus self-enhancing feedback. Individuals who are most concerned with their public behaviors would be the most likely to adopt whichever strategy will be most successful given the situational expectations present. When pure public individuals receive failure feedback that seems valid, they may doubt their ability to refute that information and, therefore, run the risk of being perceived as inconsistent. Rather than running this risk, then, they may simply adopt a self-verifying self-presentational style and all will end well (e.g., Doherty & Schlenker, 1991). If, however, there are no expectancies or the feedback the individuals receive appears to be invalid, these same individuals demonstrate a preference for self-enhancing feedback.

Abrams and Brown (1989) argue that traditional views of self-awareness suggest that group behaviors are the result of lost self-regulation and less accountability on the part of any individual within that group. Social identity theory, however, suggests that the behavior of individuals within groups is highly regulated by perceiving self as a "group member." When individuals identify with the group and, therefore, consider themselves to be group members, that identity may play a key role in regulating the behaviors those individuals will or will not choose to engage in (Abrams & Brown, 1989). Brown and Abrams (1986) suggested that intergroup similarity is perceived negatively by groups, and groups strive to establish their distinctiveness. This, of course, makes sense. Two groups would want to be seen as distinctive; otherwise individuals may wonder why two groups are needed or if one of the groups is simply trying to be like the other.

Because of this desire for intergroup distinctiveness, individuals high in private self-consciousness should be most disturbed when an outgroup expresses attitudes that are similar to those of the ingroup. Abrams and Brown (1989) report evidence to support this contention. These researchers also discovered that individuals high in public self-consciousness expressed the most positivity toward outgroups that were similar to the ingroup. Presumably this reflects the high public's desire to be perceived as personally acceptable. Showing favoritism to the ingroup would limit the high public's ability to be deemed acceptable by more than one group (Abrams & Brown, 1989). Contrary to traditional views of individuals relinquishing self-regulation in order to identify with a group, Abrams and Brown (1989) report data consistent with the hypothesis that when social identity is salient, individuals within that group will engage in systematic and organized self-regulation. Levels of self-consciousness seem to play a role in this process, with both high privates and high publics self-regulating in a fashion that is consistent with their self-consciousness level. This organized self-regulation not only allows individuals to be a successful part of the group, but also allows them to adhere to their level of self-consciousness as well.

Buss and Scheier (1976) suggest that individuals high in private self-consciousness would make more internal attributions for events than those low in private self-consciousness. Briere and Vallerand (1990) and Duval and Wicklund (1973) remind the reader that this internal attribution bias on the part of high privates is due to the direction their attention is turned. If one is attuned to internal characteristics, then it is also reasonable to assume that internal attributions will be made. Briere and Vallerand (1990), however, extend these findings by suggesting that the degree to which high privates will exhibit the internal bias of attributions may depend, in part, on the outcome. Consistent with this prediction, subjects high in private self-consciousness made more internal attributions following a successful outcome than their low private self-consciousness counterparts. In the condition with no outcome, however, no significant differences were found. Contrary to Duval and Wicklund's (1973) assumption, the direction of self-focus does not, in and of itself, determine the kind of attribution the individual will make. Briere and Vallerand's (1990) findings clearly indicate that both direction of self-focus and outcome in the situation determine whether or not the individual will make biased attributions.

Shepperd and Arkin (1989) discovered that public self-conscious subjects self-handicap more than their low public self-conscious counterparts, but only on a test they have been led to believe is valid. Again, as Doherty and Schlenker (1991) suggest, the validity of the information seems to play an important role in determining the impact that self-consciousness will have for the individual. In this vein, the high publics in Shepperd and Arkin's (1989) research purposely chose to listen to potentially performance debilitating music when the task they would be performing was labeled as self-defining. The discussion of self-handicapping already provided in this text (Chapter Ten) suggested that individuals will sometimes engage in behaviors specifically designed to make success in a situation less likely. Although intuitively this might seem odd, it is a rather sound strategy. If individuals succeed against the odds, their performance seems even more stellar. If the individuals fail, the impression is that the odds were stacked against them. This allows the individuals the pleasure of maximizing success and minimizing the impact of failure.

It makes sense that individuals scoring high in public self-consciousness would be most likely to self-handicap when the task is considered self-defining. This supports the assumption that the nature of the task plays an important role in determining the degree to which the individual will self-handicap. Taken together, these findings lead to a more precise understanding of not only the nature of self-handicapping, but of the impact of self-consciousness as well. Both individual differences and facets of tasks or situations need to be understood if one is ever truly going to understand the eclectic nature of self.

Froming, Corley, and Rinker (1990) discovered that both familiarity with an audience and individual levels of public self-consciousness combine to determine when individuals will withdraw from embarrassing situations. Interestingly enough, Froming, Corley, and Rinker (1990) found that low public self-conscious persons respond differently to close friends than they do to strangers. In the presence of friends, these individuals are less concerned about possible embarrassment and, therefore, are less likely to withdraw from the situation. In the presence of strangers, however, the low public self-conscious persons, just like their high public self-conscious counterparts, tend to withdraw from embarrassing situations. This, of course, is another example of the eclectic nature of self-related behavior. Both situational parameters (and situations certainly include the other individuals in the environment) and individual differences combine to determine the individual's actions.

Baumeister and his colleagues (e.g., Baumeister & Showers, 1986; Baumeister & Steinhilber, 1984) note that achieving a favored status in a competition can often lead to "choking under pressure." Baumeister and Showers (1986) suggest that this tendency to choke in front of the home crowd is due to the intense self-awareness that this favored status induces. Because this intense self-awareness may focus the individual's attention so much on the mechanical details of performing the task, the performance can seem lifeless and strained. Athletes can become so good at what they do that the performance becomes automatic. Under times of intense self-awareness, however, this automaticity is lost and more mistakes can be made.

Heaton and Sigall (1991) discovered an interactive relationship between self-consciousness, audience, and feedback in relationship to choking under pressure. This is an important discovery for expanding Baumeister and Showers' (1986) findings. Heaton and Sigall (1991) suggest that self-awareness alone does not determine the degree to which an individual will choke under pressure. These researchers suggest that during times of pressure, individuals high and low in self-consciousness may feel different pressures because of their differing self-presentational concerns. Persons high in self-consciousness (those persons who characteristically focus attention inward toward self) were more likely to choke when performance could have a negative impact on self-construction. Self-construction was defined as "constructing one's public self such that it becomes congruent with one's ideal self." Individuals low in self-consciousness (those persons who focus attention away from self), however, were more likely to choke when their performance could lead to a disappointment for the audience.

Given what has already been stated about self-consciousness, these findings make a great deal of sense. Individuals have different motives they are trying to fulfill in performance situations. Differing possible outcomes from their performance may lead to differing kinds of pressure. An individual who is mostly concerned with pleasing the audience would experience more pressure when audience disappointment is most likely. Add to this the degree to which the individual focuses attention toward or away from self, and the pressures can mount. An individual who tends to focus attention away from self would be more concerned with the audience's reaction than an individual who is concerned with reaching a self ideal. The individual who is concerned with constructing a public self that is as close to the ideal as possible, however, would be concerned with living up to some internal standard and, therefore, would experience the most pressure when performance is likely to have negative implications for reaching the ideal self. Individuals who are high in self-consciousness and, therefore, focus attention on self are particularly likely to be vulnerable to such pressures.

WRAPPING IT UP: WHAT DOES ALL THIS MEAN?

An eclectic approach to self has, at its very core, an awareness that self is multifaceted. But this complexity is not entirely internal. Situations exert a powerful influence on the individual and sometimes these constraints can be in direct conflict with the individual's motives. Only by understanding the interaction between internal motives, individual differences, and situational forces will we clarify the picture of what self really is. Individuals differ to the extent that they focus attention on the private or public aspects of self. Some situations, however, can be so powerful as to override the individual's predisposition and force the person to become aware of either the public or private characteristics of self.

Carver and Scheier (1985) suggest that individuals should be assessed as to whether they score as true privates or true publics. It makes sense that different behaviors might be expected from those individuals who score high on one dimension and low on the other than from those individuals who score high on both, low on both, or somewhere in between. Doherty and Schlenker (1991) use the terms pure publics and pure privates to illustrate a similar point. These researchers discovered that pure publics adopt different self-presentational styles depending on the validity and type of feedback they are receiving. When pure publics receive valid feedback of failure, they tend to engage in self-verifying, whereas these same individuals tend to self-enhance if the valid feedback they are receiving is of success. Individuals who can be labeled pure publics also alter their behaviors to conform to social norms and expectations more than do individuals either low in public self-consciousness or high in private self-consciousness (Carver & Scheier, 1985).

These findings suggest that pure publics are concerned with adopting self-presentational styles that allow them to appear to match the evaluative feedback they are receiving. Thus, by knowing the individual's level of self-consciousness, the apparent validity of evaluative feedback, and whether that feedback is of success or failure, it is possible to predict with a relatively high degree of accuracy what self-presentational style the individual will adopt. Understanding self-consciousness also allows one to challenge the traditional assumption that individuals who engage in group behaviors are doing so at the expense of self-regulation (Abrams & Brown, 1989). Abrams and Brown (1989) discovered a connection between self-consciousness, self-regulation, and social identity. Individuals who are high in private self-consciousness may value intergroup distinctiveness more than others and, therefore, should be most likely to self-regulate when that intergroup distinctiveness is challenged.

These findings, and others reported in this chapter, clarify our understanding of the relationship between individual differences such a self-consciousness and the other variables that influence self that have already been addressed in this book. Such factors as situational variables, evaluative feedback, type of feedback (e.g., positive or negative), levels of self-consciousness, anticipated situational outcomes, type of audience, and degree of pressure may all interact with self-consciousness to impact the self-concept of the individual. Given the complexity of self as a construct, it is refreshing to note that new lines of research are addressing the interconnectedness of individual difference research and other social psychological phenomena. An eclectic approach to self assumes that individuals are pushed and pulled by the list of factors just mentioned, and that to some extent these variables determine the consistency of behaviors individuals will display.

If no situational forces are present, or situational forces that are present are minimal, individuals may feel most free to express their individual motives. One must also remember, however, that whenever an individual engages in behavior, some kind of evaluative feedback will follow. The positivity or negativity of this feedback along with the perceived validity of it may determine whether the individual's own self-presentational motives will prevail or if the individual will bow to situational pressure. This increased understanding of the relationship between individual differences and the other variables that affect the self-related behaviors an individual will engage in illuminates the forces that combine to create individuals and determine their behaviors. Individuals are not always free to choose their own behaviors. Even when behavioral choices are limited, however, an eclectic approach to self delineates the manner in which the individual will make choices, fulfill situational expectations, and, if possible, still find a method by which his or her own individual self-presentational motives can be fulfilled.

CHAPTER TWELVE

Self-Monitoring

CAVEAT

Before proceeding with an examination of the self-monitoring construct, some attention should be directed toward several enduring controversies in the self-monitoring literature. First, many discuss the relative strengths and weaknesses of measuring self-monitoring (as Snyder does) using a true-false questionnaire. Although the twenty-five-item (Snyder, 1972, 1974) and eighteen-item (Snyder & Gangestad, 1986) scales meet satisfactory levels of reliability and validity, some argue that Likert Scale responses should be used rather than the either/or nature of the true-false scale. Although this controversy is certainly interesting, it is not of relevance to this chapter. The focus of this chapter is examining the differences among individuals as a function of self-monitoring level (regardless of how it is measured). To enhance further the eclectic approach to self, individual difference variables need to be understood especially as they impact the manner in which individuals processes self-related information and information about others in their social world.

Second, arguments rage about the actual psychometric nature of the self-monitoring construct. Snyder envisions self-monitoring as a unipolar continuum on which subjects can score anywhere from low to high. Others, such as Briggs, Cheek, and Buss (1980), have argued that self-monitoring actually has multiple subfactors and the individual's score on each subfactor should be taken into consideration in determining self-monitoring level for that individual. Again, although this question is of interest, it does not relate to the discussion in this chapter. Discussions of this type tend to focus on the underlying "nature" of the self-monitoring construct, but in fact, they are often measurement issues and little else. Indeed, as research presented later in this chapter will suggest, questions should not focus on whether the overall self-monitoring score should be used in research or the factor scores, but when each of these techniques would be appropriate. Of most interest to this discussion, however, are questions of how self-monitoring develops (not whether it is made up of one factor or several factors), the implications of self-monitoring for the self, and the manner in which individuals process information about the social world. Readers interested in gathering more information about either of these controversies are encouraged to examine Briggs and Cheek (1986, 1988); Briggs, Cheek, and Buss (1980); John and Block (1986); Lennox and Wolfe (1984); Snyder (1987); or Snyder and Gangestad (1986).

BACKGROUND INFORMATION

Adolescence has often been described as a time of "storm and stress." As suggested in Chapters One and Two, however, much of this storm comes from the identity negotiation process in which the individual (and many other persons in that individual's social network) are trying to answer the question "Who am I?" Psychologists have pondered questions of identity and how individuals come to know themselves for about as long as psychologists have been around. Several factors seem important in truly knowing who one is. One factor is certainty. Another is importance.

How much do people really know about themselves, and who judges the accuracy of that knowledge? Megan may feel that she really knows who she is. If her best friends see her differently, who is wrong? By its nature, "self" would seem to be something that is privately constructed, and therefore Megan would be correct. Various chapters in the text (including Chapters One, Two, Three, Five, Six, and Seven), however, discuss self as being partially socially constructed.

Many individuals seem to go through life constantly in a state of identity negotiation. They seem uncertain as to who they truly are or seem unable to convey an image of self to others that others will accept. Although identity negotiation (or striving to discover and articulate one's self) is not necessarily a negative thing, it can be. Some individuals always seem to be in the process of searching for their self without ever finding answers. This chronic uncertainty can have a profound impact on the individual. Human beings want to have predictability and consistency in their lives; contributing to this stability is knowing who they are.

Some individuals have a sense of self-certainty that signals to the world they know who they are, where they have been, and where they are going. These individuals enjoy the kind of consistency about self that allows them the freedom to try new roles, expand their horizons, ask questions about their limits, and at the same time, be able to know who they are. Self-certain individuals, however, are not always happy as they have just been portrayed. Self-certainty does not guarantee high self-esteem because the individuals can be certain that they are worthless. Although self-certainty is better than self-uncertainty, either one can be less than positive for the individual.

Another area of concern involves the importance of the characteristics the individual uses to define self. Some individuals consider particular aspects of their self to be important to their self-definition. These individuals would be more strongly influenced by feedback focusing on those important aspects of self than on ones they deem less important. It should be clear that certainty and importance may work in conjunction to determine the extent to which individuals really know their self. As mentioned in Chapter Two, certainty and importance also may determine the self-esteem level. Individuals who are certain of the attributes that define self but do not feel that those attributes are important will surely be less happy than individuals who are certain of their attributes and those attributes are important to them.

What determines which self-related attributes are important to the individual? Certainly, this is partially determined by factors already discussed in this text. Parents, peers, and society all play a role in determining what is acceptable for individuals and what is not. It should be pointed out, however, that individuals play a role in deciding who they are or would like to be. Chapter Eleven suggested that individuals may differ to the extent that they become aware of and focus on the public aspects of self or the private aspects. That chapter also discussed the implications of this kind of focus for individuals and the others in their social world.

Another difference that may impact the social world of the individual is self-monitoring. Mark Snyder (e.g., 1972, 1974, 1979, 1987) defined self-monitoring as "differences in the extent to which people monitor (observe, regulate, and control) the public appearances of self they display in social situations and interpersonal relationships" (e.g., Snyder, 1987). Snyder suggested two distinct categories of self-monitors, and a variety of behavioral differences would be expected based on which self-monitoring category the individuals falls into. High self-monitors care a great deal about the images they project in social situations, and therefore they constantly monitor these images to fit the behavioral expectations of the situation. Low self-monitors, on the other hand, value consistency between who they are on the inside and how the behave externally. Because these individuals value congruence between internal self and external behaviors, their behavior is very consistent and they are quite willing to express their attitudes and feelings even when such sentiments are not popular (Snyder, 1987).

THE DEVELOPMENT OF HIGH AND LOW SELF-MONITORING

As one might guess, self-monitoring level may play a crucial role in determining the social situations in which we find individuals, how they choose to express opinions, whom they choose as dating or activity partners, and the information they will seek before making decisions. Before the research addressing such differences between high and low self-monitors is discussed, however, it is important to discuss the possible developmental processes involved in determining one's self-monitoring level. The development of such a construct is critical to our complete understanding of the role self-monitoring level might play in the eclectic nature of the self.

Research from a variety of sources, including studies of twins, suggests that degree of genetic similarity does correlate quite strongly with self-monitoring level (e.g., Snyder, 1987). Although correlation in no way determines causality, the finding is intriguing. The possibility that genetics may play a role in predisposing individuals to develop low or high levels of self-monitoring, of course, is no guarantee that the individual will indeed develop a predictable level. Self-monitoring involves social behaviors; therefore development in an environmental context is important in determining who will and who will not engage in behaviors typical of low or high self-monitors. Certainly the parental climate can encourage or discourage the kinds of behaviors normally associated with low or high levels of self-monitoring. Parents who emphasize manners, setting an example, fulfilling an image, and "do as I say, not as I do" may be signalling to their children that the ability to adjust behaviors to situational demands is important.

Parents who, on the other hand, stress the importance of being truthful, speaking your mind, adhering to your values, being your own person, and "doing what you think is right" may send signals to their children that internal values are what matter. These comments are not meant to pass judgment on the relative merits of either parental approach. Certainly, most parents stress both sets of values, depending on the situation. Also, none of this is to say that the home learning environment will override self-monitoring level although it may play a substantial role in fostering its development. Snyder (1987) seems to suggest that it might be more fruitful to ask "How does self-monitoring develop?" rather than ponder questions of its origins. It is to this question that we will now turn.

Self-monitoring seems to involve a tendency for individuals to pay attention to different aspects of the social environment and the role they play within that environment (Snyder, 1987). In this case it doesn't matter if this difference in attention is genetically based or learned early on through experience with the social world and parental reinforcement or punishment. What matters is how this difference in attention gets translated into the very different behaviors that high and low self-monitors have been shown to engage in. What an individual attends to in the social environment has a direct impact on the information that individual receives about that environment. That information then may play a role in determining what the person believes is important to attend to within that environment. Gangestad and Snyder (1985) suggested that these tendencies to attend to differing aspects of the environment may lead over time to actual differences in an individual's knowledge base about the world. Over time, then, these subtle differences may lead to a different focus in knowledge, motives, and skills for high and low self-monitors (Gangestad & Snyder, 1985).

Surely, it is also possible that individuals seek out situations that are consistent with their self-monitoring tendencies. A child, for example, who likes to be the center of attention will seek out situations in which she is called on to play a role, entertain the grandparents, or put on a show. The individuals who witness this display may reinforce such behaviors with their responses, thereby signalling to the child that such an adjustment of behaviors to the demands of the situation was not only desired but rewarding. It is just as possible that another child who is more interested in internal tasks such as thinking may be rewarded by parents and others for being so studious and contemplative. These early displays of self-monitoring propensities then can reinforce the further development of the self-monitoring tendency and, over time, become a characteristic pattern for the individual. In this fashion, self-monitoring can develop regardless of whether its foundation is rooted in genetic predispositions or early reinforcement and punishment choices that parents and other significant others make.

Snyder (1987) suggests that parental style may play a role in influencing the child's tendency to behave in a high or low self-monitoring fashion. Children often ask why something is being asked of them. Depending on how the parent chooses to answer this question, different rationales are presented. Snyder (1987) refers to these as appealing to either "personal" or "social" considerations. Parents who appeal to the child's personal considerations phrase comments in relation to the child. The parents might encourage the child to try a sport by saying "You'll really enjoy it." Parents who appeal to social considerations, however, might say such things as "I would like you to give this a try" or "All of your friends are doing it." As one can surmise, such appeals clearly signal to the child that the parent feels that certain considerations are more important than others.

Snyder (1987) sums up his discussion of the development of self-monitoring by suggesting that self-monitors "are first born, and then made." By this, he argues that there seems to be a biological-genetic predisposition to have a particular self-monitoring level. This predisposition can be enhanced and strengthened across time and situations. Situations can promote or inhibit the individual's natural tendency to monitor the internal or external aspects of self.

IMPLICATIONS OF SELF-MONITORING LEVEL

There is more to being high or low in self-monitoring than just determining which aspects of self will be controlled in social situations. Snyder began to delineate the implications of self-monitoring for the individual and others when he suggested that self-monitoring plays a role in how individuals gather information about and build knowledge bases for self (e.g., Snyder, 1979). This, of course, is of direct relevance to an eclectic approach to self. Although Snyder was referring specifically to self-monitoring, his discussion of the implications of self-monitoring parallel the emphasis this eclectic approach to self has placed on looking not only at the development of self but also at the implications of self. According to Snyder, "rather than focusing on the antecedent processes by which individuals gain self-knowledge, theory and research on self-monitoring have turned their attention toward answering the question: 'of what consequence is this self-knowledge for what the person subsequently does?'" (Snyder, 1979).

Rather than provide an exhaustive summary of all of the implications of self-monitoring level as outlined in the literature, it would be more fruitful to focus on some of the more fundamental findings that illustrate the scope of influence that self-monitoring has on the life of the individual. Self-monitoring has been linked to differences in the choices individuals make for romantic and dating partners (e.g., Snyder, Berscheid, & Glick, 1985; Snyder & Simpson, 1984), choosing activity partners (e.g, Snyder, Gangestad, & Simpson, 1983), liking for anticipated interaction partners (e.g, Lassiter & Briggs, 1990), thinking about self and others (e.g., Snyder & Cantor, 1980), marital adjustment (e.g., Richmond, Craig, & Ruzicka, 1991), behavioral variability across interpersonal relationships (e.g., Lippa & Donaldson, 1990), control of social behavior (e.g., Snyder & Monson, 1975), political choices (Young, Osborne, & Snyder, 1994), and information processing about self and others (Osborne & Young, 1994). The following summary will provide a brief look at each of these findings to give the reader an overall feel for the magnitude of the consequences self-monitoring level has for individuals and others in their social world.

Snyder, Berscheid, and Glick (1985) examined how much time men spent studying information about the physical appearance or personality characteristic of potential dating partners. As one might suspect, high self-monitoring individuals spent significantly more time examining the photographs of the potential dating partners than did their low self-monitoring counterparts. Low self-monitors, on the other hand, spent significantly more time examining the personality descriptions of the potential dating partners than did their high self-monitoring counterparts. Snyder and Simpson (1984) discovered that high self-monitors would choose a dating partner who was physically attractive even though that individual was described as very undesirable in terms of personality. Low self-monitors, of course, were more likely to choose a dating partner who was below average in physical appearance if that individual had a desirable personality. In this unique demonstration, Snyder and Simpson (1984) were able to pit appearance against personality to see which type of characteristic high and low self-monitors would sacrifice. In these cases, self-monitoring tendencies influence the types of characteristics the individual will attend to in making choices about potential dating partners. These choices, it seems, could then have profound implications for the kinds of relationships these individuals would build with those partners.

Lassiter and Briggs (1990) discovered a relationship between self-monitoring level and liking of anticipated interaction partners. This research, striving to bridge the gap between research on self-consistency and liking, revealed a relationship between self-monitoring level, anticipation of an interaction, and degree of liking for the would be interaction partner. As Lassiter and Briggs revealed, low self-monitors alter their ratings of a target individual to show even more liking when they are led to anticipate an interaction with that individual, whereas high self-monitors do not alter their ratings. It is likely that this effect is due to the low self-monitor's motivation to maintain a sense of self-consistency, whereas high self-monitors are not as concerned with self-consistency. These findings are consistent with descriptions of self-perception theory as outlined in Chapter Five (and, indeed, Lassiter and Briggs suggest self-perception theory as a possible explanation for such findings). Perhaps low self-monitoring individuals believe that they must like someone if they are going to meet with them. This provides a sense of self-certainty that low self-monitors seem motivated to maintain.

Snyder and Cantor (1980) suggest that high and low self-monitors differ on the manner in which they structure their social experiences. These differences are suspected to have implications for the social knowledge about the world that these individuals hold. High self-monitors were found to be particularly effective at organizing social information around a prototypical other, whereas low self-monitors seem to be particularly successful at organizing social information around dispositional constructs related to self. These findings, of course, relate to discussions in Chapter Nine about the self-reference effect. It seems perfectly reasonable for the high self-monitoring individual to have a clearly articulated image of what kind of person would do what kinds of things in what kinds of situations. Low self-monitors, on the other hand, would be more likely to use self as a referent point against which other kinds of social information are processed.

Richmond, Craig, and Ruzicka (1991) found no relationship between the global construct of self-monitoring and marital adjustment of husbands, wives, and couples. When factor scores as identified by Briggs, Cheek, and Buss (1980) were analyzed, however, relationships were discovered. Husbands' extroversion and other-directedness scores contributed to marital adjustment, whereas for wives, other-directedness, extroversion, and husband's other-directedness contributed to marital adjustment. Other-directedness represents the individual's defensiveness and reflects attempts to avoid anxiety. The level of other-directedness in husbands was found to correlate negatively with husband, wife, and couple marital adjustment. The more defensive and anxiety avoiding the husband, the more poorly adjusted the relationship was. Although these findings say little about the global construct of self-monitoring, they do suggest the importance of factors that have been associated with self-monitoring.

Lippa and Donaldson (1990) address issues of behavioral variability across interpersonal relationships and self-monitoring. In an elaborate design testing methods for assessing variability, these researchers discovered significant negative correlations between variability scores and self-monitoring for four out of the five consistency measures. When behavioral consistency was measured by diary reports of behaviors, diary reports of settings, computer reports of behaviors, or computer reports of settings, the higher the self-monitoring score, the lower the consistency score. This suggests that high self-monitors are significantly less consistent (and, therefore, more variable) in their behaviors than their low self-monitoring counterparts. This, of course, makes a great degree of sense. Research already reported (e.g., Lassiter & Briggs, 1990), suggests that low self-monitors value self-consistency and, therefore, would be likely to engage in more consistency across behavioral situations. High self-monitors, on the other hand, are motivated to project an image of self that matches the demands of the situation. In this manner, the high self-monitor will act in whatever manner is necessary to be successful given the constraints of the situation.

Snyder and Monson (1975) revealed a tendency for high self-monitors to engage in more control of their social behaviors. By control, Snyder and Monson are referring to the tendency for the individual to monitor and adjust behaviors given the demands of the situation. High self-monitors are more attuned to and concerned with the situational appropriateness of their behaviors; therefore, their situational behaviors vary considerably based on situationally relevant constraints. Low self-monitors, however, seem to make behavioral choices based on relevant internal characteristics rather than external situational demands. Snyder and Monson (1975) determined that the behavior of high self-monitors could best be predicted by assessing relevant situational factors, whereas the behavioral choices of low self-monitors could best be predicted by focusing on their personal characteristics or measuring internal states (Snyder & Monson, 1975, p. 643).

Young, Osborne, and Snyder (1994) extended the findings of Snyder and Simpson (1984) to the political arena. High and low self-monitoring subjects were provided with political candidate portfolios including photographs, issue information, and minor demographic information. One candidate was rated by pilot-test subjects as looking significantly more presidential than the other. Both candidates matched subjects on important issue information that the subjects had indicated during pilot testing were important to their political choices. Subjects were asked to peruse the portfolios and decide which candidate they would be most likely to vote for in an election. As predicted, high self-monitors overwhelmingly endorsed the candidate that had been rated by pilot-test subjects as looking the most presidential. Low self-monitoring subjects, on the other hand, split their vote 50–50. This suggests that the low self-monitors saw neither candidate as preferential because both matched their stance on relevant issues. High self-monitors, on the other hand, chose the candidate that more closely fit the image of a president all other things being equal. When both candidates looked presidential but only one of them matched subjects on the issues, however, high self-monitors split their vote 50–50, whereas low self-monitors overwhelmingly endorsed the candidate that more closely matched their stance on the issues.

In a follow-up study, Young, Osborne, and Snyder (1994) pitted image versus issue. In these portfolios, one candidate matched the subject on the issues but did not look at all presidential; the other candidate looked presidential but differed significantly from the subject on issue positions. High self-monitors overwhelmingly endorsed the image candidate even though doing so would mean voting for someone who did not think as they did on the issues. Low self-monitors, however, still overwhelmingly endorsed the candidate who matched them on issues. These findings suggest that high self-monitors believe image is more important than stance on issues, at least when it comes to choosing a political candidate. Low self-monitors, on the other hand, continue to tow the line, voting for a candidate even though that person does not fit the prototypical image on what a candidate "should" look like.

Osborne and Young (1994) attempted to delineate the manner in which high and low self-monitors categorize information about self and others. In a series of studies, high self-monitors have been shown to use more physical appearance and social role descriptors to describe self and friends than low self-monitors, whereas low self-monitors have been shown to use more trait descriptors to categorize self and friends than high self-monitors. This same pattern of findings was discovered for subjects' response times to adjectives presented on a computer screen (high self-monitors responded faster to self-descriptors that describe their physical appearance and roles, whereas low self-monitors responded faster to self-descriptors that described their traits). Even on an unexpected recall test one week after viewing a stranger on a videotape, high self-monitors recalled more of the target's physical descriptors and social roles than low self-monitors, and low self-monitors remembered more of the target's trait descriptors than did high self-monitors.

WRAPPING IT UP: WHAT DOES ALL THIS MEAN?

The brief review of findings from the self-monitoring literature provides only a cursory glance at the implications of self-monitoring level for the individual. The extent to which individuals monitor and adjust their behaviors to match the demands of the situation can have profound impact on the social world of those individuals. Low self-monitors value congruence between who they are and what they do. They monitor their internal standards and do not seem as willing as high self-monitors to adjust their behaviors just because the situation is calling for it. Over the years, the impressions the literature seems to hold toward high and low self-monitors has undergone a transformation. The high self-monitor is perceived as being situationally successful (e.g., Snyder, 1974, 1979, 1987), having a greater number of friends (e.g., Snyder & Simpson, 1986), and engaging in more varied sexual activities with their partners (e.g., Snyder & Simpson, 1984). Low self-monitors, on the other hand, are less concerned with situational successes that are external in nature or based on images, seem content with a few close friends (e.g., Snyder, 1987), and adopt more traditional views of variety in sexual activities (e.g., Snyder & Simpson, 1984).

But low self-monitors are not situationally unsuccessful. Just because they do not adjust their behaviors in every situation does not mean they are situational failures. These individuals are motivated to maintain self-consistency and adhere to internal standards. Sometimes this adherence to internal standards could work to their advantage. Although high self-monitors initiate more relationships, they also tend to leave these relationships sooner and choose whom to do what activity with based on the degree to which that person can help them be successful situationally (e.g., Snyder, Gangestad, & Simpson, 1983). Young, Osborne, and Snyder (1994) note that high self-monitors make political choices based on images and who is most likely to win, whereas low self-monitors make political choices based on candidates' stances on issues and how those stances match their own internal values. Could it really be claimed, therefore, that high self-monitors always have the advantage?

Self-monitoring is not a construct that should be perceived as either good or bad. Just like any personality characteristic, in excess it can lead to trouble. Individuals who are so concerned with matching a public image or adjusting behavior to fit some external standard may run the risk of not knowing their "true" self. Likewise, low self-monitoring individuals who believe their internal standards are the only options may try to force those values on others. Some individuals migrate toward relationships, careers, or hobbies that allow them the maximum opportunity for expressing their values. Other individuals seek out relationships and situations that allow them the best outlet for demonstrating their competencies and want desperately to be a part of the "in group."

An eclectic approach to self benefits greatly from an understanding of the implications of self-monitoring level. Individuals are motivated to maintain self-consistency, but some individuals are more motivated than others. These findings help to further clarify the relationship between situational influences on behavior, internal standards or characteristics, and predicting when individuals will bow to situational pressures or stand up for their own values. These findings also further clarify what individuals would be most likely to engage in social comparisons, use self-perception to articulate self, respond to cultural demands on the self, use self-verification versus self-enhancement, or be most influenced by the reflected appraisals others direct toward self. In all of these cases, there is an integration of individual characteristics and environmental influences, an assessment of individual intentions or motives, and an analysis of the individual's goal within a particular situation.

WRAPPING IT UP: INTEGRATION OF SECTION FOUR

High self-monitors adjust their behaviors more to situational demands (or perceived situational demands) because they are motivated to be perceived as situationally successful, and fitting in is the goal. Low self-monitors, on the other hand, resist attempts to place situational constraints on their behavioral choices, especially when those constraints would be at odds with their internal standards or values. These persons are motivated to maintain self-consistency and might be more likely to self-verify than their high self-monitoring counterparts. Of course, all of this is speculation and needs to be researched further. Given the eclectic theory presented so far (especially as it is outlined in Figure 7.1), self-monitoring level must be factored into our understanding of how individuals come to be the individuals they are, and how those characteristics impact their behavioral choices.

An understanding of the role played by individual differences in the self system allows us to revise our chart of the self system for the last time. Figure 12.1 presents a final flow chart of the self system. As the text has progressed, this diagram has been expanded to incorporate the growing body of knowledge about the self, its development, its maintenance, and its refinements. Self is not static; it is dynamic and fluid. But self also is a defensive structure, and change to self comes only with great effort. Individuals are constantly in a state of self-refinement; self alteration is another matter entirely. Because individuals have a lot of time and energy invested in their self-definition, change to that definition will come only with a great deal of soul searching and effort. This, of course, is not a weakness or flaw in the self system. Self-consistency has long been argued as a foundation to mental health (e.g., Freud, 1957; Adler, 1927; Fromm 1947, 1955). This stability of self that allows change only across time and with effort actually serves to protect the individual from the emotional ups and downs that are a part of daily life.

Many mental health professionals and students ponder issues of how some individuals find the strength to endure what they do and remain relatively intact. Some individuals seem to have more of an immunity to the harsh emotional ups and downs that life some-

FIGURE 12.1 Final Flow Chart of the Self System

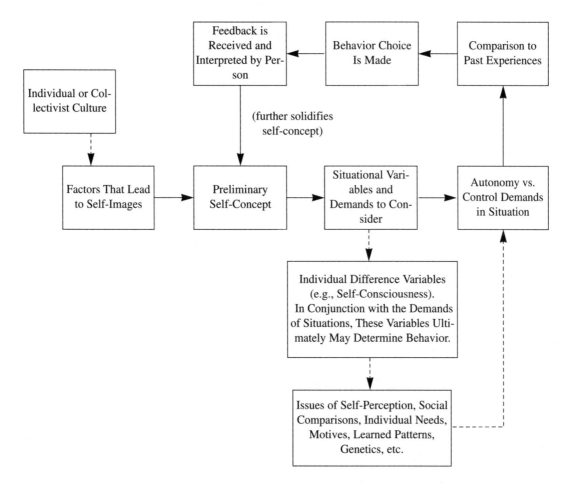

times sends their way. Other individuals seem particularly vulnerable to the effects of these ups and downs. An eclectic approach to self can address these issues to the extent that it incorporates information about the development of self, parental influences, cultural influences, the processes involved in identity negotiation, individual differences, and all of the other host of variables already discussed in this text. No two persons will experience the same traumas, tragedies, joys, or successes in their lives. Self is never completely predictable, no matter how good the foundation on which the theory has been built. However, examining individual difference variables and understanding the potential role they play in shaping self can help to clarify when self will be predictable and when it will not. The examination of individual difference variables in this chapter is not exhaustive. But self-consciousness and self-monitoring are grounded significantly in the self literature, and both seem to play a role in how individuals define their self and how those individuals react to and interact with others in their social world.

Applications of Self Theories to Everyday Life

INTRODUCTION TO SECTION FIVE

This text places a high degree of emphasis on the reasons that understanding the complexity of self is so important. All of these discussions, however, trickle down to one major underlying issue. Understanding self and its complexity is only truly useful if it can be applied to helping individuals. This section of the text is devoted to understanding some of the implications of this eclectic approach to self for the individuals that self research attempts to study. Although certainly a theory of self has far-reaching implications in many aspects of individuals' lives, this text will focus attention on three general categories of applications. First, Chapter Thirteen will address issues related to self-esteem enhancement. A major portion of this text has been geared toward illuminating the relationship between an eclectic understanding of self and self-esteem and the possibility of self-esteem enhancement. Second, attention will be devoted toward understanding the applications of self-understanding in daily life. This serves as a good focal point for discussions of applications because it touches on the importance of self for all individuals. Human beings can be described in as many different shapes, sizes, personalities, and characteristics as there are words in the English language. Despite all of these amazing differences, however, all human beings share one underlying similarity. Every one of us has a "self."

Few would deny the importance of an individual's perception of his or her self. As this book has tried to argue, however, self also is defined by the other individuals in the social world, situational constraints and demands, cultural and societal expecta-

tions, individual differences such as personality characteristics, and patterns of interpretations for success and failure. All of these must be understood within the framework of a useful self theory. In the end, however, it is the applicability of that self theory that determines its utility. Though many aspects of an individual's life may be
influenced by his or her perceptions of self, the most obvious place to center efforts is
in understanding the impact self has for the emotional and physical health of the individual. Chapter Fourteen, therefore, will present a brief summary of the applications
of self to everyday life and draw connections between these applications and the eclectic theory of self that has been outlined in this text.

Third, attention will be focused in Chapter Fifteen on the applications of self in
educational settings. Several chapters in this text (e.g., Chapters One and Two) have
presented evidence on the importance of the developmental nature of self and self-
esteem. Given that schools have been referred to as the second most influential developmental influence during middle childhood (e.g., Erikson, 1963; Seifert & Hoffnung,
1994), it is critical that our eclectic approach to self consider both the implications of
self for the educational setting and the implications of the educational setting for self.
This, of course, suggests that a pattern of reciprocal influence is at play. How the child
views his or her self will play an important role in determining his or her reaction to
the educational environment. Likewise, it is reasonable to assume that the educational environment plays an important role in shaping and molding the self. Schools not
only provide the child with a myriad of role models from which different patterns of
behavior can be adopted, but also provide almost continuous feedback about expectations, performance, success, and failure.

Children spend a significant proportion of their childhood within the walls of
schools. Within these walls, they are presented with rules to follow, expectations for
behaviors, and opportunities to explore their talents and interests. They are expected
to get along with other individuals who may be significantly different from them, are
reinforced for appropriate behaviors, are punished for inappropriate behaviors, and
receive a multitude of feedback about behaviors that indicate whether those actions are
being perceived by others as successes or failures. In short, school acts very much like
a culture to delineate normative expectations and provide incentives for adhering to
those norms and punishments when they are violated.

Whether schools explicitly realize it or not, they bear a significant portion of the
burden for socializing children to follow the rules and philosophies of the culture. Anyone who doubts this statement need only ask what happens to a school system's state
and federal funding if it does not uphold the separation of church and state. Part of the
business of teaching involves an inherent adherence to cultural standards, and this has
implications for the child's self-concept. Children, especially as they transition from
childhood into adolescence, have multiple demands placed on them by all of the forces
striving to socialize them. Parents continue to play an important, albeit somewhat dwin-
dling, role in the socialization of children as they progress into school. At this point,
the rules of the school and the authority of the teachers and administrators play an ever-
increasing role. Peers, however, must not be ignored. As children mature and struggle
to fit in with their peers, others whom they are trying to emulate play an ever-increas-
ing role in helping the children define who they are. As children age, the struggle

between defining self in one's own fashion and giving in to these socializing forces becomes more and more difficult to bear. The self that is left standing after these battles have been waged, then, is both influenced by and provides influence on the environment, whether it be the more general setting of daily life or the more specific setting of educational institutions.

CHAPTER THIRTEEN

Self-Esteem Enhancement

CHAPTER PHILOSOPHY

Most of the chapters in this text have been driven primarily by the research literature. Although that literature will be drawn on here, this chapter more than any of the others will be speculative as well. An eclectic understanding of self-concept and self-esteem provides information that may be used to understand the processes that might be involved in self-esteem enhancement. The literature surrounding self-esteem enhancement is, indeed, in its infancy. The technique outlined within this chapter is based on an extrapolation from existing literature and recent attempts to validate these processes empirically. The reader is asked to bear this in mind as self-esteem enhancement is discussed within the pages of this chapter.

Some may question the utility of placing anything within the confines of a text that is not entirely grounded in the research literature. My response to that is simple and straightforward. Every research area begins with observations, proceeds to hypotheses, generates research, and becomes integrated into theories. Self-esteem enhancement should be no different. The observations have been made and have been articulated when appropriate within the other chapters of this text. The hypotheses (as well as preliminary supportive evidence) are presented in this chapter. Once this has been accomplished, the result will be a theory of self-esteem enhancement that will be placed before one and all for consideration, further refinement, empirical examination, and if need be refutation. With such a philosophy in mind, then, let us proceed with applying the eclectic approach to self to self-esteem enhancement.

A REVIEW OF THE RELEVANT LITERATURE

Arguably, the best review of contemporary thinking about self-esteem was recently published by Baumeister (1993), providing cutting edge information on the implications of self-esteem level for the cognitions, emotions, motivations, and behaviors of individuals with low or high self-esteem. This text, however, did not have an eclectic approach to self as its driving force; little attention was paid to the ramifications of the findings being reported for a global theory of self or for methods of self-esteem enhancement. If an eclectic approach to self is to be successful, it must not only address the development and implications of the major aspects of self, but it must also address issues of self change, self-esteem enhancement, and the implications of self and self-esteem for other facets of the individual's life. Before continuing with efforts to create such an eclectic approach, however, it would be prudent to take a quick look at the picture of self-esteem painted by the theorists.

Baumeister (1993) includes significant findings from a variety of contemporary self theorists and provides summaries, making the text an extensive review of self-esteem research. The reported findings provide insights into how self-esteem should be incorporated into this eclectic approach to self as a whole. A quick summary of the major findings presented in Baumeister will provide a framework by which to answer the question "What does it really mean to have low self-esteem?" This summary of self-esteem research in combination with information on self-esteem enhancement approaches will further complement this eclectic approach to self. What follows is a brief summary of the major points addressed in each chapter of Baumeister's text, as well as suggestions for the implications that information has for strategies of self-esteem enhancement.

BAUMEISTER'S *SELF-ESTEEM: THE PUZZLE OF LOW SELF-REGARD*

Campbell and Lavallee (1993) argue that attention should be paid to both the knowledge and evaluative components of the self. One central question to understanding self-esteem is "How are the knowledge and evaluative components of self related?" Overall, these theorists provide good experimental evidence to support a longstanding assumption in the self literature that individuals with low self-esteem have less clearly articulated self-concepts (the knowledge component) than those individuals with high self-esteem. The implications of such an assumption for theories of self-esteem (the evaluative component) and self-esteem enhancement are profound. Given that low self-esteem individuals have less clearly articulated self-concepts, a possible method by which self-esteem enhancement could take place would be through a process of enhancing self-concept articulation. The more the self-concept of these individuals is clarified, the greater advancements in self-esteem one could expect.

Spencer, Josephs, and Steele (1993) suggest that the struggle for self-integrity on the part of individuals with low self-esteem may be complicated by a lack of resources with which they can build an affirmative view of self. When self-integrity is threatened, individuals who are high in self-esteem have many more aspects of self to turn to that are already positive to bolster them against the threatening information. Low self-esteem persons, on the other hand, have fewer positive aspects of self they can use to water down the impact of the threatening information. Negative information will have a more profound impact on low self-esteem persons because they cannot buffer the impact that this negative information will have. If a person fails an exam but has one hundred other examples of good grades to rely on to address her concerns about whether she is a good student, that one bad grade will have only a minor impact. If, however, the person has only mediocre grades or few prior grades on which to base questions of her ability as a student, then that one instance of poor performance will carry significantly more weight and more dramatically threaten self-esteem. Strategies designed to initiate self-esteem enhancement, then, must address this issue of differences in the amount of positive prior information the individual has to use in maintaining self-integrity. Low self-esteem persons need to minimize the impact that negative information has, and the best method for doing this is to interpret that feedback appropriately.

Because the first goal of individuals with low self-esteem in social situations is to avoid embarrassment, humiliation, failure, or rejection, such individuals do not approach situations with the same motivations as individuals who are high in self-esteem (e.g., Tice, 1991, 1993). This difference in the situational motivations of individuals with low or high self-esteem provides important clues about what issues successful self-esteem enhancement strategies should address. To the extent that low and high self-esteem individuals do not have the same motivations or goals within the same social situation, the methods by which they interpret feedback information will differ as well. This issue of feedback interpretation continues to surface as an important part of the developmental process of low self-esteem and therefore should be of major importance in self-esteem enhancement approaches.

Blaine and Crocker (1993) provide a helpful summary of the literature surrounding the use of self-serving biases by individuals with low or high self-esteem. Although the literature suggests overwhelmingly that individuals with high self-esteem engage in self-serving attributions (interpreting situational events in such a way as to bolster feelings of self-worth), individuals with low self-esteem do not. These theorists suggest that individuals with low self-esteem are either unbiased in their attributions or are self-deprecating. They provide little information to determine when the low self-esteem persons' attributions would be unbiased or when they would be self-deprecating. The information about self-esteem already provided may suggest that it depends on the degree of negativity of the persons' self-esteem. If individuals have extremely low self-esteem, it is highly likely that they will be self-deprecating in attributing feedback. These individuals would simply find it too difficult to allow for the possibility that they could be the cause of anything good that might happen to self. As such, issues of the extremity of low self-esteem must be addressed by self-esteem enhancement strategies if they are to be successful.

A review of the causes and consequences of low self-esteem by Harter (1993b) suggests that individuals with low self-esteem feel inadequate in domains in which success is valued. This point relates back to the discussion presented earlier about the factors that influence the extent to which self-images will impact self-esteem. If an individual values success in academic situations, but cannot or does not do well in such environments, the impact on self-esteem will be clear and dramatic. Perhaps one of the major goals of self-esteem enhancement, then, would be to help low self-esteem individuals shift their view of what domains are important and focus their efforts on other domains in which success is more likely. It might also be fruitful to provide the individuals with the training necessary to maximize the likelihood that they will succeed in what have been designated as important domains.

Self-esteem levels can be influenced by possibly conflicting motivational needs. Brown (1993) suggests that low self-esteem individuals face a unique bind because they have two mutually incompatible motivational needs. On the one hand, they are motivated to acquire positive information about self and, therefore, self-enhance. The same individuals, however, also are motivated by a possibly destructive need to maintain their self views. This problem of conflicting motivational demands also is discussed in a later chapter by De La Ronde and Swann (1993), who suggest that the need to self-enhance and the need to self-verify place the low self-esteem person in a difficult crossfire from which escape is difficult. De La Ronde and Swann (1993), however, do suggest that self-concept change is possible for low self-esteem individuals. Such self-concept change would be possible if the individuals' perceptions of their self as predictable could be reinforced (e.g., Hormuth, 1990), and the individuals could be placed into environments that confirm the new self-concept rather than perpetuate the old one.

This need to be perceived consistently and have self be predictable (e.g., De La Ronde & Swann, 1993; Hormuth, 1990; Osborne & Stites, 1994; Simon, 1990) has already been discussed, and the implications of the two-step nature of self-concept change suggested by De La Ronde and Swann are striking. Through differing levels of interpretation of feedback, low self-esteem persons can minimize the positive impact of success information and maximize the negative impact of failure feedback. This suggests that an important part of self-esteem enhancement would involve controlling the extremity of the positive or negative information the low self-esteem persons are receiving. To the extent that the information is wildly discrepant from the individuals' self views, they will reject it because it threatens the stability of self. The goal with successful self-esteem enhancement, then, is to provide the persons with consistently more positive information, allowing them to slowly incorporate increasingly positive information into their self-concept. The old adage that "One must walk before one can run," therefore, seems extremely appropriate.

Heatherton and Ambady (1993) remind the reader that high self-esteem is not necessarily always a good thing. This point is well taken because it is often assumed that individuals with high self-esteem have everything going for them. If it is possible, however, to have too little of this thing called "self-esteem," then it must be possible to have too much of it as well. Individuals with high self-esteem set themselves up to have high demands placed on them. To the extent that they can achieve these high expectations, more may be expected in the future. This idea reinforces a point that has been made several times throughout this text. Realistic interpretations for success and failure are crucial if self-esteem is to be healthy, stable, and comfortable. Such a point becomes relevant, again, as self-esteem enhancement strategies are pondered. If too much emphasis is placed on getting the low self-esteem person to externalize failure and internalize success, the person still will not have a realistic picture of self. Individuals who have high self-esteem that is healthy understands that they are not perfect and that sometimes good things happen whether they deserve them or not, and sometimes bad things happen despite monumental efforts to avoid them.

Kernis (1993) suggests that simply knowing whether an individual suffers from low self-esteem is not enough to understand the impact that self-esteem level has on psychological functioning. According to this researcher, one must also address questions of the stability of self-esteem level to determine the ramifications of low self-esteem. Unstable self-esteem can be considered a detriment to a person with high self-esteem because it means that the individual has feelings of self-worth that are fragile. Unstable self-esteem for the individual with low self-esteem, however, may prove to be an advantage. This means that the individual is not completely committed to the negative impressions of self and might be more amenable to self-esteem enhancement. Osborne (1993b) has already suggested that self-esteem enhancement will only occur when the low self-esteem person begins to question the self-images he or she is using to define self. As such, part of self-esteem enhancement involves becoming less certain of one's negativity and, at the same time, allowing oneself the luxury of accepting positive information.

Pelham (1993) provides a helpful summary of the research assessing the extent to which depressed persons hold positive beliefs. Although it is tempting to assume that depressed persons hold only negative beliefs toward self, such has not proved to be the case. Depressed persons may admit at some level that they have positive feelings in one or a limited number of areas (e.g., Jones, 1973; Wills, 1981), yet research also reveals that these same persons tend not to report such feelings in spontaneous self-descriptions. The main point that Pelham wants to make is that "it may be instructive to remember that, like other painful experiences (e.g., divorce, dieting, dental work), depression may occasionally have positive consequences" (Pelham, 1993, p. 194).

Although this point relates specifically to depressed individuals, the same point has been made several times earlier in this text in connection with individuals suffering from low self-esteem. The critical point to bear in mind as one contemplates self-esteem enhancement strategies is that low self-esteem individuals have very good reasons for interpreting positive and negative information the way they do. Such interpretations of feedback are not necessarily designed to make the self feel worse, but rather to protect what little esteem the individuals may have left (Osborne, 1993b, 1993c; Pelham 1991a, 1993).

The information just provided builds a strong foundation for understanding self-esteem enhancement. It is critical to bear in mind that self-esteem enhancement will involve not only emotional changes to the self-concept but also fundamental changes in the self-images that individuals use and shifts in the manner in which they will define self. As the chapters of Baumeister's book suggest, self-esteem provides an interpretive framework through which the individual processes information about self, bases future expectations about self, and garners evaluative feelings about self. Any changes to the emotionally charged aspects of self (called self-esteem) will have profound implications for all other facets of self. It has been argued that individuals tend to interpret incoming feedback in a manner that is designed to perpetuate current self-views (e.g., De La Ronde & Swann, 1993; Osborne, 1993b, 1993c; Pelham, 1991a, 1993; Swann, 1983, 1987). Individuals have a lot invested in the strategies that they use to interpret self-related feedback. This illuminates one of the most important aspects of self-esteem enhancement. Self-esteem enhancement is extremely difficult. Individual have a lot to lose if their attempts to enhance self-esteem are not successful. In order to accomplish this enhancement, individuals will have to risk the only thing they have left of self that they feel has value—its predictability. With these warnings in mind, then, let us proceed with a discussion of self-esteem enhancement strategies.

ELEMENTS OF SUCCESSFUL SELF-ESTEEM ENHANCEMENT STRATEGIES

The points made at the end of the previous section are not meant to articulate a pessimistic notion that self-esteem enhancement is not possible. Rather, these points are made in an attempt to make sure that the reader understands that self-esteem enhancement is not easy. When it is clear what one is up against in terms of trying to transform one from a sufferer of low self-esteem into a person with high self-regard, a lot of foolish mistakes can be avoided. Any person who has ever known someone with low self-esteem has experienced the biting protectiveness that comes with it. Attempts to say something nice to a low self-esteem person may be violently rejected. Why is it that low self-esteem persons will adamantly resist one's efforts to provide them with positive feedback? It all boils down to a matter of self-protection. How does it feel when someone has a drastically different impression of our self than we have? It feels extremely uncomfortable, and it motivates us to behave in ways that try to bridge the gap between the image of self we had hoped to project and the image of our self that the other person seemed to have.

It works the same way with someone who has low self-esteem. Any discrepancy between the way an individual sees his own self and the perceptions that others hold toward that self is uncomfortable (e.g., Swann, Stein-Seroussi, & Giesler, 1992b). For protective reasons, the low self-esteem person wants to reduce or eliminate discrepancies between the way he sees his self and the way others perceive his self (e.g., Osborne, 1993b; Osborne & Stites, 1994; Tice, 1993). High self-esteem individuals must resist the temptation to assume that everyone would want to feel better about self regardless of the potential cost. When the person has only one or two stable aspects of self left to rely on, he would probably be extremely unwilling to take a gamble with those and risk losing them as well. The first time someone tries to say something nice to low self-esteem persons, they get defensive, nasty, or even brutal. Why respond this way when someone was just trying to help? Most likely the negative response on the part of the low self-esteem persons is a reaction to the threat that the positive information made toward their self. If individuals are internally motivated to be seen in predictable and consistent ways, then efforts to change self-esteem level may challenge the only thing relating to the self that individuals are sure about.

Telling low self-esteem persons that they are really worthy and great is the same as telling them that they were wrong even about their impressions of their self. Do you see the problem here? For perhaps a major portion of their life, the only thing they knew they could count on was their worthlessness, and now you are telling them that they couldn't even get that right. What is the answer? Should those who would like to help others with self-esteem deficits simply throw up their hands and walk away? Absolutely not. Self-esteem enhancement is not only possible but successful as well. It is, however, challenging. Individuals that want to change must come, at some point, to trust the feedback that others are providing. If the individuals do not trust that information, will not open themselves up to more accurate interpretations of feedback, or refuse to accept some responsibility for their successes as well as failures, then self-esteem enhancement strategies will not work.

AN EARTH-CORE MODEL OF SELF-ESTEEM

Figure 13.1 displays an earth-core model of self-esteem that is meant to illustrate the self-protective nature of self-esteem. The key to successful self-esteem enhancement lies within this protective sphere. Efforts to alter a person's self-esteem level will only be successful to the extent that this protective system can be defused or the patterns of self-protection can be turned against the person to motivate self-esteem change. The inner circle of this figure represents the core feelings of self-worth that an individual holds. The feelings associated with this inner core are not specific to any particular characteristic but are a combination of one's feelings about all facets of self. This global representation of self feelings is a sum of the positive and negative characteristics that one believes defines who one is. As mentioned earlier, this sum of self-oriented feelings creates "a relatively permanent positive or negative feeling about self that may become more or less positive or negative as individuals encounter successes and failures in their daily lives."

This definition of self-esteem, combined with the idea that individual characteristics and the positive and negative feelings associated with them can influence global feelings of self-worth, suggests that there are two self-esteem levels that need to be understood. This idea was implied with Figure 1.1 but needs to be further clarified at this time. Self-images have already been shown to influence behavioral choices. Then, as a function of the feedback that one receives about those behavioral choices, the behavior can become more or less likely in the future. If the individual interprets the feedback she is receiving as indicating a success, and she accepts responsibility for that success by interpreting the feedback in internal, stable, and global ways (e.g., Abramson, Seligsman, & Teasdale, 1978; Osborne & Stites, 1994), her self-esteem in the situation will be elevated.

But such interpretations also influence the degree to which the individual will incorporate that situational success into her global feelings of self-esteem. If, however, the person interprets the success as being due to external, temporary, or specific causes (e.g., Abramson, Seligsman, & Teasdale, 1978; Osborne & Stites, 1994), her situational self-esteem may be elevated but her global level of self-esteem will not be affected. The reverse can happen if the feedback is interpreted as indicating a failure. If the individual makes internal, stable, and global interpretations for that failure, it will impact both situational feelings of self-esteem and impressions of global self-worth. Should the person decide, however, that the failure was due to external, temporary, or specific causes, situational self-esteem may suffer, but global feelings of self-worth will remain relatively untouched.

In order to initiate self-esteem enhancement, then, one must understand not only the types of interpretations the individual is making for successes and failures but also the difference between situational and global self-esteem. Global or core self-esteem, as depicted in Figure 13.1, is extremely difficult to access because of the protective nature of self-esteem and the self system as a whole. Rather than try to engage in global self-esteem change, as might be one's inclination given the seriousness of a global self-esteem level that

FIGURE 13.1 Earth-Core Model of Self-Esteem

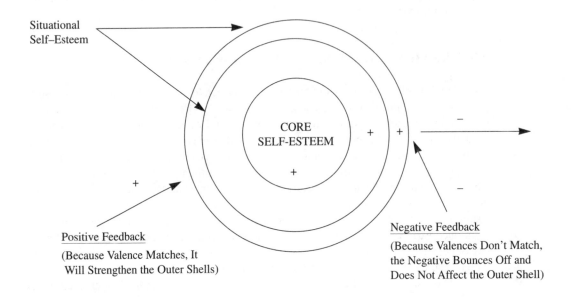

Situational
Self–Esteem

CORE
SELF-ESTEEM
+

+ +

–

–

+

Positive Feedback

(Because Valence Matches, It
Will Strengthen the Outer Shells)

Negative Feedback

(Because Valences Don't Match,
the Negative Bounces Off and
Does Not Affect the Outer Shell)

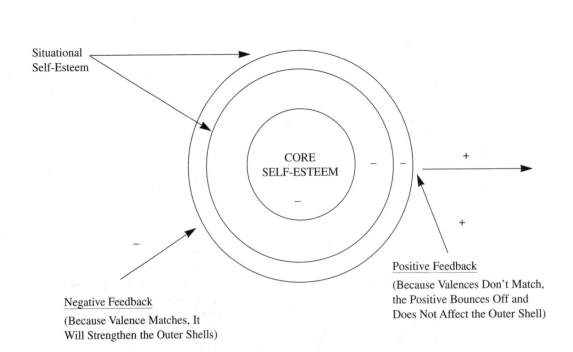

Situational
Self-Esteem

CORE
SELF-ESTEEM
–

– –

+

+

–

Negative Feedback

(Because Valence Matches, It
Will Strengthen the Outer Shells)

Positive Feedback

(Because Valences Don't Match,
the Positive Bounces Off and
Does Not Affect the Outer Shell)

is negative, the individual must create a pattern of self-esteem enhancement that is slow, steady, and predictable. A self-esteem enhancement strategy that will be successful is one that provides for the low self-esteem person the very things that are being threatened by positive information. If receiving positive information threatens the individual's self because it is too unpredictable, then only predictable positive information should be used. If the individual is resisting efforts by others to provide her with positive feedback, it may be because she feels that she is being put on a pedestal from which a fall would be devastating. This reaction, however, can be avoided if the individual takes smaller movements toward positive self-esteem.

Another important aspect of self-esteem enhancement is providing the individual with positive feedback that cannot simply be dismissed. If the person feels worthless and you tell her how nice her shoelaces look, this will probably have little impact on her global, inner feelings of self-worth. Does this mean that one should not compliment her on her shoelaces? Absolutely not. The point being made is that one cannot expect such minor compliments to turn around completely an ingrained pattern of misinterpretation of feedback tempered by a total lack of belief in anything positive that anyone ever directs toward the individual's self. It is entirely possible that the individual has used this pattern of misinterpretation of feedback to perpetuate low self-esteem for many years. If this is the case, how could one expect to turn that pattern around with one or two pieces of relatively unremarkable positive information?

Self-esteem enhancement is a time-consuming process because one must find some way to break through the outer protective shells individuals use to keep their inner core from being exposed. If an individual has learned throughout life that exposing one's self to others ends up in pain, then he will do everything possible to build a defensive structure that will minimize the likelihood that the self can be threatened by feedback from others. This also, however, makes self relatively impervious to one's own attempts to feel better about self. In order to access the core self-esteem that is hidden deep within, the individual must come to accept the information that he originally would have rejected. Low self-esteem persons tend to reject positive information because it is safer. But not all positive information will be rejected. As suggested by Spencer, Josephs, and Steele (1993), one possible method for helping individuals with low self-esteem would be to provide them with the resources they need to buffer themselves against negative information.

The resources referred to are prior positive experiences or other positive attributes. A low self-esteem person has little to fall back on when major self-attributes are called into question. Self-esteem enhancement, then, would depend on building a strong base of positive experiences that the individuals can then use to shield themselves against the negative. When the individuals understand that patterns of interpretation are affecting their self-esteem, this also will help to provide them with the foundation they need to begin accepting more positive information (e.g., Osborne, 1993d; Pelham, 1991a). In all of this, significant others take a support position in the enhancement process. Individuals who desire help with enhancing their own self-esteem will need encouragement to do so. They also will need occasional reminders about what to do and the moral support to get it done. To help them build their defenses, they must accept a lot of positive information. But positive information will only be accepted to the extent that the individuals believe the information is valid (e.g., Osborne, 1993d).

Before outlining the exact sequence involved in self-esteem enhancement, it would be beneficial to emphasize one more point about self-esteem that has already been implied. Many individuals assume that self-esteem is either negative (as bad as it can get) or positive (as good as it can get) and you are either on one end or the other or floating somewhere in between. This, however, is not the true nature of self-esteem. If it is the case that individuals value consistency and predictability in the way self is perceived, the self-uncertainty would feel worse than low self-esteem. This point about the individual wanting self to be perceived consistently has come up time and again throughout this text. Although repetition of this point may not seem absolutely necessary, the point is so critical for self-esteem enhancement that it is worth noting again.

If Joe believes that he is a worthless person and you tell him that he is wrong about that, you are threatening his self. Positive information will not push him directly toward positive self-esteem because he is not as far toward the negative end as he can get. Figure 13.2 contrasts the traditional view of the self-esteem continuum with a revised view to demonstrate the point that is being made. Low self-esteem should be visualized as being in the middle of the self-esteem continuum rather than the endpoint. Attempts to give low self-esteem persons positive feedback push them toward self-uncertainty by calling into question their views of self. Is it any wonder, then, that low self-esteem persons resist efforts to shove positive information down their throat? In order for self-esteem enhancement to work, however, low self-esteem persons must allow themselves to become self-uncertain. If the individuals are committed to taking steps toward self-esteem enhancement on their own, they are less likely to feel that they are being threatened or coerced, and self-esteem enhancement attempts are much more likely to be successful.

A STAIR-STEP APPROACH TO SELF-ESTEEM ENHANCEMENT

Remembering the old cliché that one must walk before one can run provides the right frame of orientation for dealing with self-esteem enhancement. Successful self-esteem enhancement will occur when the individuals lower their self-protective spheres and allow positive information to impact their self as strongly as the negative information has. Although this task will not be easy, the extent to which it is successful will set the tone for the entire self-esteem enhancement enterprise. What, then, does it take to get the individual to realize this and lower these shields? It takes a systematic destruction of the interpretive patterns that the person has used so successfully to perpetuate negative self-feelings. Osborne (1993) suggests that self-esteem enhancement requires eight steps.

1. The individuals must be made aware of the interpretive patterns they are using to perpetuate their negative self-views. Low self-esteem persons usually do not even realize that they are engaging in interpretive patterns that minimize successes and maximize failures. How, then, does one convince low self-esteem persons that they are perpetuating their own misery? Because the individuals may use this pattern so automatically, just pointing

FIGURE 13.2 Traditional vs. Revised Views of Self-Esteem

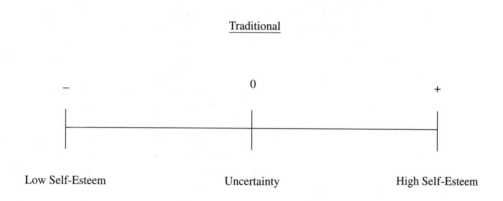

Traditional

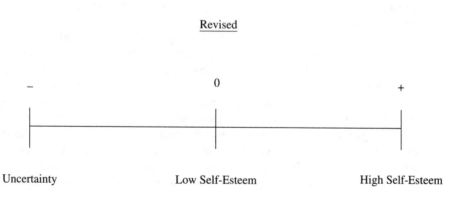

Revised

out verbally again and again that they are doing that may be quite eye opening for them. When realization sinks in, it is almost visible. This pattern of interpreting success and failure has become such a constant pattern in the individuals' life that they don't even know it is being done. Convincing them of this will not, in and of itself, alter the way the individuals feel toward self, but it is a significant first step in the right direction.

2. The persons must focus on at least one aspect of self that they feel positive about. Low self-esteem persons may not have a whole lot of positive things in their life to hold onto, but we all have at least one precious characteristic about self that we are extremely unwilling to give up (Pelham, 1993). The individuals must sift through their own efforts to

hide that characteristic and must draw it out into the open. Low self-esteem persons are extremely adept at making even their best attributes sound worthless or unimportant. Even if that attribute seems obvious to others, they may deny that they care about it. Why would they deny the importance of that characteristic to you? Because they are afraid that exposing the characteristic to you will make them vulnerable and that in some way they may lose that most precious thing. Low self-esteem persons usually turn to someone they trust before revealing that one positive attribute they believe they have.

3. Low self-esteem persons must believe that the positive characteristic discovered in step two is important and is their responsibility. Often low self-esteem persons will so adamantly resist others efforts to help them feel better that they will try to blame those other persons for whatever they can do well, or they will try to minimize the significance of what they can do. A student may feel worthless about all facets of her life and then she gets an "A" in a very hard class. She may try to minimize the impact of that "A" by saying that the test was easy, she got "lucky," "even the stupid get a break now and then," "the teacher likes me," and so on. Although it is obvious that she is doing this to minimize the potential risk to self that admitting positive information may lead to, self-esteem enhancement will only be successful when the individual is willing and able to take responsibility for both successes and failures. If individuals try to reject the seriousness of the positive characteristic, ask them why they are doing that. Don't allow them to blame you, the environment, or anyone else for the good things that occasionally happen to them. The only method by which the outer shells of negativity can be knocked down is by breaking or interrupting the pattern of misinterpretation of feedback the person has fallen into.

4. It should be kept in mind that knocking down these outer defenses will be a difficult task. Looking at Figure 13.1 suggests why this is the case. For persons with low self-esteem, the positive information is so different from what they are used to dealing with that they will reject it because it doesn't match what is known about self. Negative information, however, is readily accepted because it matches what is already known. The worst part about their willingness to incorporate the negative information readily is that it further strengthens the negative valence to these defenses, which makes it even more likely that future negative information will be accepted and future positive information will be rejected. If they admit that they have at least one self characteristic that is positive and that they are responsible for that characteristic, it provides them with one example of an appropriate interpretation for success.

5. It is critical to realize that individuals going through self-esteem change will throw a lot of garbage at people they care about. This is a disquieting but necessary part of the enhancement process. The individuals have learned not to trust anyone because trusting someone could possibly result in exposing their very fragile inner self. Anyone who sees them more positively than they see themselves may be perceived as a threat because it threatens self-stability (e.g., Osborne, 1993b). The individuals have learned across time that people who say or do nice things for them usually have some ulterior motive in mind. Such comments as "Why are you being nice to me?" or "What do hope to gain by lying and being nice to me?" will come flying from the mouth of the low self-esteem person. The consistency of the people that low self-esteem persons trust, then, will be critical to the enhancement process. Only through such consistency will a trusting relationship be established.

Once this relationship is in place, however, the low self-esteem persons are ready and willing to accept more positive views of self.

6. Successfully changing self-esteem will require knocking away the outer shells of the earth-core model, which in effect makes the person self-uncertain. The fact that self-uncertainty is uncomfortable has already been discussed. Large-scale attempts to alter self-views, therefore, will not work. Think about driving a car down the highway. Small pebbles and stones are sometimes deflected off the tires and bang against the undercarriage of the vehicle or against the windshield or sides of the car. Do these tiny pebbles ever knock the car off the road? No. Do they leave some evidence that they have been there? Yes. If you look closely at any car, you can see hundreds of tiny dents and scratches caused by these tiny projectiles. Think of positive feedback in the same manner and the trick to self-esteem enhancement becomes even more obvious. What would happen if a hundred different pebbles all slammed into the same part of the car? Major damage would eventually be done. This is exactly what needs to be done to the outer defenses of low self-esteem persons. Keep knocking away at those outer rings by hitting low self-esteem persons over the head with the one positive characteristic they admit to having. Little by little, they stop being so adamant about their worthlessness and willingly allow this one tiny piece of positive information through. Once this shell has been knocked down, the individuals are teetering on the edge of self-uncertainty because they have allowed themselves to admit that their self-esteem was not as negative and certain as they had thought.

7. It is important that the individuals quickly build upon this self-uncertainty and put forth the effort that minimizing success and maximizing failure requires. Invariably they will say that, given the chance, they wouldn't do such a thing. Once they are aware of their former methods of interpreting feedback to maintain low but predictable self-esteem, it will be difficult for them to use those old patterns again without realizing it. They must take responsibility at this point for their own self-esteem. They must decide if they are going to take the initiative and rebuild a self-esteem level that is positive, or if they are going to continue to wallow in self-pity and, therefore, never take any chances. They will try to reject what others are saying at this point because positive comments point out to them that they have been part of the cause of their own problems. Of course they are not solely responsible for their self-esteem being negative in the first place. But, through inappropriate patterns of interpretation for success and failure feedback, they did manage to guarantee that self-esteem would never get better.

8. At this point, the individuals will begin rebuilding their feelings and expectations about self. They will still continue to lean on significant others for support through this time of self-analysis. Many times the individuals will experience flashbacks of uncertainty and will need someone to provide them with a few words of encouragement. As the former low self-esteem persons rebuild self-esteem, they will come to realize that self-esteem is not just knowing what one is good at doing. Self-esteem means a healthy understanding of one's capabilities and limits. Self-esteem also means a truthful awareness of the fact that positive and negative things happen for both internal and external causes. If high self-esteem persons never admitted that failures were their fault, they would never be able to set knew goals and find realistic ways to work toward them. Likewise, constantly internalizing all successes may set up individuals for future letdown because a grandiose image of what they are capable of may result from this over-internalization of success.

The steps involved in self-esteem enhancement may sound easier than they actually are. Successful self-esteem enhancement depends on the individuals getting to a point in their understanding of self that they are willing to risk the only thing about self that they can depend on as being predictable and continuous. Self-esteem enhancement, therefore, will be neither easy nor rapid. One important key to the success of self-esteem enhancement strategies is remembering that for every aspect of self that the low self-esteem persons reject, they will need to discover within themselves a more positive aspect of self to hold onto. If they are being asked to reject a negative self-image, it must be replaced with a positive one. If this is not the case, they will not be willing to risk self by rejecting what little they do know about themselves.

WRAPPING IT UP: WHAT DOES ALL THIS MEAN?

The information provided in this chapter suggests that understanding self-esteem development plays a crucial role in understanding self-esteem enhancement. The developmental sequence that leads to the creation of self-concept and self-esteem puts the individual in a potentially unique bind. Since self-concept and self-esteem are both defensive structures, the very process that leads to their development can interfere with their enhancement or change. Self-esteem is not just a feeling toward the components of one's self, it is not just a compilation of the myriad of feelings one has that are associated with various self-images, and it is not simply a component of self-concept. Self-esteem serves as an information processing strategy that the individuals use to make their world more predictable. If that predictability means seeking out negative information, then the sense of control that comes with it is perceived by the individuals as more beneficial than the uncertainty that comes with accepting feedback that is discrepant with self-views.

Human beings find self-discrepancies to be very uncomfortable and are motivated to seek out and acquire information from others that is consistent with their own views of their self. For high self-esteem persons, this process is non-threatening, and the steady flow of positive feedback that comes in from others, or from the manner in which the individuals process that feedback, constantly reconfirms the positive feelings that are associated with self. Low self-esteem persons, however, find themselves in a position where positive feedback, because it is discrepant from self-views, is threatening. If the individuals interpret success feedback in such a way that they are admitting that they were responsible for that success, then self-consistency is threatened. In the end, the determining factor as to whether self-esteem enhancement will be successful is the extent to which the individuals believe that the potential benefit to be gained from allowing self to be called into question outweighs the potential cost to allowing the self's vulnerability to be exposed.

CHAPTER FOURTEEN

Applications of Self in Daily Life

A PERSONAL REFLECTION

I have learned so much about my own self as I have written the chapters in this text that I felt obligated (if not compelled) to share them with you, the reader. Although textbooks usually try to avoid personal reflections at all cost, I couldn't think of anything more appropriate for a book on self than giving you a feel for my own personal reflections on self. My toddler son is learning to name his body parts. I ask him to point to his ears and he does so with pride. He even stops and claps to congratulate himself each time that I praise him for a job well done. Yesterday (exactly eighteen months after his birth), I watched this interplay and thought about what it must be like to be him. When I think about this, I am usually struck by a profound awareness of my own self. It seems strange that watching this relatively common childhood interaction would initiate within me a profound sense of self-awareness, but it is true, nonetheless. My being a psychologist might explain part of the reason that such a simple interaction could seem more profound to me, but I think there is more to it than that. Each time Joseph names one of his body parts and feels pride for having done so, I wonder if he realizes that all of those parts combine into a greater whole called "self." Such situations also remind me of what Higgins, Vookles, and Tykocinski (1992) refer to as a "Gestalt perspective."

The Gestalt psychologists adopted use of the term Gestalt (which in German means a whole or form) to suggest that, at least in perception, the whole may be greater than the sum of its parts. I believe that this motto holds true for self-perception as well. As Joseph learns about the parts that make him up, he is bound to question who he is and know, at some level at least, that he is more than just a conglomeration of recognizable body parts. He can proudly point to himself when anyone asks "Where is Joseph?" but does he understand that he is fundamentally different from the person who is asking the question? Self-awareness develops gradually as the child learns to differentiate self from others and other objects in the social environment. As he begins to take pleasure in his accomplishments (as evidenced by his clapping for himself and smiling broadly when my wife and I get excited about his accomplishments), he is building self-esteem.

This awareness that his self-esteem is already beginning to form makes such interchanges between the two of us strike me as fundamentally important in his development. Self permeates every facet of our lives and isn't something that just comes and goes. We are not always aware of ourselves, but self is important in everything that we or others do. My self may not be called into question as things are running smoothly in my life, but I will become instantly aware of self if an obstacle is thrown in my path toward accomplishing my goals or if I succeed at some level that surpassed my own or others' expectations. Every interaction that we have with others, every behavior we choose or feel pressured to engage in, and every decision that we make or decide not to make can call our self into question or reconfirm it.

I see an eclectic approach to self at work within my son every day. From the way he approaches toys and objects and is amazed by his ability to cause an effect on them, to his fascination with his appearance in the mirror, I see his "self" growing to fruition. In all of his behaviors, I see a self developing and I am fearful of the responsibility I have for helping him to develop a self that is good and positive. Self is a developmental sequence that is further complicated by all the things that children must learn. Chapters One and Two focused a great deal on this developmental sequence and discussed some of the important ramifications of this developmental process as it is occurring. This chapter will focus on the ramifications of the entity called "self" once it is in place. It should be kept in mind that whenever an individual's sense of self is called into question, it is like going back to that point in childhood when our place in the world was not clear to us and we didn't know how to answer the question "Who am I?"

A very important thing to remember as this chapter addresses the applications of self to everyday life is that any attempts individuals make to define, refine, or redefine their sense of self will be met with some resistance by others within their social world. This resistance is not based on disapproval as much as it is based on the fact that our sense of self-stability is determined, in part, by the predictability of others in our social network. Such thoughts can be recognized in some of the things that individuals say in anger when others are not acting in a manner that is consistent with their past.

Statements such as "I don't know you anymore," or "You're sure not the same person I used to know and love," can be painful for the person they are leveled against, but they also reflect pain on the part of the individual saying them. When individuals try to redefine self, it calls the self of loved ones into question to the extent that part of their own self-definition is based on the self of others. If Jane's sense of self comes from her children needing her, she is going to feel lost and threatened if her children move away and seem to be branching out on their own. It is this interconnectedness among the selves of individuals that further complicates the self process. So, without further ado, this chapter will address the applications of self in daily life.

BACKGROUND INFORMATION

Part of the battle in understanding the applications of self in daily life revolves around remaining issues about what is meant by self. The eclectic approach as taken by this text places a high degree of importance on defining what is meant by self. Multiple factors have been said to influence this entity called self. This multifactorial approach, however, is not meant to give the impression that self is loosely constructed of barely tied together pieces. In fact, just the opposite seems to be true. Despite the myriad of factors, characteristics, and other individuals who strive to play a role in the person's self-definition, the self that results from the identity negotiation process is usually well articulated and tightly integrated. If this were not true of self, then the ups and downs that are part of daily life would have a much more dramatic impact on self and self-esteem than they usually do.

A self that is not well articulated or tightly integrated may make the individual particularly vulnerable to those very same daily ups and downs. Because self plays such a vital role in the daily functioning of the individual, it is very important that the impact of self on various aspects of daily life be considered. Many questions surround the role that self might play in the daily functioning of the individual. First, does the pattern of self-beliefs held by the individual impact functioning in daily life? This question centers on the fact that individuals may cluster or organize beliefs about self in a myriad of ways. Surely, the pattern adopted may impact the individual in a variety of ways. Second, what role do self-views play in the emotional and physical health of the individual? This question ponders the connection between states of mind (as represented in the self) and states of the body (as represented by physical health). Third, what role does self-esteem play in the overall wellness of the individual? This question is of critical importance because it focuses discussion on the interconnection between self-esteem and patterns of behavior by the individual that may impact overall wellness. Do low self-esteem individuals, for example, neglect other aspects of self and wellness more than do individuals with high self-esteem? Do high self-esteem individuals adopt a superhuman frame of mind that actually may lead them to take unnecessary risks?

Each of these questions will be addressed in the sections that follow. At each step of the way, however, the reader is encouraged to consider the overriding implications of daily life for an eclectic approach to self. Indeed, it seems difficult to imagine a theory of self being useful if it does not help one to understand the self in daily life or to recognize the impact of daily life on the self. If, as has already been suggested in this text (e.g., Chapter Thirteen), self-esteem can cure many of society's ills, an eclectic approach to self would be remiss if the interconnections between self and daily functioning (or dysfunction) were not understood.

SELF-BELIEF PATTERNS

Higgins, Vookles, and Tykocinski (1992) suggest that patterns of self-beliefs may have more psychological significance than the self-beliefs independently. This adoption of a Gestalt perspective further suggests that the interrelatedness among self-beliefs is more critical for understanding self than just knowing the self-beliefs the individual holds. Although this seems to make a great deal of sense, it is an important enough point to be rearticulated here. Individuals are more than just a conglomeration of self-beliefs, and the patterns of self-beliefs the individual holds are more important to self and behaviors than the individual elements (in isolation) would suggest. In order to test this assumption, Higgins, Vookles, and Tykocinski (1992) identified patterns of self-beliefs that contained an actual-self/ideal-self discrepancy and differed in how a third self-belief related to that actual/ideal discrepancy.

Their research identified and compared four self-belief patterns. The first pattern is described by the researchers as "doing less well than wished for but not less than expected." With this pattern, the individuals' ideal has not been reached, but minimum expectations for the actual self have not been violated either. The second pattern is described as, "chronically unfulfilled hopes." This represents individuals with a large discrepancy between ideal and actual selves. In addition to this, the individuals use the ideal self to define who they are. The individuals are matching what they can currently do but are constantly dissatisfied because what they cannot do represents hopes that cannot be fulfilled. The third pattern is defined as "fulfillment of one's limited potential." In this pattern the individuals' actual self matches expectations but is still perceived by the individuals as being less than the ideal. The individuals make small steps toward the ideal and realize they are making positive accomplishments, but these accomplishments fall short of the what the individuals perceive as their overall potential. The fourth pattern is described as "chronic failure to meet one's positive potential." Although this sounds similar to the second pattern, there is a significant difference. With this pattern the accomplishments do not even match the "can" self let alone come close to matching the ideal self.

As one might guess, Higgins, Vookles, and Tykocinski (1992) found different patterns of emotional and physical problems as a function of the patterns of self-beliefs just outlined. The patterns of "chronically unfulfilled hopes" and "chronic failure to meet one's positive potential" were associated with stronger degrees of suffering than the remaining patterns. In addition to the general findings that the chronic patterns predicted severity of suffering, each pattern predicted a slightly different pattern of suffering as well. Individuals who felt a chronic failure to meet positive potential were most likely to report feeling "listless," "non-driven," "unmotivated," and so forth. Those individuals who showed self-belief patterns associated with chronically unfulfilled hopes, however, were more likely to report feeling "discouraged," "hopeless," and "sad" (Higgins, Vookles, & Tykocinski, 1992).

This research is unique and of great importance to an eclectic approach to self because it suggests that self-beliefs, in and of themselves, do not determine the psychological impact on the individual. Actual/ideal self-discrepancies do not, alone, determine the suffering of the individual. When a third self-belief is added to the pattern, however, different patterns of suffering emerged. This lends credence to the hypothesis that self is multifaceted and, as such, is more complicated than each corresponding factor would suggest. Discrepancies between actual and ideal selves certainly can impact the individual, but the true degree of that impact can best be understood when other self-beliefs are added to the formula. Likewise, self can best be understood when the myriad of factors that influence its development are also understood.

SELF-PATTERNS IN EMOTIONAL AND PHYSICAL HEALTH

Higgins, Vookles, and Tykocinski (1992) provide evidence that suggests an interconnection between patterns of self-beliefs and emotional and physical health for the individual. Part of the impact that self has for the daily health of the individual comes from the fact that self is not a static construct. In other words, individuals do not view self as simply something that reflects who they are at the present. Self is dynamic and ever changing and, as such, it reflects who the individual was in the past, who the individual believes he or she is at the moment (the actual self), who the individual believes he or she could be (the can self), and who the individual (or significant others) ultimately would like the self to be (the ideal self). Discrepancies between these entities can create and foster different patterns of suffering for the individual and, as a consequence, can have profoundly different implications for the mental and physical health of the individual.

Higgins, Vookles, and Tykocinski (1992) conclude that the Gestalt motto that "the whole may be greater (or different) than the sum of its parts" can be applied to the impact of self-beliefs. By isolating self-belief patterns that contained a common self-discrepancy, these researchers could then determine what effect, if any, a third self-belief would have. This research strongly suggests that patterns of self-beliefs are better predictors of mental and physical health than just the positivity or negativity of independent beliefs. This approach envisions self-beliefs as becoming part of integrated patterns that are more impactful for the person than independent self-beliefs because these patterns may serve as knowledge structures through which the individual processes self-relevant information. As mentioned earlier in this text (e.g., Section Four), patterns of traits are more predictive of an individual's behavior than any single trait would be. The same is true for self-beliefs. The more interconnected the self-beliefs become, the more likely these constructs are to be used as cognitive structures for information processing. In fact, according to Higgins, Vookles, and Tykocinski (1992), self-beliefs can become so integrated that they operate like schemas (cognitive structures) and influence the motivational significance of psychological situations.

Because these patterns of self-beliefs can serve as knowledge structures for individuals, they are likely to influence the manner in which the individuals process self-relevant information. If the individual feels that the self-discrepancies between the actual and the ideal selves is likely to remain or get worse, then the impact on emotional health should be negative. If, however, the individual believes that the discrepancy is an isolated event or a temporary event, mental health should be fairly well insulated from any long-term negative impact from the discrepancy. Previous chapters in this text (e.g., Chapters Eight, Nine, and Ten) focused on the impact of self-knowledge. The manner in which individuals process information about self can have a profound impact on that self. Individuals who feel competent to face obstacles and overcome actual/ideal self-discrepancies would be much less likely to experience long-term negative effects from those discrepancies than would individuals who believe that overcoming those discrepancies would require monumental effort.

The concept of self-efficacy (Bandura, 1977) suggests that individuals differ in the extent to which they feel confident that they can perform the behaviors that certain situations are requiring. As one might guess, the individuals' confidence in their ability to engage in the behaviors that situations dictate could impact health related behaviors (e.g., O'Leary, 1985). If individuals believe that they play a role in their own health, then certainly they would be more likely to engage in health-related behaviors than would individuals who believed that they had no control over their health. If Rodney believes that health is all in the genes, then he is probably going to engage in fewer health related behaviors than Sydney, who believes that she is in control of her own health related destiny. Hofstetter, Sallis, and Hovell (1990) discovered that self-efficacy ratings of subjects resulted in a factor structure that "clearly reflects each behavioral domain." In other words, subjects' self-efficacy ratings clearly reflect their self-reports of behaviors in health related domains, including political self-efficacy, medical care self-efficacy, exercise self-efficacy, and diet self-efficacy. Clearly the beliefs individuals hold about their own role in their emotional and physical health relates to the very behaviors that, ultimately, may impact health in those areas. Individuals who believe that they can play a role in their own physical health tend to engage in behaviors that do, indeed, lead to healthier lives (e.g., Shunk & Carbonair, 1984).

SELF-ESTEEM AND WELLNESS

Shillingford and Shillingford-Mackin (1991) suggest that self-esteem and wellness are related, that self-esteem can enhance wellness, and that wellness programs can enhance self-esteem. Wellness for these researchers involves a concerted effort on the part of individuals to engage in a healthy lifestyle and strive to reach their unique potential. This, of course, relates directly to an understanding of how self applies to everyday life. If wellness can be enhanced through self-esteem programs (as Shillingford and Shillingford-Mackin suggest), then the connection between emotional and physical health is made even clearer. With supportive evidence from several successful school-based wellness programs at the elementary and college level, these researchers argue that a curriculum that integrates classroom teaching and physical education would greatly enhance children's self-images. This enhancement in self-image would channel directly into the eclectic theory of self outlined in Figure 12.1. As self-esteem becomes more positive, the individual would experience an increase in feelings of self-efficacy (e.g., Bandura, 1977). These increased feelings of self-efficacy also would lead to better health related behaviors as outlined by Hofstetter, Sallis, and Hovell (1990).

OTHER APPLICATIONS OF SELF TO EVERYDAY LIFE

It doesn't take a great deal of effort to discover the role that self plays in daily life. The self-related factors already presented in this text emphasize the importance of self for the individual's life. From the beginning of the self-development process, the individual is pushed and pulled by this entity called self. The significant others in a person's life all have a vested interest in how the person's self develops. Self is constantly a point of focus in childhood and is called into focus at any point in the individual's life when a major life event comes to pass. Graduating from high school makes salient all aspects of self, be they positive or negative. Individuals ponder their abilities and wonder if they are, indeed, "college material." As the monumental day called graduation draws ever closer, that inner voice becomes increasingly more insistent in wondering "What do you want to be when you grow up?" This voice, of course, also starts clamoring for attention as graduation day from college draws near, or as the individual considers marriage, having children, changing jobs, or going back to school. In each of these instances, the life change that is being considered calls all previous self-related choices into question.

Self-esteem also plays a role in motivating the individual to make certain behavioral choices and impacting how behavioral feedback is interpreted (e.g., Chapter Two). Low self-esteem persons tend to interpret failures as being due to internal, stable, and global factors and successes as being due to external, temporary, and specific factors (e.g., Osborne & Stites, 1994). Certainly, these patterns of interpretations, like patterns of self-beliefs as outlined by Higgins, Vookles, and Tykocinski (1992), perpetuate or amplify existing self-feelings. These feelings, then, also influence the future behavioral choices that the individual will make.

Individual differences in self (e.g., self-consciousness and self-monitoring) also have an impact on the daily life of the individual. These dimensions influence the manner in which individuals seek out, process, and interpret social and self-related information. These dimensions not only influence the interactions individuals will have with others in the social environment and the kinds of persons the individuals may seek out, but they also may play a role in the choices individuals will make. Young, Osborne, and Snyder (1994), for example, discovered a relationship between self-monitoring levels and the political choices that subjects made. In a review of the literature surrounding the self-monitoring construct, Snyder (1987) suggest that self-monitoring propensities play a role in individuals' decisions about dating partners, activity partners, product advertisements, coping with depression, product purchases, and jobs or careers.

An eclectic approach to self has, at a basic level, an understanding of the applications of self to daily life at its root. Referring to a self theory as an eclectic approach assumes that the resulting theory would have applicability and generalizability. Self theories, in the author's opinion, are only as useful as they are applicable. Self is evident in daily life, and to a certain extent daily life is geared toward self. Every time an individual performs an act, he or she will receive some kind of performance feedback, and that feedback inevitably will have importance for self. If Mary works very hard at her job but the boss never seems to notice, Mary may interpret that lack of interest as a signal that she is not doing enough or that her efforts don't matter. This may also influence her perceptions of how much she enjoys what she is doing. This in turn could impact Mary's feelings about herself because she may wonder why she keeps doing the same old job if she isn't good enough at it to get noticed. This cyclical nature of performance feedback flows directly into the self cycle as outlined in Figure 12.1.

Mark's boss always comments on his performance, but the feedback is always negative. When an individual receives performance feedback that is less than positive, the impact on self-esteem can be profound. When his ability is called into question, the resulting impact on self is not necessarily isolated. Depending on the patterns of interpretations that Mark is using for analyzing feedback, it could have a global impact on his self-esteem. When self-esteem becomes negative, all facets of the person's self and life can be affected. Mark may begin to question other abilities (even if those talents are not related to performance on the job). As already mentioned (e.g., Chapters Ten and Thirteen), negative self-esteem can perpetuate itself because the individual's expectations for future positive performance is diminished. Mark, then, may adopt a defeatist attitude that results in further negative performance feedback, and this will lower self-esteem even more.

Individuals are trained through socialization to adopt the normative standards of the culture. Individualistic cultures encourage (if not demand) adopting a strategy of "looking out for number one." Individuals in such cultures also perceive that they should be able to get by without help from others. If they are unable to get by without help, questions inevitably arise about what is wrong with them. A great deal of emphasis is placed on being successful, but success is defined in part by the culture. At the same time that individuals are being taught by society to take care of themselves, they are being told to fit the mold, be like everyone else, and not to stand out in a crowd. This double bind was discussed in Chapter Ten and was argued to have a profound impact on individuals and their daily life because it is impossible to fulfill both goals simultaneously. In essence, individuals must make a choice. This choice then will impact their behaviors, will influence the behavioral feedback they receive, and will impact the self of their significant others as well.

Self is evident in most things that individuals do. Although individuals do not spend a great deal of time thinking specifically about self (e.g., Csikzentmihalyi & Figurski, 1982), many events throughout the day impact self. The self becomes very relevant in daily life whenever the smooth workings of the day are challenged or when obstacles are thrown into the individual's path. Others also force self to become a salient part of daily life. If Walter's best friend walks up to him and yells "I thought we were friends. I can't believe you back-stabbed me like that," Walter's self-concept quickly becomes the focal point of his awareness. Suddenly all thought is directed toward that entity called self, and Walter may try to reconstruct his recent actions to determine what he might have done to offend his friend so deeply. Self-reflection impacts daily functioning. Walter, for example, may become so concerned about what has happened to his friend that he has a hard time concentrating, resulting in lowered performance at work.

WRAPPING IT UP: WHAT DOES ALL THIS MEAN?

The point underlying this discussion is the difficulty of establishing parameters delineating where self stops and everything else starts. Individuals cannot come into contact with each other and interact at anything beyond a rudimentary level without becoming self-aware. Once self-awareness has been initiated, then the characteristics of self will influence the images of self that individuals will project to others (e.g., reflected appraisals, discussed in Chapter Three), how the individuals' own behaviors will impact their perceptions of self (e.g., self-perception, outlined in Chapter Four), which people in the social world the individuals will choose to compare self to (e.g., social comparison processes, described in Chapter Five), the role that culture plays in the formation and maintenance of self-characteristics (e.g., culture and self, presented in Chapter Six), what needs and motives the individuals will strive to fulfill in social interactions (e.g., organismic approaches to self, discussed in Chapter Seven), the type of self-relevant feedback the individuals will seek (e.g., self-enhancement versus self-verification, outlined in Chapter Nine), and what individuals will notice about interaction partners (e.g., individual differences, detailed in Chapters Eleven and Twelve).

In essence, then, an eclectic approach to self is directed toward understanding how daily life influences the development, maintenance, and refinement of self, and how self impacts the individual's functioning, perceptions, and actions in daily life. Every factor that plays a role in defining self, then, would also be impacted by self. Culture places certain demands on the self of individuals within that culture. When individuals do not adhere to those normative standards, culture is threatened and the individuals are punished in some fashion. Laws exist to punish individuals whose patterns of behavior threaten the normative standards of the culture. If the self that has developed is deviant in some manner, the individual's daily functioning will be somehow impaired. Individuals with low self-esteem may, through their actions, perpetuate that misery. In a similar fashion, individuals who have developed a deviant set of self-characteristics will be held accountable for any violations of the normative standards of the macroculture (i.e., society) or the microculture (i.e., the family).

Further research needs to be devoted to delineating the interconnected nature of self and daily life. As suggested by Shillingford and Shillingford-Mackin (1991), this integration between self and daily life is important for understanding the relationship between self-esteem and wellness, as well as for being able to predict, control, treat, or even eliminate emotional and behavioral disorders in the school environment. It also stands to reason that self characteristics such as self-esteem, self-esteem certainty, individual motives and needs, and prior experiences will color the manner in which individuals process self-relevant and other types of social information. In the end, then, the manner in which individuals approach daily life is both a reflection of and a reflection upon self.

CHAPTER FIFTEEN

Applications of Self in Educational Settings

THE ROLE OF SCHOOLS

Few can deny the importance of schooling in the life of a child. Schools have been labeled the second most influential socialization agent in this country (Seifert & Hoffnung, 1994). Children over the age of five spend as many hours in the school environment as they do sleeping or being around the family. But what else contributes to the significant role that schools play in our children's lives? An understanding of the variety of factors that contribute to the impact that schools have on children will illuminate the role that an understanding of self and self theories will have in the educational setting. At least six reasons can be cited to explain the powerful effect that schools have on children.

First, academic success is considered an indicator on one's self-worth. Individuals who succeed academically often are considered more worthy, expected to be more successful, and given more opportunities for success than those who do not seem to perform as well in the academic setting. This text has already described the importance of expectations placed on individuals. To the extent that others expect individuals to succeed because they are seen as academically successful, self-fulfilling prophecies may ensue. Chapter Ten discussed this issue at great length and elaborated the methods by which individuals act in ways that are designed to confirm the expectations they hold for others. If Paul's teacher believes that he is and will be academically successful, she may interpret a low grade on Paul's part as being beyond Paul's control, due to an illness, or explainable in some fashion that does not call her assessment of Paul's ability into question. On the other hand, a teacher could have expectations that keep her from granting students success when they do earn it. If a teacher had the expectation that Paul would not be successful academically and he earned an "A," it might be written off by the teacher as an example of luck, an easy test, or even raise suspicions that Paul cheated.

Second, almost every child will go through some schooling and, therefore, be exposed to the school's influence. Few other social institutions will be attended by such a huge percentage of the population. For the most part, the only children that do not spend a good number of years in the school system are the home schooled. Because schools are such an important part of our society, they are expected (implicitly or explicitly) to help indoctrinate children with the norms and values of the society. Although the United States takes great efforts to separate issues of church and state, the fact that schools must go through accrediting processes guarantees that many of the values and attitudes of the culture will be reflected in the curriculum of those schools. Indeed, if a school was suspected of teaching values and attitudes that ran counter to societal views, parents and community leaders alike would be in an uproar.

Third and fourth, some behaviors are clearly expected, but other behaviors are clearly considered intolerable. An important part of what it means to be successful in school is to learn to follow directions, engage in conformative behaviors, obey the rules, and pay the price if rules are violated. Again, it is clear that the values of society will be reflected within the rules that students are asked to abide by.

Fifth, children are forced to interact with a diversity of other individuals. Children from fairly diverse backgrounds are put into the school environment and expected to get along. Many things may result from these forced interactions, including animosity, prejudice, discrimination, tolerance, acceptance, or goodwill. As children experience a diversity of other individuals, they learn something about themselves in return. The school setting provides individuals with a wealth of circumstances in which social comparisons (Chapter Five) can be made, provide a host of others off which reflected appraisals can be made (Chapter Three), and provide the types of success and failure feedback that can alter self-concept and self-esteem (e.g., Chapters One, Two, and Thirteen).

Sixth, schools play an important role in the socializing of children because of the number of hours they spend there. Because children spend so much time within its confines, the school system plays a critical role in the development of their talents, skills, flaws, biases, and misconceptions. An eclectic approach to self, of course, also addresses these issues. Understanding the applications of self in the educational environment, then, must also focus on these issues. The pages that follow in this chapter will look at how an understanding of self can be applied to the educational setting and address issues of how studying the educational system can provide insights into self and self-related issues.

ACADEMIC SUCCESS AND SELF-WORTH

Kelly (1971) uses the term "intuitive scientist" to describe human beings as rational information processing agents who seek out data that can be used to master both self and environment. Covington (1992) suggests that the notion of the intuitive scientist assumes that thoughts drive motivations and argues that three values are associated with the intuitive scientist's quest for mastery over self and environment: rationality, consistency of action, and accurate self-knowledge. The reader may recognize these terms as similar to ones that have been used many times throughout this text. These concepts are of global significance for an eclectic approach to self because they are at the very core of understanding self. Human beings pride themselves on being rational creatures, although we are not consistently rational. Nonetheless, rational thinking is considered a virtue in our society. Of even greater importance for understanding self, however, are the concepts of consistency of action and accurate self-knowledge.

The theme of consistency of action has appeared throughout this text whenever discussion turned toward the individual's need for predictability and self-consistency (e.g., Chapters One, Two, and Nine). Individuals sometimes choose their actions with the specific goal in mind of trying to confirm self. Likewise, individuals may interpret the actions of others in such a way as to maintain their own consistency of self-images. The goal of acquiring accurate self-knowledge has been a consistent theme in virtually every chapter of this text. Although it is certainly true that sometimes self-relevant choices are made with other goals than accuracy in mind (e.g., downward social comparisons as a method for enhancing self-esteem, discussed in Chapter Five), these are the exception and not the rule. More often than not, the social comparison choices individuals make, the motives that may underlie and therefore drive their behavior, and the manner in which self is manifested in everyday life will be a reflection of this underlying need for accurate information about self.

Covington (1992) described this view of the intuitive scientist as one in which the theorist believes that thoughts drive motivations. But certainly the opposite could be even more likely. If the individual values rationality, consistency of action, and accurate self-knowledge, then those values can become motives that may drive thoughts and alter or distort the individual's perceptions of success and failure. As outlined in Chapters Two and Thirteen, these patterns of interpretations for success and failure can have a profound impact on the individual's self-esteem and future behaviors the individual will choose to engage in. From this highlighted premise, then, Covington (1992) draws connections to the educational system that may provide critical information for understanding the impact that the school environment has on the child's self-worth and standards of excellence. Self-worth theory can be incorporated into the school environment to motivate students to strive toward excellence and accurately interpret successes and failures (Covington, 1992).

Self-acceptance in school comes from one's ability to achieve competitively. Students therefore may be motivated not to put forth effort toward success because, if they don't try, they can avoid the negative implications of failure. Covington describes this as "nothing ventured, nothing lost," and it may be a sad but true aspect of our educational system and school environment. Of course this is very consistent with the methods that low self-esteem individuals use to avoid feeling any worse than they already do. As described in Chapter Two, low self-esteem persons may sabotage their own performance because success may cause higher expectations to be placed on them. These high expectations place the low self-esteem persons in a particularly bad situation in which failure will hurt even more. To avoid this trap of escalating expectations, then, low self-esteem persons, or low self-esteem students, may simply refuse to try.

Self-worth theory has as its basic premise the assumption that "the protection of a sense of ability is the student's highest priority—higher sometimes even than good grades—so that students may handicap themselves by not studying because to try hard and fail anyway reflects poorly on their ability" (Covington, 1992, p. 17). This, of course, parallels the discussion of self-verification in Chapter Ten. When the individual's sense of self is threatened, the individual will adopt an information processing and behavioral strategy that is meant to reconfirm existing self-beliefs. Even if the feelings about self are negative, the individual will act in whatever way necessary to confirm them unless the individual is absolutely certain that success will follow effort. In the school environment, the same kind of cost-benefit analysis is being conducted by students on a daily basis. If the students are certain that hard work and effort will pay off with success, then energy will be expended. If, however, there is any significant danger that the effort will be followed by failure, the students will cease to expend the energy. In this fashion, failure can be dismissed as inevitable because "I don't care about school, so I didn't try."

If by some stroke of luck, however, students succeed even when no effort was put forth, they will be seen as extremely high in ability. This "defensive approach" to school serves the students well and may be a direct consequence of the manner in which our educational system has been structured. Although this suggests that America does, indeed, have a crisis in education, Covington (1992) makes several points that suggest a light at the end of this dark educational tunnel. According to Covington, this self-worth theory analysis of the educational system suggests that two areas traditionally cited as responsible for the decreasing educational performance of our children are, in fact, not responsible for the crisis. First, contrary to popular thinking, lower scores are not simply a reflection of a lack of motivation on the part of the students. As already suggested by this discussion, the students are motivated, but rather than being motivated to put forth effort, they are motivated to protect their self-esteem. Second, the self-worth theory suggests that the current crisis in the educational system is not just a matter of poor performance. Rather than seeing the lower achievement scores as the outcome of some greater societal deterioration, this suggests that lower achievement scores are merely a symptom of this crisis of motivation in schools. As Covington states it, "Once teachers alter the reasons that students learn, the symptoms should coincidentally disappear, like the breaking of a fever" (Covington, 1992, p. 17).

SOLVING THE CRISIS IN EDUCATION

Thousands of different programs could be proposed (and probably have been) for how to cure the educational crisis in this country. An eclectic approach to self, however, suggests that these attempts will be less than completely successful unless they address the issues of self that come into play in schools. Russell (1988) summarizes many of the current efforts to get the educational system back on track. Because most of these have been modestly successful at best, this text will not go into details about them. Following Russell's (1988) description of these techniques, however, it is apparent that most attempts to reform the educational system rely on a "more is better" philosophy. Most reform attempts, then, stress "more academic courses, more hours in school, more homework, more tests, more hurdles for prospective teachers, more units for graduation" (Russell, 1988, p. 4). Although these all sound like good starting points for reforming the system, they will be successful only if one extremely fundamental assumption is discovered to be accurate. If this assumption is not found to be accurate, then none of these techniques will work. The assumption underlying most contemporary efforts to reform the educational system is that the present educational system is basically a good and sound one.

If this assumption is not accurate, then other questions need to be asked about what may be the underlying flaws in the current system, how those flaws can be addressed, or the role that self-concept and self-esteem of students may play in the problem. Covington summarizes much of the motivation literature as it applies to issues of reforming the educational system and provides many insights that help to clarify further the role self plays in the educational setting. As already mentioned throughout this text, the motives or goals that individuals have or set are strong motivators on subsequent behavior. If children are coming into the school environment with motives or goals that run counter to those of education, then either the goals of education will have to be changed or those of the students. It is probably safe to assume that the goals of education will not be changed dramatically any time soon; therefore, emphasis should be placed on helping students to adopt motives and goals that more closely match those of the educational system. This should not strike anyone as particularly bothersome unless, of course, the individual believes that there is something fundamentally wrong with the goals of education.

How, then, do we help students to clarify their goals and match student goals to the goals that underlie education? Covington suggested Maslow's hierarchy of needs (1970) as one plausible step in bringing students' and teachers' goals into harmony. Maslow's theory proposed that human beings are driven to satisfy a hierarchical set of needs: (1) physiological needs, such as the need for food or water; (2) safety or security needs, including the need to feel safe in one's environment and have shelter; (3) social or belongingness needs, including a need to be a part of something or belong; (4) esteem needs, which include the need to feel competent and be respected by others; and (5) self-actualization, which is the need to reach one's unique potential. Note that Maslow used the term "hierarchy" to describe how these needs are arranged. As with any hierarchy, the lower level needs must be satisfied before one will expend the effort required to strive to fulfill the higher order needs.

As can be seen in Figure 15.1, individuals will move up and down this hierarchy as needs arise. One may be able to satisfy many of the lower order needs and, therefore, begin to focus on asking questions such as "Who am I in relation to who I am supposed to be?" "What was I placed on this earth to do?" and "Am I doing the best job I can at what I'm doing?" As one might guess, however, this kind of self-actualization contemplation is not a luxury that all persons can afford. Dorothea Dix has been quoted as saying "Nobody wants to kiss when they are hungry." Although this quote certainly predates Maslow's theory, the sentiment is appropriate. Maslow's theory suggests that individuals prioritize their needs and will be motivated to fulfill higher order needs only to the extent that the lower order needs are satisfied. Thus, the more affluent in our society and the ones who have enough of the basic things needed for survival will be the ones most likely to be able to work on satisfying the higher order needs.

Covington (1992) suggests that educators can use Maslow's theory to create a school environment that fosters striving toward more appropriate goals and allows students the freedom to focus on their higher order needs. The challenge, then, is to alter the school environment so that students can focus on becoming self-actualized rather than on beating others. When the emphasis is constantly on competition and winning, there must, by definition, be a loser. Because the students are so concerned with making sure that they are not the "losers," they adopt self-protective strategies that encourage lack of effort and minimal per-

FIGURE 15.1

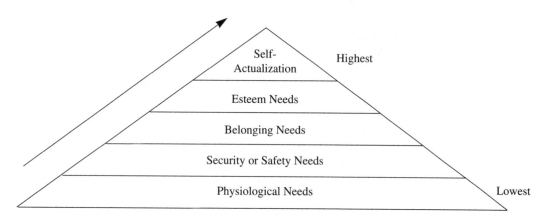

Note: The needs are arranged in a hierarchy with the lower-order needs (physiological, safety, etc.) being satisfied before the higher-order needs. If the lower-order needs are deficient, they will become the motivators behind the individual's behavior. Only if these lower-order needs are satisfied will a person be motivated to fulfill higher-order needs.

formance. Any attempt to incorporate this intriguing idea into the educational system or the societal mentality, however, will have to address the problem of getting individuals who do not have their basic needs satisfied to focus on the higher order need of self-actualization. Although Covington did not address this issue, it is a critical one if some version of Maslow's theory is to be used successfully in initiating educational reform.

Covington (1992) suggests that progress in changing the mentality of the students could be achieved by changing their focus from extrinsic to intrinsic motivation. This, of course, ties into Maslow's hierarchy of needs because some motives (such as the need for self-esteem) are partially dependent on external resources, whereas others (such as fulfilling one's unique potential) may be more intrinsic in nature. An educational environment that stresses competency and higher order goals will pull attention away from the goals of competition and "beating others." If students are encouraged to do their best, then beating others becomes less relevant. A word of caution is in order, however, if this is to be successful. Telling a child to "do your best" can be very problematic if the child assumes that that means "be perfect." "Best" is a word that needs to be defined and separated from other terms such as "success" and "failure."

Other efforts have been centered on establishing more success in the classroom by enhancing student self-esteem. One such program, the Mind Fitness Program for Esteem and Excellence, was created by Caron Goode and Joy Lehni Watson (1992). This program follows the basic philosophy that effective learners must be able to construct knowledge for themselves. Bringing students to a point from which they can construct knowledge, however, requires that the students believe they are competent and capable of playing such an active role in the educational environment. An eclectic approach to self assumes that individuals play a role in developing their own self and that the self being developed also impacts other areas of the individual's life. Individuals who have high self-esteem and trust in their own competencies may approach the educational environment with more of a "take charge" attitude. Students who do not feel competent and capable or do not understand the skills that are required to gain competency may develop a "learned helplessness" attitude toward education. This relates to Covington's description of the student who feels that effort will not be rewarded with success or fears the consequences if the effort does not pay off. In this fashion, the individual may avoid effort rather than risk the embarrassment and ridicule of working hard and "failing."

Goode and Watson (1992) propose four goals that they believe can accomplish the mission of helping students to achieve the skills necessary for academic excellence and discovering their human potential. These goals include fostering and promoting self-esteem, encouraging and training for optimal learning, inspiring attitudes of excellence, and promoting positive and productive actions. In order to accomplish these goals, the Mind Fitness program organizes lessons into four basic units: self-worth, self and relationships, self and environment, and self-discovery (Goode and Watson, 1992). The driving force behind this approach is the assumption that feelings of self-esteem or self-worth are a necessary precursor for helping the student strive toward excellence. Excellence, as is consistent with the themes of this eclectic approach, means doing your best. It should never be assumed that anything less than complete success is considered a failure, although some students and parents seem to make this assumption. Students are encouraged to discover their talents and understand and control their emotions so they are free to be creative and strive toward personal goals.

Chapters Three and Seven of this text stressed the importance of understanding the relationship between individuals' motives and goals and their self-esteem. The same can be said of the classroom. Students who feel that they are being asked to do things for reasons external to themselves may not feel ownership for the material and, therefore, may not feel compelled to strive to perform at their highest possible level. Goode and Watson (1992) urge teachers to allow students to articulate their goals and motivations and integrate those individual needs into the educational environment. Of course all of this may be easier said than done, but Covington's comments as well as the information provided by Goode and Watson strongly suggest that the outcome will be more than worth the effort. The discussion of interpretations for success and failure in Chapter Two of this text also suggest that individuals who do not feel competent and have low self-esteem may not be willing to try new things or put forth effort because they do not feel those efforts will pay off. In this manner, these individuals are quite vulnerable about self and are unwilling to risk any further damage to self by trying something that might lead to failure.

In order to get individuals (or students) to believe that effort is in and of itself a success, the individuals must be ready to engage in appropriate interpretations for success and failure. In this fashion, self-esteem enhancement strategies or educational and curricular programs that foster and promote self-worth may provide the students with opportunities to try things simply because they seem interesting, without fear of the implications of failure. If the students feel capable of constructing knowledge and have the skills to analyze and solve problems, they may approach the educational environment with a more positive outlook and may perpetuate their own success, rather than initiating their own failure. As mentioned in Chapters One, Two, and Ten of this text, individuals who feel incompetent are less likely to put forth the effort that success would require and are more likely to engage in actions and thoughts that confirm the negative expectancies they hold about their self.

Isser and Schwartz (1985) suggest that developing and encouraging individual competencies may be one successful weapon schools can use to combat the lower self-esteem of minority students. Educational and curricular programs that promote group standards run the risk of damaging the self-esteem of minority students if those standards are created from the normative beliefs of a white middle-class mentality. Programs and methods such as those suggested by Covington, Goode and Watson or the previous fourteen chapters of this text that stress the importance of self-esteem, individual motives and goals, and taking ownership for education, all promote excellence based on individual standards. This is not to say that students can decide what they believe merits an "A," but it does stress the fact that not all students are good at, or even interested in, the same things. Students who are average in math but excellent in history should be praised as much as students who are great in science but not so hot in art.

Excellence, therefore, does not mean perfection. Helping students to believe that they can be successful without expecting perfection relieves a lot of the stress students may be feeling. As Virginia Dickens (1992) suggests in her foreword to Jones's (1992) text on enhancing self-concepts of handicapped students, "We have long been aware that unless we, to some degree, appreciate and understand ourselves, it is most difficult to relate to the world around us." This sentiment, of course, can be applied to understanding and relating to the other individuals in the world around us as well. Helping students to discover who they are and appreciate that uniqueness also fosters an acceptability of others and their individual uniqueness. When this appreciation of others is in place, individuals may be less fearful of putting forth effort because they are accountable more to their individual standards than the standards of others. All of this, of course, could be suggested as only being possible in a perfect world. But self-esteem enhancement and stressing individual competencies and standards do not require a perfect world to be successful. However, they do require alternative teaching methods and commitment from faculty members (Goode & Watson, 1992).

Jones (1992) suggests that increasing the achievement of students with mild disabilities (including the learning disabled, mildly mentally retarded, and behavior disordered) may be directly linked to enhancing self-concepts. Jones (1992) also suggests assessment and program planning techniques as well as developing strategies that educators can use to encourage positive images of the body, the social self, the emotional self, and the cognitive self as well as a positive overall self-concept. Although a summary of these curricular strategies is beyond the scope of this text, they do suggest the importance of incorporating an understanding of self in the educational environment as a tool for enhancing student outcomes and achievement.

Schunk and Meece (1992) provide an edited volume addressing issues of student perceptions in the classroom. This text stresses the importance of both teacher and student expectations for performance on actual performance as well as the influence of peers, gender, and perceptions of efficacy of student achievement. Zimmerman and Schunk (1989) provide an edited volume stressing the connection between self-regulated learning and academic achievement. Echoing the sentiments of Covington (1992), Goode and Watson (1992), Dickens (1992), and Jones (1992), Zimmerman (1989) states, "contributors to this volume share a belief that students' perceptions of themselves as learners and their use of various process-es to regulate their learning are critical factors in analyses of academic achievement." Self-regulated learning may best be described as a process of working with students to discover their motives and goals. It encourages an educational environment that has expected out-comes but that also provides multiple paths by which those outcomes can be achieved. This allows students to work at individual paces, and encourages additional work in areas in which students need particular enhancement (e.g., Zimmerman & Schunk, 1989).

A SOCIAL-COGNITIVE VIEW OF SELF-REGULATED LEARNING

Schunk (1989a) draws a connection between Bandura's (1986) social-cognitive learning theory and student perceptions and learning in the educational environment. Bandura's (1986) theory suggests that human information processing consists of the reciprocal influ-ence of cognitive/personal factors, environmental variables, and behaviors. According to this view, only understanding the mutual influence of all three factors allows one access to the complexities of human information processing. Also of great importance, howev-er, according to Schunk (1989a) is Bandura's notion of perceived self-efficacy. Perceived self-efficacy reflects the individual's belief that he or she possesses the skills or capabil-ities necessary to carry out the actions that are required for success in a given situation. Schunk (1989b) showed that students' self-efficacy beliefs influence a host of achieve-ment oriented behaviors, including persistence, skills acquisition, choice of task, and amount of effort expended.

Noting the effects of perceived self-efficacy on achievement related behaviors, then, is similar to the discussion of self-fulfilling prophecies in Chapter Ten. If students believe that their efforts will not be successful, they will become less likely to expend that effort. This, of course, also parallels Covington's (1992) suggestion that students may cease to put forth effort if failure will hold significant consequences. Other individuals, however, may turn to students' perceptions of their own abilities to make judgments about those students as well. If Kathy continues to provide information about herself that suggests she feels worthless, other individuals may assume that she must know herself and, therefore, maybe she is worthless. This pattern is definitely disturbing, but it also makes perfect sense. Impres-sion formation and making attributions of others is an effortful process (e.g., Bargh & Thein, 1985; Gilbert, Pelham, & Krull, 1988). Given this fact, it seems reasonable that individu-als might accept, without much question, the feedback others are providing about their self. If Jarred tells me that he is worthless, why would I bother to gather the information that would be needed to discover if he is correct?

A negative-expectancy cycle can quickly be established if the teacher accepts the stu-dents' perceptions of their own ability. If the teacher then (possibly through the use of self-fulfilling prophecies as described in Chapter Ten) acts in a manner that reconfirms the children's own expectations, the children's feelings of self-efficacy are diminished. Schunk (1989a) suggests that self-regulated learning may be especially useful and successful because it engages students in enactive learning and not just vicarious learning (e.g., Bandura, 1986). Students, like tennis players or gourmet chefs, cannot acquire competency in all the fine nuances that success requires simply by observing the actions of others. Teachers who adopt a "do as I do" philosophy are not allowing students the maximum benefit that comes from interacting with the material and receiving corrective feedback.

As Schunk points out, the social-cognitive view of learning is fundamentally different from traditional views because it assumes that simple reinforcement and punishment do not account for all behavioral changes. In this view, individuals learn from the consequences of their actions, and these actions affect the cognitions they have (or the way they process information about) those behaviors. These behavioral consequences, then, are assumed to serve as sources of both information and motivation for the individual. As already suggested in this text, the motives and needs of individuals can strongly influence their behavioral choices and, thus, impact their perceptions of self and future expectations for that self.

According to Schunk (1989a), the social-cognitive perspective views self-regulation as a consequence of three underlying processes: self-observation, self-judgment, and self-reaction (e.g., Kanfer & Gaelick, 1986). Schunk stresses the interrelated nature of these subprocesses by stating "These subprocesses are not mutually exclusive but rather interact with one another. While observing aspects of one's own behavior, one may judge them against standards and react positively or negatively. One's evaluations and reactions, then, set the stage for additional observations, either of the same behavioral aspects or others" (Schunk, 1989a, p. 88). The classroom environment, then, that will most successfully use self-regulation as a method for enhancing student self-concepts and academic achievement must help students to articulate their beliefs (including both learning goals and self-efficacy) as well as promote the self-regulatory subprocesses as suggested by the social-cognitive theory (Schunk, 1989a).

ASSESSMENT AND OTHER ISSUES OF SELF

Assessment is gaining increasing attention and considered to be of increasing importance in education. Programs that promote self-regulated learning and other attempts to alter the traditional educational format must have assessment policies and procedures in place before they are instituted within the curriculum. Schunk (1989a) argues that "people cannot regulate their own actions if they are not fully aware of them." It is important to note that Schunk suggests that assessment of self-regulated student learning should not be limited to assessment of student outcomes. Students also must be encouraged to assess their own work on quality, quantity, originality, and rate of self-regulated behaviors. In this fashion, both teacher and student are involved in assessment and play a role in defining the criteria that will be used to make assessment decisions. Although some teachers may cringe at the thought of giving that much control to the student, it is important to remember that the teacher is the one who defines the parameters and minimum expectations for performance.

Schunk (1989a) reminds the reader that there is a difference between absolute and normative standards. Standards that are defined numerically are usually absolute standards, such as expecting students to complete six math problems in twenty minutes. Normative standards may not be quite as easy to define. The discussion of social comparison theory in Chapter Six stressed the importance that individuals place on normative standards. Students and teachers alike may make judgments about other students based on such normative comparisons as who finished the work first or if the teacher looked at the work and said "Good" without actually having graded it. Consistent with organismic approaches to self as outlined in Chapter Seven, standards motivate individuals by allowing comparisons to set goals and provide information about the student's progress toward the goal. Schunk (1987) suggests that normative goals may promote the kind of self-efficacy that Covington (1992) and others have suggested is important to student achievement in educational settings. If students compare themselves to similar others and discover that these individuals were successful, it can promote self-efficacy because the student can say, "If Helen can do this, and she and I are so much alike, I can do this too."

But normative standards (just like social comparisons) can be detrimental if the student makes comparisons to inappropriate targets. If Aaron constantly compares himself to the brightest student in the class, his average performance will seem comparatively worse than if he chose to compare himself to others more like him. That's not to say that Aaron couldn't or shouldn't use the brighter student as a target for ideal comparisons, but comparisons that are used for day to day evaluations of performance (in order to keep them from impacting negatively on self-esteem and possibly reducing future effort) should be made to similar comparison others. As already mentioned in this text (and included in Schunk's 1989a discussion of self-regulated learning), Weiner (1985) suggests that the perceived causes of successes and failures can have a dramatic impact on performance expectancies (what the students believe will be the outcome of their performance), behaviors (what the students choose to do), and emotional reactions (how the students respond to or feel about the actual performance when it is carried out).

The concept of self-regulated learning and related issues (such as self-determination, self-efficacy, and intrinsic motivation) have profound implications for students and the overall functioning of the education system. But one must resist the temptation to assume that self-regulation, self-determination, self-efficacy, and intrinsic motives will drive all students to perform in the same fashion or even value the same outcomes. Although a discussion of all these issues is beyond the scope of this text, mention should be made of a few of the notable works that students may want to consider for further information gathering. In a comprehensive text on the education of self, the media, and popular culture, Schostak (1993) discusses the changing nature of self and the changing roles of the media, family, and the culture as the individual grows and matures. Senese (1991) analyzes self-determination and the social education of Native Americans. At issue are questions of the impact of self-determination on school reform and where self-determination should come from. Yates (1982) addresses the issues of self-concept and other variables to the work value orientation of inner-city, African-American, female students. These issues remind the reader that a myriad of variables, besides just the curricular framework of a particular school, can effect not only the philosophy of the educational system but also the motives and needs that may drive the students' educational choices.

WRAPPING IT UP: WHAT DOES ALL THIS MEAN?

This chapter does not attempt an exhaustive or even comprehensive analysis of the variables that influence the relationships between self and the educational curriculum. This chapter does, however, attempt to introduce the concept of integrating the self-literature into the educational system and addresses a couple of suggestions as to how information within this text could be used to make curricular adjustments that foster students' self-determination and ownership for their education. A recurring theme throughout this text has been the importance of feelings of self-efficacy, that one is an entity capable of actions, and that those actions have consequences. If one loses this sense of self-efficacy, negative moods such as learned helplessness, low self-esteem, or even depression could result. Students who have been taught (implicitly or explicitly) that effort is rewarding only if it results in success may come to be unwilling to put forth that effort because of the inherent risk involved (e.g., Covington, 1992).

Students who are allowed to express their learning goals and motives may be more willing to put forth the effort that success would require because they can immediately see the relevance of what they are doing. If students ask a teacher "Why do I need to know this?" they deserve an answer. Putting expectations upon our students is not, in and of itself, a bad thing. These expectations, however, can be very detrimental if students are not provided either a motivation for achieving that level of performance or a path by which that success can be attained. Many implicit assumptions are made by parents, educators, and administrators about how and why children should be taught the particular things they are. Certainly guidelines are needed to ensure some uniformity of learning by students, but allowing students the freedom to set some of their own goals promotes a sense of ownership that makes learning something the student is willing to invest in.

From the moment the child is born, older children and adults are providing nearly constant feedback about expectations, duties, and correct and incorrect ways to do things. In the March 1994 issue of *The Atlantic Monthly*, Bruno Bettelheim suggests that children are even restricted from playing with toys in a fashion that would maximize their ability to learn from play. Children acquire many skills and advantages from playing (including but not limited to expression of thoughts, expression of feelings, problem solving, and the complex notions of past, present, and future). Left to their own devices, most children will develop these skills with little effort. If, however, playtime becomes another time of explanation and correction, the spontaneity and magnitude of learning is lost. Parents who constantly correct a child for using a toy remote control as a car on the carpet are thwarting the child's imagination more than they are helping the child to create and refine schemas. In this fashion, the parents are taking the initiative in determining what the child will learn from that play. A more self-directed approach to play (and to learning) allows the child (within reason) to decide how each toy will be played with.

David Elkind (1981, 1986) suggests that applying educational programs designed for school-age children to younger children may be doing a disservice to the younger children. Because young children often learn so differently from older children, the methods that work when they are eight years old may not work in Kindergarten. Elkind probably sums it up best by arguing that successful educators must adapt the educational setting to the different learning modes of younger children. If younger children are taught using the same methods and same expectations as older children, issues of self-perceptions and self-esteem become very relevant. Feelings of self-efficacy are so crucial to the early development of the child that learning environments which stress the skills that children are most successful with will promote feelings of positive belief expectancies, stable self-concept, and positive self-esteem. A major implication in this text is that enhancing self-esteem can have a profound impact on many facets of the individual's life. To a high degree, positive self-esteem keeps many of these other issues (e.g., learned helplessness, negative belief expectancies, lack of effort, fear of success and failure) from becoming relevant. In the end, then, we may discover that self-esteem is the most significant vaccine for curing not only society's ills (California Task Force to Promote Self-Esteem and Personal and Social Responsibility, 1990), but also many of the ailments within the educational system as well.

A Few Final Mental Morsels

WHERE HAS ALL THIS TAKEN US?

As this text comes to a close, I feel compelled to add a few final thoughts. Perhaps this need is more a matter of not wanting to let go than anything else, but I feel that some closure is needed. One is not given a lot of room in a textbook to "chat" with the reader, although that is the writing style that I hope I have used successfully within this text. I believe I know my own self a little better having written these chapters, and a few main points stand out in my mind as being particularly poignant. As the pages of this text come to a close, I'd like you to ponder these issues with me. An awareness of these points summarizes, in essence, my eclectic approach to self.

After fifteen chapters summarizing many aspects of the self literature and trying to integrate the sometimes complex theories of others, it seems fitting to provide a brief summary of the smorgasbord that has been put before us. Many key thoughts have been articulated on these pages and within the theories of the individuals cited herein. The reader may have felt that too many things were labeled as "fundamental," "critical," "significant," "paramount," and "far reaching," but such is the case with the topic. Few would disagree that self is one of the foundations on which social interactions are built. Many successful contemporary social psychology textbooks (including but not limited to Brehm & Kassin, 1993; Deaux, Dane, & Wrightsman, 1993; Aronson, Wilson, & Akert, 1994) now present an understanding of self as an issue that should be discussed prior to or simultaneously with discussions of understanding others.

Feelings about self have an impact on aspects of individuals' social functioning, including (but not limited to) their perceptions of self (e.g., reflected appraisals, discussed in Chapter Three, or self-perception, outlined in Chapter Four), choices about toward whom self comparisons should be made (e.g., social comparison, outlined in Chapter Five), how one fits into the culture (e.g., culture and self, discussed in Chapter Six), serving as a basis against which others will be compared (e.g., the self-reference effect, covered in Chapter Eight), or the manner in which expectations may lead to confirming behaviors (e.g., self-fulfilling prophecies, presented in Chapter Ten).

As the chapters have unfolded in this text, the reader has moved from global chapters discussing the myriad of factors that influence the development of self (Chapter One) and chapters covering specific issues such as when individuals will choose to enhance their impressions of self or verify existing impressions, be they positive or negative (Chapter Nine), to more applied chapters focusing on how the eclectic approach to self could be used to better the lives of others (Chapters Fourteen and Fifteen). The reader has now come full circle. If one were asked to present the eclectic theory to someone else, could it be done? The answer is probably an uncertain "Maybe" or even a more honest "I don't know." The eclectic approach outlined in this text is not something that can easily be summarized with a few leading questions or boxes on a flow chart. The very nature of an eclectic approach suggests that self and all its subtle nuances are not that simple. Self is a dynamic, ever-changing entity. Individuals have a core that adequately defines who they are regardless of who is asking, when they are being asked, or how the questions are phrased. But self also includes the fluid, dynamic aspects that change as often as moods or the other persons present.

If Jerry teaches for a living, is he the same person at home that he is in the classroom? The question may not be as easy to answer as one might first think. Many people automatically think "No" when they read the question. This, of course, is based on the intuitive notion that people put on different hats in different situations because each situation places unique demands on the person. Certainly, this is true. But Jerry may have a specific number of reasons why he became a teacher in the first place, and surely these reasons reflect a more fundamental underlying philosophy that colors other things he does. If he believes in being stern and strict at home, will he run an open and permissive classroom? Probably not. Individuals have characteristic values, beliefs, attitudes, and philosophies that are born out of what it was like to grow up being them. These characteristics permeate most aspects of the self that has developed across time.

SELF DEVELOPS AND CHANGES ACROSS THE LIFE SPAN

Many references have been made in this text to a developmental sequence in self. Perhaps it would be more appropriate to discuss a "life span approach to self." Just as the developmental literature (and the corresponding textbooks on the market) have moved toward a fundamental emphasis on a life span approach to development, so, too, should the self literature address the issue of how and why self changes across time. Markus and Wurf (1987) refer to the "dynamic" self-concept to emphasize the fluid and changing nature of the self. Should it really be that difficult to reconcile the fact that self is both static and dynamic at the same time? Several chapters in this text have made the point that individuals are motivated to maintain current self-conceptions, almost at any cost. At the same time, however, individuals are trying on new hats, adopting new roles, and forcibly altering self to adjust to the demands of other persons and other situations. Perhaps we could be said to truly have an "identity" once we come to realize and accept the fact that we are both driven by the desire to change and held back by the fear of it.

I was watching my son the other day and marvelling at his mastery of the English language. I realized while watching and listening to him that his word choices sometimes very clearly indicate his way of thinking. He willingly repeats (many times ad nauseam) "Mommy" and "Daddy" to any who care to listen. I ask him "Where is your daddy?" and he will proudly point to me. I then ask him "Where is Joseph?" and he will proudly point to himself. His understanding of his self as an entity, however, becomes more apparent if the questions are asked in a slightly different manner. Rather than asking "Where is Joseph?" I asked him "Who is Joseph?" His response was incredible. He simply pointed to himself and said "Me."

Although any non-parent reading this might question if I have enough work to do if I sit around and ponder my child's use of personal pronouns, the implications for his developing sense of self are profound. The phrasing of the question "Where is someone?" indicates that the questioner is interested in that person's location in physical space. To this end, my son points to the person as if to indicate geographic location. When the wording of the question, however, centers on who a person is, his use of "me" to indicate his self suggests very strongly to me that he has experienced self-efficacy. The reader will recall that self-efficacy is defined as an individual's "awareness that he or she is an entity capable of action and that those actions have consequences." As children explore the environment and initiate actions, they will observe the consequences of those actions and associate those consequences with self. Learning such an association is as natural as learning to engage in certain activities because they cause positive responses from Mother and Father.

None of this is meant to assume, however, that self-efficacy is somehow limited to the first few years of life. It has already been stated that self is a dynamic and ever-changing construct. As such, individuals may go through several self-related challenges in their lives. The stability of our self can be called into question whenever major life changes are chosen or thrust upon us. Just a few examples of such major changes would include moving away to college, graduating from college, changing jobs, getting married, having children, getting divorced, or the death of a spouse. Each of these events calls into question the sense of self that the individual may have come to feel comfortable with. After being married for over nine years myself, it is obvious to me that a large part of my self-definition is intricately dependent on my wife. If she were no longer a part of my life for whatever reason, major portions of my self would be called into question and I would be forced to renegotiate who I think I am.

WE CAN'T ESCAPE THE ROLE THAT OTHERS PLAY

Self does not develop in a vacuum; it is intricately linked with the significant others who play a role in our lives. Just as I am defining a sense of self that is partially dependent on these other persons, so, too, are these individuals defining themselves in a manner that is partially dependent on me. Most individuals have experienced concern when someone who is an important part of their life changes. When an individual utters the phrase "I just don't know who you are anymore," this comment is of utmost significance. It indicates that the individual has become, to some degree, dependent on the other being stable and predictable. If that other person then changes, the individual's own sense of self is called into question. If my spouse decides to cut her hair short, buy a black leather jacket, and drive a Harley, those changes will call my own sense of self into question. How could I not look at those changes and wonder where I fit into this new image that she is trying to portray. What room is there in her new identity for a mild-mannered, bespectacled college professor? In this fashion, when those whom we are close to attempt to make changes in their own identities, they call ours into question as well.

Individuals may resist the efforts by others to engage in self-analysis because they do not wish to alter their own self. Rather than alter my own self to be more in line with my wife's new identity, then, I would try very hard to bring her back into the old mold that I had for her. If she, however, resists these efforts, conflict will probably arise. There is something very contradictory about the whole concept of self. On one hand, we have a very private intimate thing that is extremely personal. On the other hand, however, we have something that other persons want to play a key role in helping us to define. Where does an individual draw the line? If I decide to listen only to my own values, thoughts, ideals, and goals in articulating my sense of self, I may alienate the others that are so important to me. If, on the other hand, I allow these same persons to create my sense of self for me, then I have no ownership for it nor any control over it. Many dangers are inherent in such a case. Potentially the most disastrous side of not having ownership for one's self is the fact that one cannot then own any successes that come one's way, nor can one own up to or learn from any of the failures.

CAN HIGH SELF-ESTEEM LEAD TO EGOMANIA?

Self-esteem enhancement is not predicated on the idea that only success can lead to high self-esteem. If high self-esteem were simply a matter of number of successes, every person would be on very shaky self-esteem ground. Self-esteem is also partially a matter of having or taking control for one's own actions and knowing when not to assign blame to self if things go wrong. In short, then, self-esteem is contingent upon having ownership for self and accurately interpreting successes and failures. Accepting responsibility for all successes and rejecting responsibility for all failures is really not that much better than rejecting responsibility for all successes and accepting responsibility for all failures. Both conditions may make a person just as lonely and just as miserable. Egomaniacs are lonely because no one can possibly compete with their greatness, and therefore most persons choose not to be around them. Low self-esteem persons are lonely because they can make others feel as if they are being pulled down into the gutter of misery right along with them. How many times have you heard someone say something like "I've got to get away from Sally. She's bringing me down"?

Is it ever possible to have too much self-esteem? It is sometimes difficult to resist the temptation to assume that someone who is labeled an egomaniac simply has too much self-esteem. At first this may seem a perfectly reasonable assumption. In reality, however, the egomaniac may be doubting his self a great deal. Numerous methods are available for dealing with self-doubt. First, the individuals could choose to seek out self-related information in an effort to make a decision about who they are. Second, the individuals could put forth an image of what they would most like to be and then do everything in their power to convince other people that the image being projected is accurate. The real problem with this method is that individuals usually go overboard. If they want to be seen as worthy, they tell the world every chance they get that they are already worthy. If they want the world to see that they are great, they are always the first to mention it. Those who come into contact with these individuals may misinterpret these actions as narcissism, self-love, or egomania when, in fact, they may be very clear indicators of uncertain or even low self-esteem. The main difference between the individual with egomania and the person with low self-esteem may simply be a matter of certainty. Low self-esteem persons are certain that they are worthless, whereas egomaniacs are afraid that they might be.

In the whole scheme of things, then, who is worse off? Chapter Thirteen already mentioned that low self-esteem persons are particularly sensitive to the impact of positive feedback because it questions the consistency with which they have viewed themselves in the past. In this case, it may be better to wallow in misery than have to face up to the fact that you don't know yourself as well as you thought you did. Egomaniacs, who in order to hide such great uncertainty about self act as if they are God's gift to the world, may be suffering more. Every single moment that feedback is not received to confirm their greatness can be quite frightening because it may cause them to have to fess up to their true feelings about self. As also mentioned, one of the reasons that self-esteem enhancement can be so difficult (and also why low self-esteem persons may resist self-esteem enhancement attempts so strongly) is that low self-esteem can only be changed to high self-esteem by first going through a transition period of self-concept and self-related uncertainty. Given how uncomfortable such self-related uncertainty can be, individuals may simply opt to wallow in the predictable low self-esteem.

The cliché says that misery loves company. In actuality, misery loves miserable company. It has also been said that only a drunk could love a drunk. These phrases all reflect the sentiment that we don't usually want to be around people who are in a dramatically different mood than we are in. High self-esteem persons may find it uncomfortable to be around someone with low self-esteem, and vice versa. Many students have told me that the hardest thing for them to accept about my lectures on self-esteem and self-esteem enhancement is the notion that low self-esteem persons do not want positive feedback. This may be a counterintuitive notion. But one must remember that people want only accurate feedback if they are self-seeking. High self-esteem persons want only negative feedback when they are self-seeking; otherwise, positive feedback would probably be preferred. Likewise, low self-esteem persons want only positive feedback if they feel they can definitely trust that feedback and that it does not have the potential for setting them up for future failure. If either the information doesn't seem trustworthy or it runs the risk of placing higher expectations on them in the future, the low self-esteem persons would probably prefer negative feedback.

KNOWING WHO YOU ARE AND WHO YOU ARE NOT

Another fundamental lesson to learn from all of this is the importance of the concept "not-me." Many individuals assume that self-esteem enhancement involves taking the person from labeling most things as "bad-me" to labeling most things as "good-me." This assumption, however, misses the mark. Self-esteem isn't just being aware of what you are good or bad at. It also involves an awareness of who you are as well as who you are not. I am not a basketball player. Does this bother me? Absolutely not. In this case, labeling myself as "not a basketball player" helps me to define and differentiate more clearly who I am. Most self-related attributes are known to us as a matter of comparison. How do I know if I am tall unless I compare myself to someone I believe to be either average in height or even short. How do I know if I am making a decent income unless I compare myself to someone else? These dichotomous comparisons allow individuals to place themselves on a scale that signals to self and others where they fall on the dimension of interest. In this fashion, I not only come to realize who I am and what I am good and bad at, but also who I am not.

I realize that I do not have to be all things to all people, and part and parcel with this realization is an understanding that there are simply things out there that I am not good at. If high self-esteem is ever to be possible, however, I must also realize that just because I am not good at something does not require me to label myself as "bad-me." In the case of basketball ability, I simply choose not to incorporate that as part of the repertoire of characteristics I use to define who I am. We tell our children "You don't have to be good at everything." But this isn't enough. We also need to remind them that they should be proud to express their limits as part of their uniqueness. I am proud of the fact that I am a nerd. Rather than looking at all of the things that I don't do well (like mechanical things or athletic things or even musical things), I use such things as guides for helping others to understand just exactly who I am.

WHAT DOES HIGH SELF-ESTEEM REALLY MEAN?

One final thing to note about self-esteem involves having a better understanding about what it means to say someone has high self-esteem. As self-esteem is discussed, it is quite obvious that anyone would prefer to have high self-esteem than low. But high self-esteem doesn't mean that one's life will be perfect or that one believes there is no room or need for self-related growth. The high self-esteem person is aware of the "good, the bad, and the ugly" associated with being who they are. They have self-related uncertainties, and they have good and bad self-esteem days. The real difference between high self-esteem individuals and low self-esteem individuals is less a matter of current feelings about self and more a matter of future outlook. Even on a bad day, individuals with high self-esteem believe that tomorrow will be better. Even when self-doubt or even self-disgust are present, individuals with high self-esteem trust self enough to know that they can do what it takes to make amends, correct errors, or make a better impression the next time around.

References

Abrams, D., & Brown, R. (1989). Self-consciousness and social identity: Self-regulation as a group member. *Social Psychology Quarterly*, *52*, 311–318.

Adler, A. (1927). *Understanding human nature*. Garden City, NY: Doubleday Anchor.

Adler, A. (1969). *The science of living*. Garden City, NY: Doubleday Anchor.

Affleck, G., & Tennen, H. (1991). Social comparison and coping with major medical problems. In J. Suls & T. A. Wills (Eds.), *Social comparison: Contemporary theory and research* (pp. 369–393). Hillsdale, NJ: Erlbaum.

Affleck, G., Tennen, H., Pfeiffer, C., Fifield, J., & Rowe, J. (1987). Downward comparison and coping with serious medical problems. *American Journal of Orthopsychiatry*, *57*, 570–578.

Alicke, M. D. (1985). Global self-evaluation as determined by the desirability and controllability of trait adjectives. *Journal of Personality and Social Psychology*, *49*, 1621–1630.

Amabile, T. M. (1983). *The social psychology of creativity*. New York: Springer-Verlag.

Anderson, C. A., Lepper, M. R., & Ross, L. (1980). Perseverance of social theories: The role of explanation in the persistence of discredited information. *Journal of Personality and Social Psychology*, *39*, 1037–1049.

Andrews, J. D. W. (1991). *The active self in psychotherapy: An integration of therapeutic styles*. Boston: Allyn & Bacon.

Arkin, R. M. (1981). Self-presentation styles. In J. T. Tedeschi (Ed.), *Impression management theory and social psychological research* (pp. 311–333). New York: Academic Press.

Backman, C. W. (1985). Interpersonal congruency theory revisited: A revision and extension. *Journal of Social and Personal Relationships*, *2*, 489–505.

Backman, C. W. (1988). The self: A dialectical approach. In L. Berkowitz (Ed.), *Advances in experimental social psychology* (pp. 72–93). New York: Academic Press.

Baldwin, J. M. (1897). *Social and ethical interpretations in mental development: A study in social psychology*. New York: Macmillan.

Bandura, A. (1977). Self-efficacy: Toward a unifying theory of behavioral change. *Psychological Review*, *84*, 191–215.

Bandura, A. (1982). The self and the mechanisms of agency. In J. Suls (Ed.), *Psychological perspectives on the self* (Vol. 1). Hillsdale, NJ: Lawrence Erlbaum.

Bandura, A. (1986). *Social foundations of thought and action: A social cognitive theory.* Englewood Cliffs, NJ: Prentice-Hall.

Banks, J. H., & Wolfson, J. H. (1967, April). *Differential cardiac response of infants to mother and stranger.* Paper presented at the Eastern Psychological Association meeting, Boston.

Bargh, J. A., & Thein, R. D. (1985). Individual construct accessibility, person memory, and the recall–judgment link: The case of information overload. *Journal of Personality and Social Psychology, 49,* 1129–1146.

Baumeister, R. F. (1986). *Public self and private self.* New York: Springer.

Baumeister, R. F. (1990). Suicide as escape from self. *Psychological Review, 97,* 90–113.

Baumeister, R. F. (1993). *Self-esteem: The puzzle of low self-regard.* New York: Plenum Press.

Baumeister, R. F., & Showers, C. J. (1986). A review of paradoxical performance effects: Choking under pressure in sports and mental tests. *European Journal of Social Psychology, 16,* 361–383.

Baumeister, R. F., & Steinhilber, A. (1984). Paradoxical effects of supportive audiences on performance under pressure: The home field disadvantage in sports championships. *Journal of Personality and Social Psychology, 47,* 85–93.

Baumeister, R. F., Tice, D. M., & Hutton, D. G. (1989). Self-presentational motivations and personality differences in self-esteem. *Journal of Personality, 57,* 547–579.

Baumgardner, A. H. (1990). To know oneself is to like oneself: Self-certainty and self-affect. *Journal of Personality and Social Psychology, 58,* 1062–1072.

Baumgardner, A. H. (1991). Claiming depressive symptoms as a self-handicap: A protective self-presentation strategy. *Basic and Applied Social Psychology, 12,* 97–113.

Beggan, J. K. (1992). On the social nature of nonsocial perception: The mere ownership effect. *Journal of Personality and Social Psychology, 62,* 229–237.

Bellah, R. N., Madsen, R., Sullivan, W. M., Swidler, A., & Tipton, S. M. (1985). *Habits of the heart.* New York: Harper & Row.

Bellezza, F. S. (1987). Mnemonic devices and memory schemas. In M. McDaniel & M. Pressley (Eds.), *Imagery and related mnemonic processes* (pp. 34–55). New York: Springer-Verlag.

Bellezza, F. S., & Hoyt, S. K. (1992). The self-reference effect and mental cueing. *Social Cognition, 10,* 51–78.

Bem, D. J. (1965). An experimental analysis of self-persuasion. *Journal of Experimental Social Psychology, 1,* 199–218.

Bem, D. J. (1972). Self-perception theory. In L. Berkowitz (Ed.), *Advances in experimental social psychology* (Vol. 6, pp. 1–62). New York: Academic Press.

Bem, D. J. (1981). Assessing situations by assessing persons. In D. Magnusson (Ed.), *Toward a psychology of situations: An interactional perspective* (pp. 245–257). Hillsdale, NJ: Lawrence Erlbaum.

Berglas, S. (1986). *The success syndrome: Hitting bottom when you reach the top.* New York: Plenum Press.

Berglas, S. (1988). The three faces of self-handicapping: Protective self-presentation, a strategy for self-esteem enhancement, and acharacter disorder. In S. L. Zelen (Ed.), *Self-representation: The second attribution-personality conference* (pp. 133–169). New York: Springer-Verlag.

Berglas, S., & Jones, E. E. (1978). Drug choice as a self-handicapping strategy in response to non-contingent success. *Journal of Personality and Social Psychology, 36,* 405–417.

Bernstein, D. A., Roy, E. J., Srull, T. K., & Wickens, C. D. (1991). *Psychology* (2nd ed.). Boston: Houghton-Mifflin.

Bettelheim, B. (1987, March). The importance of play. *Atlantic Monthly.*

Blaine, B., & Crocker, J. (1993). Self-esteem and negative self-serving biases in reactions to positive and negative events: An integrative review. In R. F. Baumeister (Ed.), *Self-esteem: The puzzle of low self-regard.* New York: Plenum Press.

Bower, G. H., & Gilligan, S. G. (1979). Remembering information related to one's self. *Journal of Research in Personality, 13,* 420–432.

Brehm, S. S., & Kassin, S. M. (1993). *Social psychology.* Boston: Houghton Mifflin.

Brickman, P., & Bulman, R. J. (1977). Pleasure and pain in social comparison. In J. M. Suls & R. L. Miller (Eds.), *Social comparison processes: Theoretical and empirical perspectives* (pp. 149–186). Washington, DC: Hemisphere.

Briere, N. M., & Vallerand, R. J. (1990). Effect of private self-consciousness and success outcome on causal dimensions. *Journal of Social Psychology, 130,* 325–331.

Briggs, S. R., & Cheek, J. M. (1986). The role of factor analysis in the development and evaluation of personality scales. *Journal of Personality, 54,* 107–148.

Briggs, S. R., & Cheek, J. M. (1988). On the nature of self-monitoring: Problems with assessment, problems with validity. *Journal of Personality and Social Psychology, 54,* 663–678.

Briggs, S. R., Cheek, J. M., & Buss, A. H. (1980). An analysis of the self-monitoring scale. *Journal of Personality and Social Psychology, 38,* 679–686.

Brockner, J. (1983). Low self-esteem and behavioral plasticity: Some implications. In L. Wheeler & P. Shaver (Eds.), *Review of Personality and Social Psychology* (Vol. 4, pp. 237–271). Newbury Park, CA: Sage.

Bronson, G. W. (1972). Infants' reactions to unfamiliar persons and novel objects. *Monographs of the Society for Research in Child Development, 47*(3), Serial No. 148.

Brown, J. D. (1993). Motivational conflict and the self: The double-bind of low self-esteem. In R. F. Baumeister (Ed.), *Self-esteem: The puzzle of low self-regard.* New York: Plenum Press.

Brown, J. D., Collins, R. L., & Schmidt, G. W. (1988). Self-esteem and direct versus indirect forms of self-enhancement. *Journal of Personality and Social Psychology, 55,* 445–453.

Bruner, J. S. (1964). The course of cognitive growth. *American Psychologist, 19,* 1–15.

Bruner, J. S., & Tagiuri, R. (1954). Person perception. In G. Lindzey (Ed.), *Handbook of social psychology* (Vol. 2, pp. 634–653). Reading, MA: Addison-Wesley.

Buss, A. H. (1980). *Self-consciousness and social anxiety.* San Francisco: Freeman.

Buss, A. H., & Scheier, M. F. (1976). Self-consciousness, self-awareness, and self-attribution. *Journal of Research in Personality, 10,* 463–468.

California Task Force to Promote Self-esteem and Personal and Social Responsibility (1990). *Toward a state of self-esteem.* Sacramento: California State Department of Education.

Campbell, J. D., & Lavallee, L. F. (1993). Who am I? The role of self-concept confusion in understanding the behavior of people with low self-esteem. In R. F. Baumeister (Ed.), *Self-esteem: The puzzle of low self-regard.* New York: Plenum Press.

Cantor, N., & Mischel, W. (1979). Prototypes in person perception. In L. Berkowitz (Ed.), *Advances in experimental social psychology* (Vol. 12, pp. 3–52). New York: Academic Press.

Carpenter, S. L. (1988). Self-relevance and goal-directed processing in the recall and weighing of information about others. *Journal of Experimental Social Psychology, 24,* 310–332.

Carver, C. S., & Scheier, M. F. (1981). *Attention and self-regulation: A control-theory approach to human behavior.* New York: Springer-Verlag.

Carver, C. S., & Scheier, M. F. (1985). Aspects of self, and the control of behavior. In B. R. Schlenker (Ed.), *The self and social life* (pp. 146–174). New York: McGraw-Hill.

Chow, S. L. (1988). An examination of Jussim's (1986) three-stage model of self-fulfilling prophecies. *Journal of Psychology, 122*(1), 95–99.

Cialdini, R. B., Borden, R. J., Thorne, A., Walker, M. R., Freeman, S., & Sloan, L. R. (1976). Basking in reflected glory: Three (football) field studies. *Journal of Personality and Social Psychology, 34,* 366–375.

Cialdini, R. B., & De Nicholas, M. E. (1989). Self-presentation by association. *Journal of Personality and Social Psychology, 57,* 626–631.

Combs, A. W., & Snygg, D. (1959). *Individual behavior.* New York: Harper & Row.

Cooley, C. H. (1902). *Human nature and the social order.* New York: Scribner's.

Cooley, C. H. (1902/1964). *Human nature and the social order.* New York: Schocken Books.

Coopersmith, S. (1981). *The antecedents of self-esteem.* Palo Alto, CA: Consulting Psychologists Press.

Covington, M. V. (1992). *Making the grade: A self-worth perspective on motivation and school reform.* New York: Cambridge University Press.

Craik, F. I. M., & Lockhart, R. S. (1972). Levels of processing: A framework for memory research. *Journal of Verbal Learning and Verbal Behavior, 11,* 671–684.

Cross, S., & Markus, H. (1991a). *Cultural adaptation and the self: Self-construal, coping, and stress.* Paper presented at the 99th annual convention of the American Psychological Association, San Francisco.

Cross, S., & Markus, H. (1991b). Possible selves across the life span. *Human Development, 34,* 230–255.

Csikzentmihalyi, M., & Figurski, T. J. (1982). Self-awareness and aversive experiences in everyday life. *Journal of Personality, 50,* 15–28.

Darley, J. M., & Goethals, G. R. (1980). People's analyses of the causes of ability-linked performances. In L. Berkowitz (Ed.), *Advances in experimental social psychology* (Vol. 13, pp. 1–37). New York: Academic Press.

Darley, J. M., & Gross, P. H. (1983). A hypothesis-confirming bias in labeling effects. *Journal of Personality and Social Psychology, 44,* 20–33.

Deci, E. L. (1971). Effects of externally mediated rewards on intrinsic motivation. *Journal of Personality and Social Psychology, 18,* 105–115.

Deci, E. L. (1992). On the nature and functions of motivations theories. *Psychological Science, 3,* 167–171.

Deci, E. L., & Ryan, R. M. (1980). The empirical exploration of intrinsically motivated processes. In L. Berkowitz (Ed.), *Advances in experimental social psychology* (Vol. 13). New York: Academic Press.

Deci, E. L., & Ryan, R. M. (1985). Intrinsic motivation and self-determination in human behavior. New York: Plenum Press.

Deci, E. L., & Ryan, R. M. (1986). The dynamics of self-determination in personality and development. In R. Schwarzer (Ed.), *Self-related cognitions in anxiety and motivation.* Hillsdale, NJ: Lawrence Erlbaum.

Deci, E. L., & Ryan, R. M. (1987). The support of autonomy and the control of behavior. *Journal of Personality and Social Psychology, 53,* 1024–1037.

Deci, E. L., & Ryan, R. M. (1991). A motivational approach to self: Integration in personality. In R. Dienstbier (Ed.), *Nebraska Symposium on Motivation: Vol. 38. Perspectives on motivation* (pp. 237–288). Lincoln: University of Nebraska Press.

DeGree, C. E., & Snyder, C. R. (1985). Adler's psychology (of use) today: Personality history of traumatic life events as a self-handicapping strategy. *Journal of Personality and Social Psychology, 48,* 1512–1519.

De La Ronde, C., & Swann, W. B., Jr. (1993). Caught in the crossfire: positivity and self-verification strivings among people with low self-esteem. In R. F. Baumeister (Ed.), *Self-esteem: The puzzle of low self-regard.* New York: Plenum Press.

Deutsch, M., & Solomon, L. (1959). Reactions to evaluations by others as influenced by self-evaluations. *Sociometry, 22,* 70–75.

De Vos, G. A. (1990). *Differential minority achievement in cross-cultural perspective: The case of Koreans in Japan and the United States.* Unpublished manuscript.

De Vos, G. A., & Orozco, M. S. (1990). *Status inequality: The self in culture.* Vol. 15, Cross-Cultural Research and Methodology Series. Newbury Park, CA: Sage.

Dickens, V. J. (1992). Foreword. In C. Jones, *Enhancing self-concepts and achievement of mildly handicapped students.* Springfield, IL: Charles C. Thomas, Publisher.

Dion, K. K., Berscheid, E., & Walster, E. (1972). What is beautiful is good. *Journal of Personality and Social Psychology, 24,* 285–290.

Dipboye, R. L. (1977). A critical review of Korman's self-consistency theory of work motivation and occupation choice. *Organizational Behavior and Human Performance, 18,* 108–126.

Doherty, K., & Schlenker, B. R. (1991). Self-consciousness and strategic self-presentation. *Journal of Personality, 59,* 1–18.

Duval, T. S., Duval, V. H., & Mulilis, J. P. (1992). Effects of self-focus, discrepancy between self and standard, and outcome expectancy favorability on the tendency to match self to standard or to withdraw. *Journal of Personality and Social Psychology, 62,* 340–348.

Duval, S., & Wicklund, R. A. (1972). *A theory of objective self-awareness.* New York: Academic Press.

Duval, S., & Wicklund, R. A. (1973). Effects of objective self-awareness on attribution of causality. *Journal of Experimental Social Psychology, 9,* 17–31.

Eagly, A. H., Ashmore, R. D., Makhijani, M. G., & Longo, L. C. (1991). What is beautiful is good, but . . .: A meta-analytic review of research on the physical attractiveness stereotype. *Psychology Bulletin, 110,* 107–128.

Ehrlich, H. J. (1973). *The social psychology of prejudice.* New York: Wiley.

Elkind, D. (1986, May). Formal education and early childhood education: An essential difference. *Phi Delta Kappan.*

Erdelyi, M. H. (1984). The recovery of unconscious (inaccessible) memories: Laboratory studies of hypermnesia. In G. H. Bower (Ed.), *The psychology of learning and motivation* (Vol. 18). New York: Academic Press.

Erikson, E. H. (1963). *Childhood and society.* (2nd ed.). New York: Norton.

Fazio, R. H., Effrein, E. A., & Falender, Y. J. (1981). Self-perceptions following social interaction. *Journal of Personality and Social Psychology, 41,* 232–242.

Fazio, R. H., Zanna, M. P., & Cooper, J. (1977). Dissonance and self-perception: An integrative view of each theory's proper domain of application. *Journal of Experimental Social Psychology, 13,* 464–479.

Felson, R. B. (1981). Ambiguity and bias in the self-concept. *Social Psychology Quarterly, 44,* 64–69.

Felson, R. B. (1989). Parents and the reflected appraisal process: A longitudinal analysis. *Journal of Personality and Social Psychology, 56*(6), 965–971.

Fenigstein, A. (1979). Self-consciousness, self-attention, and social interaction. *Journal of Personality and Social Psychology, 37,* 75–86.

Fenigstein, A., Scheier, M. F., & Buss, A. H. (1975). Public and private self-consciousness: Assessment and theory. *Journal of Consulting and Clinical Psychology, 43,* 522–527.

Festinger, L. (1954a). A theory of social comparison processes. *Human Relations, 7,* 117–140.

Festinger, L. (1954b). Motivation leading to social behavior. In M. R. Jones (Ed.), *Nebraska Symposium on Motivation: Vol. 2* (pp. 191–218). Lincoln: University of Nebraska Press.

Festinger, L. (1957). *A theory of cognitive dissonance.* Stanford, CA: Stanford University Press.

Filipp, S.-H. (1979). Entwurf eines heuristischen Bezugsrahmens fur Selbstkonzept-Forschung: Menschliche Informationsverarbeitung und naive Handlungstheorie. In S.-H. Filipp (Ed.), *Selbstkonsept-Forschung* (pp. 129–152). Stuttgart: Klett-Cotta.

Filipp, S.-H., Aymanns, P., & Braukmann, W. (1986). Coping with life events: When the self comes into play. In R. Schwarzer (Ed.), *Self-related cognitions in anxiety and motivation* (pp. 87–109). Hillsdale, NJ: Lawrence Erlbaum.

Fodor, J. (1983). *The modularity of the mind*. Montgomery, VT: Bradford.

Frank, R. (1985). *Choosing the right pond: Human behavior and the quest for status*. Oxford, England: Cambridge University Press.

Frankel, A., & Prentice-Dunn, S. (1990). Loneliness and the processing of self-relevant information. *Journal of Social and Clinical Psychology, 9*(3), 303–315.

Freedman, J. L., & Fraser, S. C. (1966). Compliance without pressure: The foot-in-the-door technique. *Journal of Personality and Social Psychology, 4*, 195–202.

Freud, S. (1938). Totem and taboo. In A. A. Brill (Ed.), *The basic writings of Sigmund Freud* (pp. 807–930). New York: Random House.

Freud, S. (1957). *A general introduction to psychoanalysis* (J. Riviere, Trans.). New York: Permabooks.

Friend, R. M., & Gilbert, J. (1973). Threat and fear of negative evaluation as determinants of locus of comparison. *Journal of Personality, 41*, 328–340.

Froming, W. J., Corley, E. B., & Rinker, L. (1990). The influence of public self-consciousness and the audience's characteristics on withdrawal from embarrassing situations. *Journal of Personality, 58*, 603–622.

Fromm, E. (1947). *Man for himself*. New York: Holt, Rhinehart & Winston.

Fromm, E. (1955). *The sane society*. New York: Holt, Rhinehart & Winston.

Funder, D. C., & Colvin, R. C. (1991). Explorations in behavioral consistency: Properties of persons, situations, and behaviors. *Journal of Personality and Social Psychology, 60*, 773–794.

Gangestad, S., & Snyder, M. (1985). To carve nature at its joints: On the existence of discrete classes in personality. *Psychological Review, 92*, 317–349.

Gibbons, F. X., & Gerrard, M. (1991). Downward comparison and coping with threat. In J. Suls & T. A. Wills (Eds.), *Social comparison: Contemporary theory and research* (pp. 317–345). Hillsdale, NJ: Erlbaum.

Gibbons, F. X., & McCoy, S. B. (1991). Self-esteem, similarity, and reactions to active versus passive downward comparison. *Journal of Personality and Social Psychology, 60*, 414–424.

Gilbert, D. T., & Cooper, J. (1985). Social psychological strategies of self-deception. In M. W. Martin (Ed.), *Self-deception and self-understanding* (pp. 75–94). Lawrence: University Press of Kansas.

Gilovich, T. (1983). Biased evaluation and persistence in gambling. *Journal of Personality and Social Psychology, 40*, 797–808.

Goethals, G. R., & Darley, J. (1977). Social comparison theory: An attributional approach. In J. Suls & R. L. Miller (Eds.), *Social comparison processes: Theoretical and empirical perspectives* (pp. 259–278). Washington, DC: Hemisphere.

Goode, C. B., & Watson, J. L. (1992). *The mind fitness program for esteem and excellence*. Tucson, AZ: Zephyr Press.

Gordon, C. (1968). Self-conceptions: Configurations of content. In C. Gordon & K. J. Gergen (Eds.), *The self in social interaction*. New York: Wiley.

Greenwald, A. G. (1980). The totalitarian ego: Fabrication and revision of personal history. *American Psychologist, 35*, 603–618.

Greenwald, A. G., & Banaji, M. R. (1989). The self as a memory system: Powerful but ordinary. *Journal of Personality and Social Psychology, 57*, 41–64.

Greenwald, A. G., Bellezza, F. S., & Banaji, M. R. (1988). Is self-esteem a central ingredient of the self-concept? *Personality and Social Psychology Bulletin, 14*, 34–45.

Hakmiller, K. L. (1966). Threat as a determinant of downward comparison. *Journal of Experimental Social Psychology, 2* (Suppl. 1), 32–39.

Hall, G. S. (1904). *Adolescence: Its psychology and its relations to physiology, anthropology, sociology, sex, crime, religion and education.* New York: Appleton.

Harris, M. J., & Rosenthal, R. (1985). Mediation of interpersonal expectancy effects. *Psychological Bulletin, 97*, 363–386.

Harris, R. N., & Snyder, C. R. (1986). The role of uncertain self-esteem in self-handicapping. *Journal of Personality and Social Psychology, 51*, 451–458.

Harter, S. (1985). Competence as a dimension of self-evaluation: Toward a comprehensive model of self-worth. In R. L. Leahy (Ed.), *The development of the self* (pp. 55–121). London: Academic Press.

Harter, S. (1986). Processes underlying the construction, maintenance, and enhancement of the self-concept in children. In J. Suls & A. G. Greenwald (Eds.), *Psychological perspectives on the self* (Vol. 3, pp. 137–181). Hillsdale, NJ: Lawrence Erlbaum.

Harter, S. (1988). Developmental and dynamic changes in the nature of the self-concept: Implications for child psychotherapy. In S. Shirk (Ed.), *Cognitive development and child psychotherapy. Perspectives in develomental psychology* (pp. 119–160). New York: Plenum.

Harter, S. (1990). Causes, correlates and the functional role of global self-worth: A life-span perspective. In J. Kolligan & R. Sternberg (Eds.), *Perceptions of competence and incompetence across the life span* (pp. 43–70). New York: Springer-Verlag.

Harter, S. (1993a). Visions of self: Beyond the me in the mirror. In J. E. Jacobs (Ed.), *Nebraska symposium on motivation: Vol. 40. Developmental perspectives on motivation. Current theory and research in motivation* (pp. 99–144). Lincoln: University of Nebraska Press.

Harter, S. (1993b). Causes and consequences of low self-esteem in children and adolescents. In R. F. Baumeister (Ed.), *Self-esteem: The puzzle of low self-regard.* New York: Plenum Press.

Harter, S., & Marold, D. B. (1991). A model of the determinants and mediational role of self-worth: Implications for adolescent depression and suicidal ideation. In G. Goethals & J. Strauss (Eds.), *The self: An interdisciplinary approach.* New York: Springer-Verlag.

Hass, R. G. (1984). Perspective taking and self-awareness: Drawing an E on your forehead. *Journal of Personality and Social Psychology, 46*, 788–798.

Hattie, J. (1992). *Self-concept.* Hillsdale, NJ: Erlbaum.

Heatherton, T. F., & Ambady, N. (1993). Self-esteem, self-prediction, and living up to commitments. In R. F. Baumeister (Ed.), *Self-esteem: The puzzle of low self-regard.* New York: Plenum Press.

Heaton, A. W., & Sigall, H. (1991). Self-consciousness, self-presentation, and performance under pressure: Who chokes, and when? *Journal of Applied Social Psychology, 21*, 175–188.

Heider, F. (1958). *The psychology of interpersonal relations.* New York: Wiley.

Higgins, E. T. (1987). Self-discrepancy: A theory relating self and affect. *Psychological Review, 94*, 319–340.

Higgins, E. T. (1989). Self-discrepancy theory: What patterns of self-beliefs cause people to suffer? In L. Berkowitz (Ed.), *Advances in experimental social psychology* (Vol. 22, pp. 93–136). New York: Academic Press.

Higgins, E. T., & Bargh, J. A. (1987). Social cognition and social perception. *Annual Review of Psychology, 38*, 369–425.

Higgins, E. T., Bind, R. N., Klein, R., & Strauman, T. (1986). Self-discrepancies and emotional vulnerability: How magnitude, accesibility, and type of discrepancy influence affect. *Journal of Personality and Social Psychology, 51*, 5–15.

Higgins, E. T., Vookles, J., & Tykocinski, O. (1992). Self and health: How patterns of self-beliefs predict types of emotional and physical problems. *Social Cognition, 10*(1), 125–150.

Hiroto, D. S. (1974). Locus of control and learned helplessness. *Journal of Experimental Psychology, 102,* 187–193.

Hofstede, G. (1980). *Culture's consequences: International differences in work-related values.* Newbury Park, CA: Sage.

Hofstetter, C. R., Sallis, J. F., & Hovell, M. F. (1990). Some health dimensions of self-efficacy: Analysis of theoretical specificity. *Social Science and Medicine, 31*(9), 1051–1056.

Hormuth, S. E. (1990). *The ecology of the self: Relocation and self-concept change.* Cambridge, England: University Press.

Horney, K. (1950). *Neurosis and human growth.* New York: Norton.

Isser, N., & Schwartz, L. L. (1985). *The American school and the meltingpot: Minority self-esteem and public education.* Bristol, IN: Wyndham Hall Press.

James, W. (1890). *Psychology.* New York: Holt.

James, W. (1892). *Psychology: The briefer course.* New York: Henry Holt.

Jones, C. J. (1992). *Enhancing self-concepts and achievement of mildly handicapped students.* Springfield, IL: Charles C. Thomas, Publisher.

Jones, E. E. (1986). Interpreting interpersonal behavior: The effects of expectancies. *Science, 234,* 41–46.

Jones, E. E. (1990). *Interpersonal perception.* New York: Freeman.

Jones, E. E., & Gerard, H. B. (1967). *Foundations of social psychology.* New York: Wiley.

Jones, E. E., & Nisbett, R. E. (1971). *The actor and the observer: divergent perceptions of the causes of behavior.* Morristown, NJ: General Learning Press.

Josephs, R., Larrick, R., Steele, C., & Nisbett, R. (1992). Protecting the self from the consequences of risky decisions. *Journal of Personality and Social Psychology, 62,* 26–37.

Jussim, L. (1986). Self-fulfilling prophecies: A theoretical and integrative review. *Psychological Review, 93,* 429–445.

Jussim, L., & Eccles, J. S. (1992). Teacher expectations II: Construction and reflection of student achievement. *Journal of Personality and Social Psychology, 63,* 947–961.

Kahan, T. L., & Johnson, M. K. (1992). Self effects in memory for person information. *Social Cognition, 10,* 30–50.

Kanfer, F. H., & Gaelick, K. (1986). Self-management methods. In F. H. Kanfer & A. P. Goldstein (Eds.), *Helping people change: A textbook of methods* (3rd ed., pp. 283–345). New York: Pergamon.

Katz, A. N. (1987). Self-reference in the encoding of creative-relevant traits. *Journal of Personality, 55,* 97–120.

Kelley, H. H. (1967). Attribution theory in social psychology. In D. Levine (Ed.), *Nebraska Symposium on Motivation: Vol. 15* (pp. 192–240). Lincoln: University of Nebraska Press.

Kelly, G. A. (1955). *The psychology of personal constructs.* New York: Norton.

Kenny, D. A., & Albright, L. (1987). Accuracy in interpersonal perception: A social relations analysis. *Psychological Bulletin, 102,* 390–402.

Kernis, M. H. (1993). The roles of stability and level of self-esteem in psychological functioning. In R. F. Baumeister (Ed.), *Self-esteem: The puzzle of low self-regard.* New York: Plenum Press.

Kernis, M. H., Cornell, D. P., Sun, C., Berry, A., & Harlow, T. (1993). There's more to self-esteem than whether it is high or low: The importance of stability of self-esteem. *Journal of Personality and Social Psychology, 65*(6), 1190–1204.

Kihlstrom, J. F., Cantor, N., Albright, J. S., Chew, B. R., Klein, S. B., & Niedenthal, P. M. (1988). Information processing and the study of the self. In L. Berkowitz (Ed.), *Advances in experimental social psychology* (Vol. 21, pp. 145–178). New York: Academic Press.

Klein, S. B., Loftus, J., & Burton, H. A. (1989). Two self-reference effects: The importance of distinguishing between self-descriptiveness judgments and autobiographical retrieval in self-referent encoding. *Journal of Personality and Social Psychology, 56,* 853–865.

Kuiper, N. A., & Rogers, T. B. (1979). Encoding of personal information: Self–other differences. *Journal of Personality and Social Psychology, 37,* 499–514.

Langer, E. J., & Rodin, J. (1976). The effects of choice and personal responsibility for the aged: A field experiment in an institutional setting. *Journal of Personality and Social Psychology, 34,* 191–198.

Langlois, J. H. (1986). From the eye of the beholder to behavioral reality: Development of social behaviors and social relations as a function of physical attractiveness. In C. P. Herman, M. P. Zanna & E. T. Higgins (Eds.), *The Ontario Symposium: Vol. 3. Physical appearance, stigma, and social behavior* (pp. 23–51). Hillsdale, NJ: Erlbaum.

Lassiter, G. D., & Briggs, M. A. (1990). Effect of anticipated interaction on liking: An individual difference analysis. *Journal of Social Behavior and Personality, 5,* 357–367.

Lecky, P. (1945). *Self-consistency: A theory of personality.* New York: Norton.

Lee, D. (1976). *Valuing the self: What we can learn from other cultures.* Englewood Cliffs, NJ: Prentice-Hall.

Lennox, R., & Wolfe, R. (1984). Revision of the self-monitoring scale. *Journal of Personality and Social Psychology, 46,* 1349–1364.

Lepper, M. R., Green, D., & Nisbett, R. E. (1973). Undermining children's intrinsic interest with extrinsic reward: A test of the "overjustification" hypothesis. *Journal of Personality and Social Psychology, 28,* 129–137.

Lewicki, P. (1983). The self-image bias in person perception. *Journal of Personality and Social Psychology, 45,* 384–393.

Lewicki, P. (1984). Self schema and social information processing. *Journal of Personality and Social Psychology, 47,* 1177–1190.

Lewin, K. (1935). *A dynamic theory of personality.* New York: McGraw-Hill.

Lewis, M. (1979). The self as a developmental concept. *Human Development, 22,* 416–419.

Lewis, M. (1982). The social network systems model: Toward a theory of social development. In T. Field, A. Huston, H. Quay, L. Troll, & G. Fritz (Eds.), *Review of human development.* New York: Wiley.

Lewis, M. (1992). The role of the self in social behavior. In F. S. Kessel, P. M. Cole, & D. L. Johnson (Eds.), *Self and consciousness: Multiple perspectives* (pp. 19–44). Hillsdale, NJ: Lawrence Erlbaum.

Lippa, R., & Donaldson, S. I. (1990). Self-monitoring and idiographic measures of behavioral variability across interpersonal relationships. *Journal of Personality, 58,* 465–479.

Luhtanen, R., & Crocker, J. (1991). Self-esteem and intergroup comparisons: Toward a theory of collective self-esteem. In J. Suls & T. A. Wills (Eds.), *Social comparison: Contemporary theory and research* (pp. 211–234). Hillsdale, NJ: Erlbaum.

Lutz, C. (1992). Culture and consciousness: A problem in the anthropology of knowledge. In F. S. Kessel, P. M. Cole, & D. L. Johnson (Eds.), *Self and consciousness: Multiple perspectives.* Hillsdale, NJ: Erlbaum.

Major, B., Testa, M., & Bylsma, W. H. (1991). Responses to upward and downward comparisons: The impact of esteem-relevance and perceived control. In J. Suls & T. A. Wills (Eds.), *Social comparison: Contemporary theory and research* (pp. 237–260). Hillsdale, NJ: Erlbaum.

Markus, H. (1977). Self-schemata and processing information about the self. *Journal of Personality and Social Psychology, 35,* 63–78.

Markus, H. (1983). Self-knowledge: An expanded view. *Journal of Personality, 51,* 543–565.

Markus, H. (1990). Unresolved issues in self-representation. *Cognitive Therapy and Research, 14*(2), 241–253.

Markus, H., & Kitayama, S. (1991). Culture and self: Implications for cognition, emotion, and motivation. *Psychological Review, 98,* 954–969.

Markus, H., & Nurius, P. (1986). Possible selves. *American Psychologist, 41,* 954–969.

Markus, H., & Sentis, K. (1982). The self in social information processing. In J. Suls (Ed.), *Psychological perspectives on the self* (Vol. 1). Hillsdale, NJ: Erlbaum.

Markus, H., Smith, J., & Moreland, R. L. (1985). Role of the self-concept in the perception of others. *Journal of Personality and Social Psychology, 49,* 1494–1512.

Markus, H., & Wurf, E. (1987). The dynamic self-concept: A social psychological perspective. *Annual Review of Psychology, 38,* 299–337.

Maslow, A. H. (1970). *Religions, values, and peak-experiences.* New York: Viking.

Mayeroff, M. (1971). *On caring.* New York: Harper & Row.

McFarlin, D. B., & Blascovich, J. (1981). Effects of self-esteem and performance feedback on future affective preferences and cognitive expectations. *Journal of Personality and Social Psychology, 40,* 521–531.

McKay, M., & Fanning, P. (1987). *Self-esteem: The ultimate program for self-help.* New York: MJF Books.

McGuire, W. J., & McGuire, C. V. (1988). Content and process in the experience of self. In L. Berkowitz (Ed.), *Advances in experimental social psychology* (Vol. 21, pp. 97–144). New York: Academic Press.

McGuire, W. J., McGuire, C. V., & Winton, W. (1979). Effects of household sex composition on the salience of one's gender in the spontaneous self-concept. *Journal of Experimental Social Psychology, 15,* 77–90.

McGuire, W. J., & Padawer-Singer, A. (1976). Trait salience in the spontaneous self-concept. *Journal of Personality and Social Pscyhology, 33,* 743–754.

Mead, G. H. (1934). *Mind, self, and society.* Chicago: University of Chicago Press.

Merton, R. (1948). The self-fulfilling prophecy. *Antioch Review, 8,* 193–210.

Merton, R., & Rossi, A. S. (1957). Contributions to the theory of reference group behavior. In R. Merton (Ed.), *Social theory and social structure* (pp. 279–333). New York: Free Press.

Mettee, D. R., & Smith, G. (1977). Social comparison and interpersonal attraction: The case for dissimilarity. In J. M. Suls & R. L. Miller (Eds.), *Social comparison processes: Theoretical and empirical perspectives* (pp. 69–102). Washington, DC: Hemisphere.

Miller, D. T., Turnbull, W., & McFarland, C. (1988). Particularistic and universalistic evaluation in the social comparison process. *Journal of Personality and Social Psychology, 55,* 908–917.

Miller, D. T., Turnbull, W. & McFarland, C. (1990). Counterfactual thinking and social perception: Thinking about what might have been. *Advances in Experimental Social Psychology, 23,* 305–331.

Mischel, W. (1968). *Personality and assessment.* New York: Wiley.

Monson, T., Tanke, E., & Lund, J. (1980). Determinants of social perception in a naturalistic setting. *Journal of Research in Personality, 14,* 104–120.

Mueller, J. H. (1982). Self-awareness and access to material rated as self-descriptive and nondescriptive. *Bulletin of the Psychonomic Society, 19,* 323–326.

Nagata, D., & Crosby, F. (1991). Comparisons, justice, and the internment of Japanese-Americans. In J. Suls & T. A. Wills (Eds.), *Social comparison: Contemporary theory and research* (pp. 347–368). Hillsdale, NJ: Erlbaum.

Neisser, U. (1992). The development of consciousness and the acquisition of self. In F. S. Kessel, P. M. Cole, & D. L. Johnson (Eds.), *Self and consciousness: Multiple perspectives* (pp. 1–18). Hillsdale, NJ: Lawrence Erlbaum.

Neuberg, S. L. (1989). The goal of forming accurate impressions during social interactions: Attenuating the impact of negative expectancies. *Journal of Personality and Social Psychology, 56,* 374–386.

Neuberg, S. L., Judice, N. T., Virdin, L. M., & Carrillo, M. A. (1993). Perceiver self-presentational goals as moderators of expectancy influences: Ingratiation and the disconfirmation of negative expectancies. *Journal of Personality and Social Psychology, 64,* 409–420.

Nisbett, R., Caputo, C., Legant, P., & Maracek, J. (1973). Behavior as seen by the actor and as seen by the observer. *Journal of Personality and Social Psychology, 27,* 154–165.

Nissen, H. W. (1954). Comments on Professor Festinger's paper. In M. R. Jones (Ed.), *Nebraska Symposium on Motivation: Vol. 2* (pp. 219–223). Lincoln: University of Nebraska Press.

O'Leary, A. (1985). Self-efficacy and health. *Behavior Research Therapy, 4,* 437–451.

Olson, J. M. (1990). Self-inference processes in emotion. In J. M. Olson & M. P. Zanna (Eds.) *Self-inference processes: The Ontario Symposium* (Vol. 6, pp. 17–42). Hillsdale, NJ: Erlbaum.

Osborne, R. E. (1990). The influence of interactional goal familiarity on recovery from the effects of perceiving while busy. (Doctoral dissertation, University of Texas at Austin, 1989). *Dissertation Abstracts International, 51,* 3615.

Osborne, R. E. (1993a). Self-concept development and assessment. In *Magill's survey of the social sciences: Psychology.* Salem Press.

Osborne, R. E. (1993b). Self-esteem. In *Magill's survey of the social sciences: Psychology.* Salem Press.

Osborne, R. E. (1993c). *A word from the nerd.* New York: McGraw-Hill.

Osborne, R. E. (1993d). *A word from the nerd: Instructor's manual.* New York: McGraw-Hill.

Osborne, R. E., & Gilbert, D. T. (1992). The preoccupational hazards of social life. *Journal of Personality and Social Psychology, 62,* 219–228.

Osborne, R. E., Karlin, J. E., Baumann, D., Osborne, M. E., & Nelms, D. (1993). A social comparison perspective of treatment seeking by the homeless. *Journal of Social Distress and the Homeless, 2,* 135–153.

Osborne, R. E., Samborsky, J., & Marsh, G. (1994). *The impact of need for cognition on recovering from biased first impressions.* Unpublished data, Indiana University East.

Osborne, R. E., & Stites, L. R. (1994). *Perpetuating low self-regard: Self-esteem and interpretations for success and failure.* Unpublished data, Indiana University East.

Osborne, R. E., & Young, J. R. (1994). *Different I's of different beholders: Self-monitoring and the categorization of self and others.* Unpublished manuscript, Indiana University East.

Patterson, C. H. (1959). *Counseling and psychotherapy: Theory and practice.* New York: Harper & Row.

Pelham, B. W. (1991a). On confidence and consequence: The certainty and importance of self-knowledge. *Journal of Personality and Social Psychology, 60,* 518–530.

Pelham, B. W. (1991b). On the benefits of misery: Self-serving biases in the depressive self-concept. *Journal of Personality and Social Psychology, 61,* 670–681.

Pelham, B. W. (1993). On the highly positive thoughts of the highly depressed. In R. F. Baumeister (Ed.), *Self-esteem: The puzzle of low self-regard.* New York: Plenum Press.

Pelham, B. W., & Swann, W. B., Jr. (1989). From self-conceptions to self-worth: On the sources and structure of global self-esteem. *Journal of Personality and Social Psychology, 57,* 672–680.

Peterson, C., & Seligman, M. E. P. (1987). Explanatory style and illness. *Journal of Personality, 55,* 237–265.

Piaget, J. (1954). *The construction of reality in the child.* New York: Basic Books.

Piaget, J. (1959). *The language and thought of the child* (3rd ed.). M. Gabain & R. Gabain (Trans.). London: Routledge and Kegan Paul.

Pittman, T. S., & Heller, J. F. (1987). Social motivation. *Annual Review of Psychology, 38,* 461–489.

Plant, R. W., & Ryan, R. M. (1985). Intrinsic motivation and the effects of self-consciousness, self-awareness, and ego-involvement: An investigation of internally controlling styles. *Journal of Personality, 53,* 435–449.

Richmond, L. D., Craig, S. S., & Ruzicka, M. F. (1991). Self-monitoring and marital adjustment. *Journal of Research in Personality, 25,* 177–188.

Rodin, J. (1986). Aging and health: Effects of the sense of control. *Science, 233,* 1271–1276.

Rogers, T. B. (1983). Emotion, imagery, and verbal codes: A closer look at an increasingly complex interaction. In J. Yuille (Ed.), *Imagery, memory, and cognition* (pp. 285–305). Hillsdale, NJ: Erlbaum.

Rogers, T. B., Kuiper, N. A., & Kirker, W. S. (1977). Self reference and the encoding of personal information. *Journal of Personality and Social Psychology, 35,* 677–688.

Rosenthal, R., & Jacobson, L. (1968). *Pygmalion in the classroom: Teacher expectation and pupil's intellectual development.* New York: Holt, Rinehart, and Winston.

Ross, L., Greene, D., & House, P. (1977). The "false consensus effect": An egocentric bias in social perception and attribution processes. *Journal of Experimental Social Psychology, 13,* 279–301.

Rotter, J. B. (1954). *Social learning and clinical psychology.* Englewood Cliffs, NJ: Prentice-Hall.

Rubin, D. C. (1986). *Autobiographical memory.* New York: Cambridge University Press.

Russell, W. J. (1988, March). Editorial: Presidential campaigns and educational policy. *Educational Researcher, 17*(2).

Rutter, M. (1980). *Changing youth in a changing society: Patterns of development and disorder.* Cambridge, MA: Harvard University Press.

Salovey, P. (1991). Social comparison processes in envy and jealousy. In J. Suls & T. A. Wills (Eds.), *Social comparison: Contemporary theory and research* (pp. 261–285). Hillsdale, NJ: Erlbaum.

Sande, G. N. (1990). The multifaceted self. In J. M. Olson & M. P. Zanna (Eds.), *Self-inference processes: The Ontario symposium* (Vol. 6, pp. 1–16). Hillsdale, NJ: Erlbaum.

Schacter, S. (1959). *The psychology of affiliation.* Stanford, CA: Stanford University Press.

Schacter, S. (1964). The interaction of cognitive and physiological determinants of emotional state. In L. Berkowitz (Ed.), *Advances in experimental social psychology* (Vol. 1, pp. 49–80). New York: Academic Press.

Scheier, M. F., & Carver, C. S. (1988). A model of self-regulation: Translating intention into action. In L. Berkowitz (Ed.), *Advances in experimental social psychology* (Vol. 21, pp. 303–347). New York: Academic Press.

Scheier, M. F., Carver, C. S., & Gibbons, F. X. (1979). Self-directed attention, awareness of bodily states, and suggestibility. *Journal of Personality and Social Psychology, 37,* 1576–1588.

Schlenker, B. R., & Trudeau, J. V. (1990). The impact of self-presentations on private self-beliefs: Effects of prior self-beliefs and misattribution. *Journal of Personality and Social Psychology, 58,* 22–32.

Schlenker, B. R., Weigold, M. F., & Hallam, J. R. (1990). Self-serving attributions in social context: Effects of self-esteem and social pressure. *Journal of Personality and Social Psychology, 58,* 855–863.

Schostak, J. (1993). *Dirty marks: The education of self, media and popular culture.* Boulder, CO: Pluto Press.

Schunk, D. H. (1987). Peer models and children's behavioral change. *Review of Educational Psychology, 11,* 347–369.

Schunk, D. H. (1989a). Social cognitive theory and self-regulated learning. In B. J. Zimmerman & D. H. Schunk (Eds.), *Self-regulated learning and academic achievement: Theory, research, and practice.* New York: Springer-Verlag.

Schunk, D. H. (1989b). Self-efficacy and cognitive skill learning. In C. Ames & R. Ames (Eds.), *Research on motivation in education* (Vol. 3, pp. 13–44.). Orlando, FL: Academic Press.

Schunk, D. H., & Carbonair, J. P. (1984). Self-efficacy models. In J. D. Matarazzo et al. (Eds.), *Behavioral health: A handbook of health enhancement and disease prevention* (pp. 230–247). New York: Wiley.

Schunk, D. H., & Meece, J. L. (Eds.). (1992). *Student perceptions in the classroom*. Hillsdale, NJ: Erlbaum.

Sedikides, C., & Skowronski, J. J. (1993). The self in impression formation: Trait centrality and social perception. *Journal of Experimental Social Psychology, 29*, 347–357.

Seligman, M. E. P., & Maier, S. F. (1967). Failure to escape traumatic shock. *Journal of Experimental Psychology, 74*, 1–9.

Senese, G. B. (1991). *Self-determination and the social education of Native Americans*. New York: Praeger.

Shepperd, J. A., & Arkin, R. M. (1989). Self-handicapping: The moderating roles of public self-consciousness and task importance. *Personality and Social Psychology Bulletin, 15*, 252–265.

Showers, C. (1989). *The organization of positive and negative components of the self*. Unpublished manuscript, Barnard College, New York.

Shrauger, J. S. (1975). Responses to evaluation as a function of initial self-perceptions. *Psychological Bulletin, 82*, 581–596.

Shillingford, J. P., & Shillingford-Mackin, A. (1991). Enhancing self-esteem through wellness programs. *Elementary School Journal, 91*(5), 457–466.

Singer, J. E. (1966). Social comparison: Progress and issues. *Journal of Experimental Social Psychology, 2* (Suppl. 1), 103–110.

Snyder, C. R., & Higgins, R. L. (1988). Excuses: Their effective role in the negotiation of social reality. *Psychological Bulletin, 104*, 23–35.

Snyder, C. R., Lassegard, M. A., & Ford, C. E. (1986). Distancing after group success and failure: Basking in reflected glory and cutting off reflected failure. *Journal of Personality and Social Psychology, 51*, 382–388.

Snyder, M. (1972). Individual differences and the self-control of expressive behavior (Doctoral dissertation, Stanford University, 1972). *Dissertation Abstracts International, 33*: 4533A–4534A. (University Microfilms No. 73–4598)

Snyder, M. (1974). The self-monitoring of expressive behavior. *Journal of Personality and Social Psychology, 30*, 526–537.

Snyder, M. (1979a). Cognitive, behavioral, and interpersonal consequences of self-monitoring. In P. Pliner, K. R. Blankstein, & I. M. Spigel (Eds.), *Advances in the study of communications and affect: Vol. 5. Perception of emotion in self and others*. New York: Plenum.

Snyder, M. (1979b). Self-monitoring processes. In L. Berkowitz (Ed.), *Advances in experimental social psychology* (Vol. 12, pp. 85–128). New York: Academic Press.

Snyder, M. (1984). When belief creates reality. In L. Berkowitz (Ed.), *Advances in experimental social psychology* (Vol. 18, pp. 248–305). Orlando, FL: Academic Press.

Snyder, M. (1987). *Public appearances, private realities: The psychology of self-monitoring*. New York: W. H. Freeman.

Snyder, M. (1992). Motivational foundations of behavioral confirmation. In L. Berkowitz (Ed.), *Advances in experimental social psychology* (Vol. 25, pp. 67–114). New York: Academic Press.

Snyder, M., Berscheid, E., & Glick, P. (1985). Focusing on the exterior and the interior: Two investigations of the initiation of personal relationships. *Journal of Personality and Social Psychology, 48*, 1427–1439.

Snyder, M., Berscheid, E., & Matwychuk, A. (1988). Orientations toward personnel selection: Differential reliance on appearance and personality. *Journal of Personality and Social Psychology, 54*, 972–979.

Snyder, M., Campbell, B., & Preston, E. (1982). Testing hypotheses about human nature: Assessing the accuracy of social stereotypes. *Social Cognition, 1*, 256–272.

Snyder, M., & Cantor, N. (1980). Thinking about ourselves and others: Self-monitoring and social knowledge. *Journal of Personality and Social Psychology, 39*, 222–234.

Snyder, M., & Gangestad, S. (1981). Hypothesis-testing processes. In J. H. Harvey, W. Ickes, & R. F. Kidd (Eds.), *New directions in attribution research* (Vol. 3, pp. 171–196). Hillsdale, NJ: Erlbaum.

Snyder, M., & Gangestad, S. (1986). On the nature of self-monitoring: Matters of assessment, matters of validity. *Journal of Personality and Social Psychology, 51,* 125–139.

Snyder, M., Gangestad, S., & Simpson, J. A. (1983). Choosing friends as activity partners: The role of self-monitoring. *Journal of Personality and Social Psychology, 45,* 1061–1072.

Snyder, M., & Monson, T. C. (1975). Persons, situations, and the control of social behavior. *Journal of Personality and Social Psychology, 32,* 637–644.

Snyder, M., & Simpson, J. A. (1984). Self-monitoring and dating relationships. *Journal of Personality and Social Psychology, 47,* 1281–1291.

Snyder, M., & Simpson, J. A. (1986). Orientations toward romantic relationships. In S. Duck & D. Perlman (Eds.), *Intimate relationships: Development, dynamics, and deterioration.* Newbury Park, CA: Sage.

Snyder, M., & Swann, W. B., Jr. (1978). Behavioral confirmation in social interaction: From social perception to social reality. *Journal of Personality and Social Psychology, 36,* 1202–1212.

Spencer, S. J., Josephs, R. A., & Steele, C. M. (1993). Low self-esteem: The uphill struggle for self-integrity. In R. F. Baumeister (Ed.), *Self-esteem: The puzzle of low self-regard.* New York: Plenum Press.

Stouffer, S. A., Suchman, E. A., DeVinney, L. C., Star, S. A., & Williams, R. M. (1949). *The American soldier: Adjusting during army life* (Vol. 1). Princeton, NJ: Princeton University Press.

Strauman, T. J. (1989). Self-discrepancies in clinical depression and social phobia: Cognitive structures that underlie emotional disorders? *Journal of Abnormal Psychology, 98,* 5–14.

Strauman, T. J. (1992). Self-guides, autobiographical memory, and anxiety and dysphoria: Toward a cognitive model of vulnerability to emotional distress. *Journal of Abnormal Psychology, 101,* 87–95.

Strenta, A., & DeJong, W. (1981). The effect of a prosocial label on helping behavior. *Social Psychology Quarterly, 44,* 142–147.

Strube, M. J., Lott, C. L., Le-Xuan-Hy, G. M., Oxenberg, J., & Deichmann, A. K. (1986). Self-evaluation of abilities: Accurate self-assessment versus biased self-enhancement. *Journal of Personality and Social Psychology, 51,* 16–25.

Sullivan, H. S. (1947). *Conceptions of modern psychiatry.* Washington, DC: White Psychiatric Foundation.

Sullivan, H. S. (1953). *The interpersonal theory of psychiatry.* New York: Norton.

Suls, J., & Wills, T. A. (1991). *Social comparison: Contemporary theory and research.* Hillsdale, NJ: Erlbaum.

Swann, W. B., Jr. (1983). Self-verification: Bringing social reality into harmony with the self. In J. Suls & A. G. Greenwals (Eds.), *Social psychological perspectives on the self* (Vol. 2, pp. 33–66). Hillsdale, NJ: Erlbaum.

Swann, W. B., Jr. (1985). The self as architect of social reality. In B. Schlenker (Ed.), *The self and social life* (pp. 100–125). New York: McGraw-Hill.

Swann, W. B., Jr. (1987). Identity negotiation: Where two roads meet. *Journal of Personality and Social Psychology, 53,* 1038–1051.

Swann, W. B., Jr. (1990). To be adored or to be known: The interplay of self-enhancement and self-verification. In R. M. Sorentino & E. T. Higgins (Eds.), *Motivation and cognition* (Vol. 2, pp. 408–448). New York: Guilford Press.

Swann, W. B., Jr., & Ely, R. J. (1984). A battle of wills: Self-verification versus behavioral confirmation. *Journal of Personality and Social Psychology, 46,* 1287–1302.

Swann, W. B., Jr., Griffin, J. J., Predmore, S. C., & Gaines, B. (1987). The cognitive–affective crossfire: When self-consistency confronts self-enhancement. *Journal of Personality and Social Psychology, 52*, 881–889.

Swann, W. B., Jr., Hixon, J. G., & De La Ronde, C. (1992a). Embracing the bitter "truth": Negative self-concepts and marital commitment. *Psychological Science, 3*(2), 118–121.

Swann, W. B., Jr., Hixon, J. G., Stein-Seroussi, A., & Gilbert, D. T. (1990). The fleeting gleam of praise: Cognitive processes underlying behavioral reactions to self-relevant feedback. *Journal of Personality and Social Psychology, 59*, 17–26.

Swann, W. B., Jr., Pelham, B. W., & Chidester, T. R. (1988). Change through paradox: Using self-verification to alter beliefs. *Journal of Personality and Social Psychology, 54*, 268–273.

Swann, W. B., Jr., Pelham, B. W., & Krull, D. S. (1989). Agreeable fancy or disagreeable truth? Reconciling self-enhancement and self-verification. *Journal of Personality and Social Psychology, 57*, 782–791.

Swann, W. B., Jr., & Read, S. J. (1981). Self-verification processes: How we sustain our self-conceptions. *Journal of Experimental Social Psychology, 17*, 351–372.

Swann, W. B., Jr., Stein-Seroussi, A., & Giesler, B. J. (1992b). Why people self-verify. *Journal of Personality and Social Psychology, 62*, 392–401.

Taylor, S. E., & Brown, J. (1988). Illusion and well-being: A social psychological perspective on mental health. *Psychological Bulletin, 103*, 193–210.

Taylor, S. E., & Lobel, M. (1989). Social comparison activity under threat: Downward evaluation and upward contacts. *Psychological Review, 96*, 569–575.

Taylor, S. E., & Mettee, D. R. (1971). When similarity breeds contempt. *Journal of Personality and Social Psychology, 20*, 75–81.

Tedeschi, J. T. (Ed.). (1981). *Impression management theory and social psychological research.* New York: Academic Press.

Tellegen, A. (1991). Personality traits: Issues of definition, evidence, and assessment. In D. Cicchetti & D. M. Grove (Eds.), *Thinking clearly about psychology* (Vol. 2, pp. 10–35). Minneapolis: University of Minnesota Press.

Tennen, H., & Affleck, G. (1993). The puzzles of self-esteem: A clinical perspective. In R. F. Baumeister (Ed.), *Self-esteem: The puzzle of low self-regard.* New York: Plenum Press.

Tennen, H., Herzberger, S., & Nelson, H. F. (1987). Depressive attributional style: The role of self-esteem. *Journal of Personality, 55*, 631–660.

Tesser, A. (1988). Toward a self-evaluation maintenance model of social behavior. In L. Berkowitz (Ed.), *Advances in experimental social psychology* (Vol. 21, pp. 181–227). New York: Academic Press.

Tesser, A., & Campbell, J. (1983). Self-definition and self-evaluation maintenance. In J. Suls & A. G. Greenwald (Eds.), *Psychological perspectives on the self* (Vol. 2, pp. 1–31). Hillsdale, NJ: Lawrence Erlbaum.

Tesser, A., & Cornell, D. P. (1991). On the confluence of self processes. *Journal of Experimental Social Psychology, 27*(6), 501–526.

Tice, D. M. (1991). Esteem protection or enhancement? Self-handicapping motives and attributions differ by trait self-esteem. *Journal of Personality and Social Psychology, 60*, 711–725.

Tice, D. M. (1993). The social motivations of people with low self-esteem. In R. F. Baumeister (Ed.), *Self-esteem: The puzzle of low self-regard.* New York: Plenum Press.

Tice, D. M., & Baumeister, R. F. (1990). Self-esteem, self-handicapping, and self-presentation: The strategy of inadequate practice. *Journal of Personality, 58*, 443–464.

Tomasello, M. (1993). Infants' knowledge of self, other, and relationship. In U. Neisser (Ed.), *The perceived self: Ecological and interpersonal sources of self-knowledge.* New York: Cambridge University Press.

Trevarthen, C. (1993). The self born in intersubjectivity: The psychology of an infant communicating. In U. Neisser (Ed.), *The perceived self: Ecological and interpersonal sources of self-knowledge*. New York: Cambridge University Press.

Valins, S. (1966). Cognitive effects of false heart-rate feedback. *Journal of Personality and Social Psychology, 4*, 400–408.

Vallacher, R. R., & Wegner, D. M. (1987). What do people think they're doing. Action identification and human behavior. *Psychological Review, 94*, 3–15.

Vygotsky, L. (1978). In M. Cole (Ed.), *Mind in society: The development of higher psychological processes*. Cambridge, MA: Harvard University Press.

Weiner, B. (1985). An attributional theory of achievement motivation and emotion. *Psychological Review, 92*, 548–573.

Weiner, B. (1986). *An attributional theory of motivation and emotion*. New York: Springer-Verlag.

Wertsch, J. V. (1991). *Voices of the mind: A sociocultural approach to mediated action*. Cambridge, MA: Harvard University Press.

Wheeler, L. (1991). A brief history of social comparison theory. In J. Suls & T. A. Wills (Eds.), *Social comparison: Contemporary theory and research* (pp. 3–21). Hillsdale, NJ: Erlbaum.

Wicklund, R. A., & Gollwitzer, P. M. (1982). *Symbolic self-completion*. Hillsdale, NJ: Lawrence Erlbaum.

Wills, T. A. (1981). Downward comparison principles in social psychology. *Psychological Bulletin, 90*, 245–271.

Wills, T. A. (1991). Similarity and self-esteem in downward comparison. In J. Suls & T. A. Wills (Eds.), *Social comparison: Contemporary theory and research* (pp. 1–21). Hillsdale, NJ: Erlbaum.

Wood, J. V., & Taylor, K. L. (1991). Serving self-relevant goals through social comparison. In J. Suls & T. A. Wills (Eds.), *Social comparison: Contemporary theory and research* (pp. 23–49). Hillsdale, NJ: Erlbaum.

Wylie, R. C. (1974). *The self-concept: A review of methodological considerations and measuring instruments* (rev. ed., Vol. 1). Lincoln: University of Nebraska Press.

Wylie, R. C. (1979). *The self-concept: Theory and research on selected topics* (rev. ed., Vol. 2). Lincoln: University of Nebraska Press.

Yates, S. G. (1982). *The relationship of self-concept and other variables to the work value orientation for black females enrolled in inner city vocational schools*. Palo Alto, CA: R & E Research Associates.

Young, J. R., Osborne, R. E., & Snyder, M. (1994). *Personality and politics: The role of self-monitoring and the use of issues and images in political choices*. Unpublished manuscript, Hunter College.

Zimmerman, B. J. (1989). Models of self-regulated learning and academic achievement. In B. J. Zimmerman & D. H. Schunk (Eds.), *Self-regulated learning and academic achievement: Theory, research, and practice*. New York: Springer-Verlag.

Zimmerman, B. J., & Schunk, D. H. (Eds.). (1989). *Self-regulated learning and academic achievement: Theory, research, and practice*. New York: Springer-Verlag.

Zuckerman, M. (1979). Attribution of success and failure revisited, or: The motivational bias is alive and well in attribution theory. *Journal of Personality, 47*, 245–287.

Index